T0331066

"Few institutions have been more complicit in the care and feeding of shareholder capitalism than business schools over the past 40 years. The challenge – and opportunity – is to usher in a new dominant model of business education that aims to regenerate natural capital, avert the climate disaster, lift the poor, and foster racial justice, all while making money to accelerate the process. The contributors to this important book help point the way to reinventing business education for a truly sustainable future."

Stuart L. Hart, author of *Beyond Shareholder Primacy* and co-founder of the Sustainable Innovation MBA Program at University of Vermont

"As the consensus that business education should radically change grows in light of the current socio-ecological crises, it becomes ever more critical to articulate what this change could look like. This book provides a very practical response to this challenge, offering a range of examples, stories and perspectives that can inspire educators in business schools and beyond."

Anne Touboulic, Associate Professor in Operations Management, Chair of the Social and Environmental Responsibility Group, Nottingham University Business School

"Addressing the global sustainability crisis requires actions from everybody, but especially from the business sector. This book is a must-read to understand how we must reform business education to prepare businesses to support the transition to a resilient, prosperous, and sustainable society. With an excellent theoretical foundation, leading educators share their experiences in an inspiring way."

Rupert J. Baumgartner, Director, Christian-Doppler-Research Laboratory for Sustainable Product Management, University of Graz

BREAKTHROUGHS IN SUSTAINABLE BUSINESS EDUCATION

Around the globe, faculty and higher education leaders are actively changing what they teach to create a sustainable world. This book shares how to transition to programs and courses that teach sustainable business management practices critical for success.

Students are demanding more than the same business courses taught for half a century. Faculty are wondering if they have the expertise to include sustainable business practices. Easy to read and relatable, this book provides tactical ideas for transitioning from current business curriculum to courses for a sustainable future. It compiles insights and recommendations from 28 global experts who have put ideas into practice. Each chapter addresses integration of sustainability topics into existing subject areas and offers ideas for adding new courses or concepts to ground business in the context of the global socio-environmental community.

The book offers actionable ways that administrators and faculty can immediately begin transitioning their business curriculum to one that is socially and environmentally sustainable.

Morgane Fritz, PhD and HDR, is Full Professor in Sustainable Supply Chain Management. She researches and teaches about sustainable and ethical supply chain management and acts as author, editor and reviewer for various peer-reviewed journals and books. She is a member of Global Movement Initiative.

James Weichert is a serial entrepreneur and the founder of www.livingconservancy.org. He is Project Manager of the Global Movement Initiative and a doctoral candidate in sustainable economics. He is a member of Global Movement Initiative.

Isabel Rimanoczy is the convener of PRME Working Group on Sustainability Mindset and co-developer of the Sustainability Mindset Indicator (www.SMindicator.com). She has authored and edited 28 books, about sustainability, learning, poetry, and children's books.

Linda Irwin developed MBA Strategy and Marketing courses and is passionate about transforming business education for sustainability. She is CEO of SeeComm Group, and she is a member of Global Movement Initiative.

The Principles for Responsible Management Education Series

Since the inception of the UN-supported Principles for Responsible Management Education (PRME) in 2007, there has been increased debate over how to adapt management education to best meet the demands of the 21st-century business environment. While consensus has been reached by the majority of globally focused management education institutions that sustainability must be incorporated into management education curricula, the relevant question is no longer why management education should change, but how.

Volumes within the Routledge/PRME book series aim to cultivate and inspire actively engaged participants by offering practical examples and case studies to support the implementation of the Six Principles of Responsible Management Education. Books in the series aim to enable participants to transition from a global learning community to an action community.

Responsible Business
Foundations of Ethical and Sustainable Management, 3rd Edition
Alex Hope and Oliver Laasch

Responsible Management Education and Business School Practices
Walking the Talk
Wolfgang Amann

Breakthroughs in Sustainable Business Education
Change-makers in Action
Edited by Morgane Fritz, James Weichert, Isabel Rimanoczy and Linda Irwin

For more information about this series, please visit: www.routledge.com/The-Principles-for-Responsible-Management-Education-Series/book-series/PRME

BREAKTHROUGHS IN SUSTAINABLE BUSINESS EDUCATION

Change-makers in Action

Edited by Morgane Fritz, James Weichert,
Isabel Rimanoczy and Linda Irwin

LONDON AND NEW YORK

Designed cover image: ID 15530329 © Ajijchan | Dreamstime.com

First published 2025
by Routledge
4 Park Square, Milton Park, Abingdon, Oxon OX14 4RN

and by Routledge
605 Third Avenue, New York, NY 10158

Routledge is an imprint of the Taylor & Francis Group, an informa business

British Library Cataloguing-in-Publication Data
A catalogue record for this book is available from the British Library

ISBN: 978-1-032-86210-1 (hbk)
ISBN: 978-1-032-83238-8 (pbk)
ISBN: 978-1-003-52183-9 (ebk)

DOI: 10.4324/9781003521839

Typeset in Galliard
by Apex CoVantage, LLC

CONTENTS

CONTRIBUTORS

Ricardo Barretto is an invited professor at FGV and psychotherapist. He conducts extensive work in communications focused on socio-environmental issues. He holds degrees in Sustainability and Digital Networks and Psychology.

Alejandro Beltrán-Duque, PhD, is Dean of the School of Management at Universidad Externado de Colombia and Full-time Professor in Strategy.

Unique Brathwaite is Faculty of Bard Sustainability MBA and Chief External Affairs Officer at Community Resource Exchange. He is also a Doctoral Student at Fielding Graduate University in Organizational Development and Change.

Fernanda Cassab Carreira, PhD, directs the Education Program at the Center for Sustainability Studies (FGVces). She is on the Advisory Board of the Network for Business Sustainability (NBS).

Pavana Kiranmai Chepuri is Head of Strategic Initiatives and Growth at Woxsen University and serves as university legal counsel. She leads Ethics, Responsibility, and Sustainability (ERS) initiatives and teaches Business Law.

Brad Clauss is Facilities Director at Chatham University Eden Hall Campus. He has 20 years of experience in sustainability and energy management at Johnson & Johnson Consumer Companies Inc.

Thomas Dyllick, PhD, is Director of Institute for Business Sustainability in Lucerne and served as Managing Director of the Institute for Economy and Environment, Dean, and Vice President at University of St. Gallen.

Michael J. Garanzini, SJ, PhD, was President of Loyola University Chicago and taught at St. Louis University, the Gregorian University in Rome, and Georgetown University. He founded the Association of Jesuit Universities and is currently president.

Eban Goodstein, PhD, is Director of Bard Sustainability Graduate Programs, Vice President for Social and Environmental Leadership at Bard College, and author of *Economics and the Environment 10e* and *Jobs and the Environment*.

Lauren E. Graham is Faculty of Bard Sustainability MBA, environmentalist working in sustainability, strategic communications, and creative media for public engagement, and Founder of Velvet Frame, a social impact strategy and communications consultancy.

Ayako Huang, PhD, is Associate Professor and Program Director of the Sustainable MBA at Maharishi International University and holds ACSTH certifications in Shared Leadership Team Coaching. She promotes sustainability education globally.

Anu Jossan, PhD, Senior Fellow in Higher Education UK, leads Business Analytics at QFBA Northumbria University. She champions technology, business, and sustainability. She is a leader, economist, and data science professional.

Kristin Kusanovich is Founding Director of tUrn Climate Action and Professor in the Theatre/Dance and Child Studies Departments at Santa Clara University. She specializes in transdisciplinary collaboration and critical, arts-based research.

John (Jed) Lindholm, PhD, teaches leadership through operationalizing ESG practices at Worcester Polytechnic Institute. He taught at Penn State, Clark University, WPI, and internationally in China, Singapore, Israel, and Poland.

Walter Link is Executive Chair of NOW Partners Foundation and Future Economy Forum. He co-founded the first sustainable business alliance across Europe and the Americas. He scales regenerative farming approaches internationally.

J. Renay Loper is Faculty of Bard Sustainability MBA. She is a strategist of cross-sector partnerships that shift systems. She advises on Justice Equity Diversity and Inclusion and hosts the *Impact Report* podcast.

L. Hunter Lovins, JD, is Managing Partner of NOW Partners, President of Natural Capitalism Solutions, and Innovative Professor. She received numerous environmental awards and Newsweek dubbed her *Green Business Icon*.

Chahat Mishra is Head of International Relations and Strategic Development at Woxsen University. He holds an MBA and is a certified NLP Practitioner and is featured in international and national magazines.

Mario Monzoni, PhD, is Coordinator of the Center for Sustainability Studies at FGV-EAESP (FGVces). He holds master's degree from the Columbia University School of International and Public Affairs.

Katrin Muff, PhD, is Director of Institute for Business Sustainability and Professor at LUISS Business School. She was Dean of Business School Lausanne and has 20 years of intercontinental management experience.

Ilijana Petrovska, PhD, is Full Professor at University American College Skopje (UACS), Visiting Professor, and Consultant. She led MSc in Digital Marketing at QFBA Northumbria, Qatar, and is an author and speaker.

Michael Pirson, PhD, is a co-founder of the Humanistic Management Network and serves on Boards of social enterprises. He is Full Professor at Fordham University and a Research Fellow at Harvard University.

Carlos Alberto Restrepo-Rivillas, PhD, is Economist and Research Director of the School of Management at Universidad Externado de Colombia. He is Director, Professor, and Research Group Leader of Business Environment and Sustainability.

Abigail B. Schneider, PhD, is Director of the Sustainable Economic and Enterprise Development (SEED) Institute at Regis University's Anderson College of Business. She is Associate Professor of Marketing and conducts research on disinformation.

Maria Clara Araujo Secall, BA in Public Administration (FGV-EAESP), is Strategic Planning Analyst at Sociedade Beneficente Israelita Brasileira Albert Einstein.

Janice Shade is Faculty of Bard Sustainability MBA, Systems Entrepreneur, Financial Innovator, and author with 30+ years' experience building brands, businesses, and movements. She is Founder/Executive Director of Capital Innovation Lab.

Robert Sroufe is Falk Chair of Socially Responsible Business and Professor at Chatham University, with expertise in sustainable business practices, energy systems, high-performance buildings, sustainable supply chains, and decarbonization.

James A. F. Stoner, PhD, is Professor Emeritus of Fordham University, author, and founder of Global Movement Initiative to transform global business education into a leading force for creating a sustainable world.

Sandra Waddock is Galligan Chair of Strategy, Scholar of Corporate Responsibility, and Professor of Management at Boston College's Carroll School of Management, and Faculty Associate at BC's Shiller Institute for Integrated Sciences.

Gustavo Yepes-López, PhD, is Director of Research line in CSR, Director of Management and Social Responsibility, and Director of Initiatives for Sustainable Development at Universidad Externado de Colombia.

FOREWORD

John North

Dear Reader,

Since this book does not come with a consumer warning or disclaimer on the cover, I have the privilege of opening the foreword with a friendly forewarning.

There is more on offer here than bare descriptions of individual and institutional efforts to foster and strengthen sustainable business education. The breakthroughs described reveal significant and transformative strides within, across, and beyond business education to help ensure a sustainable and regenerative future for us all. The rich, personal perspectives bring practical insight and guidance on how transformative change can be initiated and offer a behind-the-scenes look at the change agents and the motivation driving their tireless efforts. In its totality, the contributions to this volume animate a vibrant, emerging collective effort that is proactively recasting business education as an enabler for serving the common good.

> *Warning: Venturing beyond this paragraph will immerse you in the work that lies ahead.*

Aside from taking inspiration from the invaluable and practical learnings discovered here, reading *Breakthroughs in Sustainable Business Education* moved me to reflect on some of the breakthroughs (and breakdowns) I have witnessed in the business and responsible management education landscape in recent years.

What? the work

"The work" deals with preparing the ground for an abundance of positively radical business education breakthroughs to emerge and scale. Equally important is doing "the work" in a way that is congruent with the type of future we hope for. I have been associated with the Globally Responsible Leadership Initiative (GRLI) since 2009, and without recounting its entire history, I will point to a few milestones, moments, and actions associated with GRLI's part of "the work" as a reference for this reflection.

It has been two decades since the global business school community was called upon to reflect on its role as a "collective" that may positively alter the course toward our common future. In 2003, the United Nations (represented by the Global Compact) and a globally recognized standard bearer for business school accreditation, EFMD Global (then European Foundation for Management Development), issued an open and joint *invite* to CEOs and business school deans across their respective networks to address the question: "How to develop the next generation of globally responsible leaders?" The invitation resulted in an inquiry that has been at the heart of catalyzing breakthrough initiatives in business and management education since.

In 2006, building on the UNGC/EFMD agreement, a number of academic institutions responded to another invitation to co-develop and steward a set of Principles for Responsible Business Education (later PRME) that would complement the Global Compact's ten principles in the areas of human rights, labor, environment, and anti-corruption. The intention was to have 1,000 business schools voluntarily committed by 2015 and to create a tipping point of commitment and sharing of learning across the 13,000+ business schools globally by the end of that decade, again an *invite* to which a collective responded and resulted in many inspiring initiatives held by PRME chapters around the globe.

In 2009, I had the opportunity to experience firsthand the *invite-inquire-initiate* mode of peer-based and whole-person learning, which still underpins the work of the GRLI. The "Blue Sky Business School" inquiry was starting to gather momentum and interest in the question: "What might a business school look like if people and planet truly mattered?" We soon joined forces with a temporary coalition of business school deans, UN PRME as a co-convener and secured sponsorship from 16 institutional co-authors. The invitation was to co-develop and launch a manifesto and vision for business and management education at the RIO+20 Earth Summit. The resulting 50+20 Agenda and the vision Management Education FOR the World (launched in 2012 and a book published in 2013) added significant momentum to embedding ethics, responsibility, and sustainability into global accreditation standards.

From 2012 onward, GRLI "calls to action" (including the 50+20 Agenda) inspired open invitations, collective inquiries, and experimental initiatives – some of which are described in more detail in this book. A non-exhaustive sample of attempts at facilitating breakthroughs catalyzed by or incubated in the context of GRLI through our partners and allies in the landscape includes the following:

- Asking what it might look like if we assessed the sustainability literacy of students and prototyping what is today known as Sulitest.
- Convening a regional 50+20 event at Hong Kong Polytechnic University to explore the new research agenda and necessary approaches, leading to the formation of the Responsible Research in Business & Management initiative (RRBM Network).
- Ensuring continued dialogue between higher education institutions, student networks, and UN bodies under the umbrella of the UN Higher Education Sustainability Initiative. By helping set up an informal "Global Alliance," major national and international networks established an SDG Accord and ensured that the collective voice of higher and further education was heard at COP21.
- Asking how innovative pedagogical methods (such as Appreciative Inquiry) may be leveraged to uncover and celebrate business innovations aligned with the UN Global Goals, leading to AIM2Flourish as championed by the Fowler Center for Business as an Agent of World Benefit at the Weatherhead School of Management – Case Western Reserve University.
- Asking what it might look like if we measured the positive impact of business schools, leading to the development of the Positive Impact Rating.
- Inviting and supporting a facilitated global process of co-learning and co-creation among more than 100 business school deans and directors since 2017, leading to numerous institutional, bilateral, and collective initiatives.

So what? some observations

Looking back on the small contribution made by an initiative such as the GRLI and considering the scale and depth of work required going forward, a few observations and suggestions on sustaining breakthroughs in sustainable business education emerge. An ongoing, inclusive, and collective call for deep systemic change remains crucially important and needs to span at least three broad domains: How we *live* and make a living together on one finite, flourishing planet; how we *learn* and facilitate learning in service of that life; and how we *lead* individually and collectively to enable both. Being consciously connected to our individual humanity, to others through meaningful relationships, and to the planet in a regenerative way appears to be prerequisites for making deep systemic change a reality. Thinking, acting, and being "globally responsible" therefore require a radical shift in perception, purpose, and practice to span and integrate across the "I," the "We," and the "All of Us" levels. More succinctly, integrative work is needed at individual, collective, and systemic levels.

It is encouraging to witness the growth and growing impact of the Responsible Management Education movement, now comprising a global system of networks, platforms, and initiatives. Simultaneously, we have to acknowledge the lack of coordination across the landscape of networks and initiatives, the persistence of a dominant competitive logic, and the prevalence of outdated approaches to building scale adopted by those very initiatives called to dismantle the status quo.

As seen from the milestones described earlier, it helps tremendously when egos and logos are left at the door, and the indefinite survival or continued visibility of those helping create the change becomes of lesser importance. Incidentally, the GRLI continues to keep 2030 in sight as a symbolic sunsetting opportunity, should our work and ways of working be fully absorbed by the wider business education landscape. "Preparing the ground," as mentioned previously, invokes the idea of nutrient cycling – a key ecological process whereby decomposers and dead organic matter return essential nutrients to the soil, which in turn supports the growth of new plants. The GRLI's symbolic decomposition reinforces our view that a living systems perspective and approach to our work is essential. What else, then, might we learn from nature in the context of creating further breakthroughs in sustainable business education?

Now what?

> Large-scale problems do not require large-scale solutions; they require small-scale solutions within a large-scale framework.
>
> David Fleming

Perhaps the time is ripe for the Responsible Management Education ecosystem to look into the mirror. What are our blind spots? What might an inclusive and shared agenda for globally responsible and sustainable education look like? What are the possibilities for enhanced collaboration and coordination of effort across differing and shifting contexts? How might we enable an ongoing, future-oriented, and systems-level dialogue about "the work" involving global, regional, and local networks, associations, and institutions?

I don't have the answers to these but am committed to holding the questions. What I do know for certain is that you and I are co-conspirators in "the work" unfolding.

We have a wise and helpful companion in the form of this book, packed with invitations, ideas, inquiries, and initiatives to help with co-creating the next wave of breakthroughs in sustainable business education – for all of us.

John North
Executive Director, Globally Responsible Leadership Initiative
George, South Africa

INTRODUCTION

Linda Irwin

Most higher education institutions and academics do not pursue their profession for wealth or fame. They gravitate to the field to help students succeed and improve their communities. Most businesses are created to solve problems and serve customers. Many business leaders strive to conduct their work in ways that provide enough return for the business to continue to thrive in the future while supporting their family and employees.

In spite of those motivations, academics and businesspeople have also contributed to what some call a global "polycrisis":

- Over the past century, business education taught millions how to maximize growth and profit for stakeholders or CEOs but have not addressed the impact of "taking" from our planet's finite resources, "polluting" our water, air, and atmosphere, or abusing other humans and societies for gain and growth.

  - The 26 richest people in the world held as much wealth as half of the global population of 3.8 billion people (https://policy-practice.oxfam.org/resources).

- The climate crisis is literally reshaping our ecosystems and the ability for humans to live on this planet.

  - The ten warmest years in the 174-year record have all occurred during the last decade (2014–2023) and sea ice coverage dropped to record lows in 2023 (https://www.noaa.gov/news/2023-was-worlds-warmest-year-on-record-by-far).

DOI: 10.4324/9781003521839-1

- Business continues to create new technologies that make it easier and faster to benefit or harm human rights.

  - Human rights suppression and wartime atrocities are increasing and adding to global chaos (https://www.hrw.org/world-report/2024).

We are human. We fear change. But we are at a point where we **must** change to survive.
The polycrisis is upon us **now**.

Considering this urgent situation, what are business educators doing to help students and communities survive and succeed in an uncertain future?

- Sadly, some are doing nothing but implementing the same practices that contributed to today's polycrisis.
- Others have initiated conversations, task forces, research, and small projects to test new ideas. Or they are seeking donors to fund studies. Unfortunately, such efforts do not produce the help needed right now by students and businesses.
- Fortunately, some universities, individual educators, students, and associations are implementing change in courses, programs, and integration with communities right now. They have forged ahead because they, and we, **must**. There is no time to follow paths from the past.

This book shares the stories of how some innovators have made real *breakthroughs* in business education so that we can create a sustainable future. These stories represent **action** and hope. Some ideas may resonate with you and inspire you to use them wherever you have influence and ability.

- Some chapters describe how entire universities or business schools changed – or are continuing to change – what they teach and how they operate to address the challenges we face.
- Other chapters describe how each of us must first understand our own purpose and commitment so that we can guide students in forming theirs as they face an uncertain world.
- Some chapters offer specific tools and tactics to transform typical business courses so that students will change business practices going forward.

The world needs our help in dealing with an uncertain future. Business schools and educators must act – right now. Change a course, change a student's view, change your own view, change a policy, or change a university! These chapters offer ideas from those who are already making breakthroughs for a sustainable future and aim at inspiring many others to stimulate a global movement in business education.

Business needs your help.
Students are demanding more help in shaping an uncertain world.
It is difficult but we can and *must* do better. Read, then do!

1

CHANGING MANAGEMENT EDUCATION

Tapping into the forgotten power of the mindset

Isabel Rimanoczy

Abstract

This chapter shares some snapshots from a professional journey that parallels my own personal shift – the development of a framework and the emergence of a movement. This journey took me from the exploration of leaders' behaviors to what educators could do to teach and to intentionally develop a new generation of conscious business leaders. It also led to the realization that this was not something to be taught – but that can be developed. I will share how an exploratory path led me to identify the core aspects of the sustainability mindset, how to develop and assess it, and importantly, to discover how the mindset is an underutilized lever to accelerate our evolutionary transformation, balancing the progress of AI with the intentional growth of our profound humanness.

Introduction

I have experienced most of my institutional learning as a one-directional transfer of knowledge. I sat in classrooms, large and small, where an expert speaks, sharing their knowledge. What I remember most from these experiences are endless accounts of theories from other experts, which we were expected to write down, memorize, and cite in a future test. These were classes where I had strategies for staying awake, like lighting a cigarette (yes, smoking in a classroom was common), eating candy, or doodling. Needless to say, I did not retain the memorized theories for very long and would be hard-pressed to cite them today. There were notable exceptions – especially when the expert referred to his/her personal experience. These experts became storytellers, and they captured my attention. Their passion made an impression, leaving me

DOI: 10.4324/9781003521839-2

with lasting memories, not of the lesson taught, but of the power of passion, and of finding a path to convert passion into action and a profession.

These educational experiences sparked my interest in different pedagogical approaches and led me to explore a learning methodology developed in Scandinavia in the late 1970s, called Action Reflection Learning. In collaboration with two colleagues, Boris Drizin and Paul Roberts, we codified the methodology, identifying ten principles that explained its power (Rimanoczy & Turner, 2012). I then used this framework to design and facilitate corporate leadership development interventions.

However, it wasn't until my late forties, while doing my doctoral studies at Teachers College, Columbia University, that I experienced, as a student myself, a more holistic and student-centered pedagogical approach. Although there were still conceptual frameworks and theories to be learned, I was able to make them relevant by bringing them into the context of my research focus: How do individuals transform their behaviors? How do our narratives and worldviews condition our actions? How do we shift our perspectives of self, of each other, and of the world? Is that the main goal of learning? What is the role of learning in this transformation? How can educators prompt or facilitate such learning, and such transformations? Is it possible? And especially, *how do individuals become the best they can be, for themselves and for the world?* I had coaches and corporate trainers in mind when I asked these questions, those who could inspire their clients to use their business to make a positive difference.

This journey took me from the exploration of leaders' behaviors to what educators could do to teach and to intentionally develop a new generation of conscious business leaders. I share how an exploratory path led me to identify the core aspects of the sustainability mindset, how to develop and assess it, and importantly, to discover how the mindset is an underutilized lever to accelerate our evolutionary transformation, balancing the progress of AI with the intentional growth of our profound humanness. To begin, let's start in 2003.

The disorienting dilemma

In 2003, I was working as a corporate team coach in leadership development programs. At a coach training session, we were invited to do an exercise called "The amazing achievement award." Designed as a visioning exercise, we had to write an acceptance speech for an award we would receive in seven years for some amazing achievement we would have accomplished. In less than 30 minutes, I entered a sort of midlife crisis, realizing I was unable to imagine that anything I was doing could deserve such a special award. I was a competent professional, but I didn't see anything "for the greater good" that would merit such recognition. This moment was what Mezirow (2008) calls "the disorienting dilemma," a simple situation or event that ruptures a stable worldview, leaving the individual confused and in uncertainty, and faced with pieces of their own life that somehow must be put back together again, and reorganized. The exercise brought up for me profound questions: *Who am I? What am I doing, why am I doing what I'm doing? Am I living my purpose? If not, what is missing? Do I know what my purpose is, anyway?*

In hindsight, this exercise was a turning point, which led me to decide that I wanted to become a "legacy coach" focusing on leaders interested in making a difference for the greater good. But to do that, I had to go back to school and to study how conventional "business-as-usual" leaders become champions for the greater good through their work. As it often happens, this "medicine" for myself became the core of my new profession.

Ecoliteracy increasing the disorientation

After enrolling in the doctoral program at Teachers College, Columbia University, I encountered for the first-time texts and stories about our current social and environmental challenges. As I began uncovering new perspectives to investigate our world, I also realized that these topics resonated with concerns I had many decades ago, as a teenager with an activist mind, and which I had kept to myself to survive the military dictatorship in Argentina, in the 1970s. The knowledge I was absorbing was more than mere information to me; I was emotionally engaged, shaken to my heart by the sudden discovery of people's suffering, injustice, the destruction of our ecosystem, the loss of species from extinction caused by human activities, and climate change, all resulting from a lifestyle that up until then had seemed perfectly acceptable, even attractive and progressive to me.

The complexity of the interconnections between what appeared to be disconnected actions started to become visible to me, and I discovered that decisions made in the past had consequences decades later, and for populations that were not part of the decisions to begin with. This new awareness was profoundly disturbing to me, as I sat in my reading chair, with tears rolling down my cheeks. *I have to do something. Do others know about this? I cannot **not** do something.* This experience confirmed that I was on the right track with my purpose to work with leaders wanting to make a difference. I just needed to discover how. How do you teach or coach individuals for such a transformation? The world needed it.

Learning from pioneers

I started seeking out some of these exceptional leaders who were actually making a difference, to learn from them. What did they know? What made them shift from business as usual and broaden their purpose for the benefit of community and environment? Not coincidentally, this was in 2006 around the time that Al Gore was starting to point to the dire trends of climate change that we were in midst of but still barely noticing it.

As I was coding many pages of my lengthy interviews, I noticed some common themes. In different contexts and circumstances, each leader had learned about some negative impacts caused by their business practices. They were not illegal practices but seemed to have long-term consequences on the health of workers, on their communities or ecosystems (Anderson, 2009). This discovery – of unintended harm – was not just a new intellectual understanding: It emotionally disturbed them. As Ray Anderson, one of my interviewees, said: "We were not bad people! We had values, grandchildren."

They not only felt compelled to do something but also realized that there were no quick fixes. Changing how their business operated required a total transformation, and the introduction of new practices that were non-existent in the industry. Moreover, if the processes had to be reinvented, everyone had to be involved, particularly the leaders of the organization. This was unchartered territory that required imagination, sensitivity, and collaborative action. Some also realized that they needed to engage people around a vision that felt meaningful. Profit shouldn't be sacrificed, but it was not an either/or question. Business had to do less harm and be profitable. The evolution of our collective understanding has changed how responsibility is seen nowadays, 20 years later. What used to be an ambitious goal – to do less harm – is now no longer seen as acceptable. Today responsibility includes restoring lost ecosystems, stopping extinction, creating sustainable cities and industries, and as in the Sustainable Development Goals and their 167 targets, creating a flourishing world that works for all. The ethical standards of what constitutes acceptable business practices have changed faster than the regulatory frameworks.

After months of pondering my notes, their words, and the common aspects of their stories, some patterns began to emerge. I noticed a profound personal shift in how these individuals saw themselves, others, and the world. They had each developed a new worldview that informed how they looked at information. Systems perspective became the lens through which they analyzed data; they began looking for how they were themselves part of the problem, realizing the complexity of the interconnections and impacts beyond the here-and-now of their decisions.

They reflected on how they were using natural resources and became aware of a collective myopia: That of not accepting that humans, business, and planet are all part of the same ecosystem. When asked what caused the transformation of their perspective, they mentioned moments when they wondered what their purpose was, and when they asked why they were doing what they were doing, who they wanted to be and how they wanted to be remembered. I ended my interviews by asking them what advice they had for educators, and one person said, "I wish someone would have asked me when I was in college, what my purpose was. I wouldn't have had an answer, but I would have started my journey seeking that answer decades ago, not in my midlife crisis."

I thought that was a question we could easily ask students.

It's the mindset, Watson

The transcripts of the interviews added a wealth of new information to a field that was then totally unexplored: The motivations and knowledge of business leaders pioneering corporate transformations in sustainability. Analyzing the key and common aspects that could be intentionally developed, I grouped them into four categories: ecological worldview, systems perspective, and emotional and spiritual intelligence (see Figure 1.1) and called them the "sustainability mindset."

The sustainability mindset is defined as *a particular way of thinking and being for results in behaviors for the greater good*. The components of the sustainability mindset later stated as the Sustainability Mindset Principles (SMPs) are clearly defined and powerful paths to develop the mindset.

Here is a further breakdown:

Ecoliteracy: Understanding the state of the planet allows us to be more fully aware of the challenges and the complexity of how each is linked to the other. We also explore what these challenges mean to us emotionally, expanding consciousness and creating higher levels of engagement.

My contribution: When we identify the ways in which we are unintentionally contributing to the problems, we have a chance to do something about it. This expands our consciousness and develops social sensitivity. It also empowers the individual, which is important in times of overwhelming circumstances.

Long-term thinking: Every action has consequences that are not immediately visible. Considering the long term when analyzing situations and making decisions can have a positive impact on global sustainability. Most of us are trained in short-term thinking and just need to balance our analysis with a consideration of what long-term impacts there might be, before making decisions.

Both+and thinking: Both+and thinking gives us the perspective to understand paradoxes and find solutions that are inclusive of all stakeholders. In our polarized world, this is a critical skill, with an impact on our daily

FIGURE 1.1 Four content areas and 12 sustainability mindset principles.

interactions, negotiations, and decisions. It is essential for building peace, developing resilient communities, and restoring ecosystems.

Cyclical flow: There are no linear processes in nature; everything flows in cycles of birth, growth, death, and rebirth. Many aspects of man-made unsustainability on our planet are the result of a misconception that we are not governed by this law of nature. *Take-make-waste* is a practice that has created many of the problems we are now faced with. We have trapped ourselves collectively in linear growth models on a planet with limits.

Interconnectedness: When we begin to see interconnectedness, we start to understand the importance of diversity, and our decisions and actions become more inclusive, contributing to the sustainability of the whole.

Reflection: Reflective practice helps to pause and to ponder a situation and its implications before jumping into action. Most of our unsustainable behaviors are unintentional, automatic habits, which we don't take the time to scrutinize before acting.

Self-awareness: Mindsets are a set of values and beliefs that form the source of our thinking and shape our actions. They are the result of our inherited worldviews, reinforced by our social interactions, and shape our identity. When we explore our personal values, assumptions, and motivations, we gain greater control over our actions, giving us the ability to see new alternative and more sustainable behaviors.

Creative innovation: Resilience is based on constant creativity, innovation, and experimentation. When we neglect our creative and intuitive wisdom, our solutions lack this critical information and may subsequently have negative impacts on the ecosystem and society.

Oneness with nature: Understanding that we are one with nature, a species within a species, is a powerful spiritual experience and can shape behaviors leading to a more harmonious relationship with each other and with all beings.

Mindfulness: Mindfulness is being fully present, experiencing connectedness with all that is. Mindfulness enhances awareness and compassion and predisposes us to social and environmental actions.

Purpose: Defining our purpose provides an unconscious compass, and when grounded in the values of our higher self, it helps us actively shape a better world.

Leaders are formed not only in management education institutions

In 2009, I was presenting the preliminary results of my research at the Transformative Learning Conference in Bermuda, when a participant asked me if I had a course to develop the sustainability mindset, since I had identified the core elements of it. This became another turning point, after Dr. Aixa Ritz invited me to create and teach such a course to students in the Masters in Hospitality and Tourism program at Fairleigh Dickinson University, New Jersey, USA.

Using the elements of the sustainability mindset as learning outcomes, I reverse-engineered a semester of classes with the Scandinavian Action Reflection Learning methodology as a pedagogical framework (Rimanoczy, 2016). The course started by explaining the holistic, self-directed pedagogical approach – unusual for the students in many aspects – as well as the self-grading process. We started with ecoliteracy to grasp the seriousness and complexity of the challenges while making room for the expression of emotions. We also explored the personal contributions to these problems, followed by reflections on what could be done differently. Students were asked to identify a personal passion project, something they could feel proud of, to be completed during the semester, and that would make a positive contribution to the world. For example, one student worked on developing ecoliteracy at her workplace, bringing new information and ideas to her colleagues and bosses. Another student developed a voluntary professional oath for the school, where graduating students committed to act professionally with a sustainability mindset.

We played games to experience interconnectedness and explored our automatic either/or polarized thinking patterns. We also analyzed newspapers to discover where long-term thinking was missing, which stunned the students, realizing how pervasive the unsustainable mindset was. We reflected on our fast-paced life and the unscrutinized values of our society that anchor us in unsustainability, including growth, comfort, competition, independence, and our fascination with speed. We had conversations delving into topics that hadn't been addressed in other classes, yet were profoundly relevant to who they were, who they wanted to be, and why. We reflected on the meaning of purpose for each student, and we even did the Amazing Achievement Award exercise.

I don't have data on what became of this group and the many students who have since participated in this program, but the reflective essays they wrote during the course are a testament to journeys of profound transformation. Using the same pedagogical approach and learning outcomes across different course designs and activities, I have taught students in higher education institutions in the United States, Canada, Spain, the UK, France, Indonesia, and Morocco. I have repeatedly witnessed the power of addressing the mindset as an accelerator for personal transformation, leading to engaged and passionate actions for the greater good. I have learned that all professionals can become inspiring leaders of this new mindset: engineers, hospitality and tourism professionals, musicians, teachers, architects, agronomists, nutritionists, nurses, etc. – not just business school graduates.

Going broader

Several years into developing the sustainability mindset with students, I realized that it was becoming urgent and critical to respond to increasingly visible challenges, both environmental and social. In 2013, I decided to create a community of practice, inviting academic colleagues interested in a holistic approach to prepare the next generation with resilience and imagination through the sustainability mindset. I named the network LEAP! (**L**everage resources, **E**xpand awareness, **A**ccelerate change and **P**artner), as the mindset was a powerful way to create engagement and prompt proactive behaviors, *leaping* forward.

Today, the network has close to 300 members in 58 countries from over 250 institutions. They are scholars and professors teaching in business schools, as well as in schools of engineering, architecture, aerospace, nursing, education, information technology, agriculture, hospitality and tourism, and the liberal arts. At the time of writing this chapter, members are from Argentina, Australia, Austria, Azerbaijan, Bangladesh, Belgium, Brazil, Canada, Czech Republic, Chile, China, Colombia, Costa Rica, Denmark, Ecuador, Egypt, Estonia, Finland, France, Germany, Ghana, Hong Kong, Hungary, India, Indonesia, Ireland, Italy, Japan, Kazakhstan, Lebanon, Lithuania, Malaysia, Mexico, Netherlands, New Zealand, Nigeria, Norway, Pakistan, Peru, Philippines, Poland, Portugal, Russia, Saudi Arabia, Singapore, Slovenia, South Africa, South Korea, Spain, Sri Lanka, Sweden, Switzerland, Thailand, Turkey, Vietnam, UAE, UK, and the United States.

These academics promote the sustainability mindset at their institutions and engage in research within their context and culture, writing papers, and presenting at conferences. In this community of scholars, members collectively and intentionally develop the sustainability mindset in over 32,000 students each year. They have published their stories in several edited books (Irwin et al., 2023; Ivanova & Rimanoczy, 2021; Kassel & Rimanoczy, 2018; Ritz & Rimanoczy, 2021; Sunley & Leigh, 2017). A growing number of doctoral students are also researching the sustainability mindset across the globe and the sustainability mindset indicator (www.smindicator.com) is now being used as a research tool to compare the mindset of incoming and outgoing students, to assess the impact of teaching in developing a sustainability mindset. Several university centers for the sustainability mindset and corporate responsibility have been created in India, Russia, and Indonesia, as well as programs/master's on the sustainability mindset.

As sustainability is becoming increasingly a component of all higher education programs, the focus is on the *external* aspects: information, benchmarks, regulatory frameworks, innovations, skills, and competencies to be mastered. The sustainability mindset framework addresses the *inner* dimensions and has become the scaffolding for further development and exploration of the paradigms and narratives underlying our unsustainable behaviors, and how to prompt transformation. More importantly, it has ignited a movement that is increasing awareness on the power of our inner dimensions.

The underutilized leverage of transformation

It has long been pointed out that changes in behavior will lag until we pay attention to the mindset that created the problems, and that the key to transformation lies in our mindset. Donella Meadows refers to it as the most effective lever for change in a system (1997). Interest in the inner dimensions has been increasing over the past decade, using a different terminology: mindset, inner development goals, our narrative, paradigm, and collective worldview. The report for the 30th anniversary of the UNDP indicates that "Nothing short of a wholesale shift in mindsets, translated into reality by policy, is needed to navigate the brave new world of the Anthropocene, to ensure that all people flourish while easing planetary pressures" (UNDP, 2020).

The current environmental, social, and political landscape has resulted in loud, disorienting dilemmas. And it raises the question "How did we get here?" which prompts scientists from different disciplines to search for the causes. While some are focusing on the technological solutions that may help us reduce climate impact, restore lost ecosystems, and address social inequities, those analyzing the mindset/paradigm that got us here are finding both causes and remedies. We have become attached to automatic habits of thinking and doing inherited without scrutiny and thoughtlessly adopted. The feedback we are getting, however, indicates that something is not working and will continue manifesting until we pay attention to it. There is a disconnect between the way we currently make meaning in the world and the feelings and wisdom anchored in our bodies. From there, we can start revising the inherited and shared beliefs shaping our unsustainable paradigm.

If we add to this that we are entering an era of unpredictable expansion of AI into all domains of our life, as well as unpredictable feedback loops and climate tipping points resulting in unpredictable impact on economies and society, what do educators need to focus on to prepare a new generation to be resilient and to thrive? With Teilhard de Chardin's *noosphere* becoming a reality, and any imaginable information accessible at our fingertips, what is the new goal and purpose of education (Fuchs-Kittowski & Krüger, 1997)?

Extensive lists of sustainability competencies are being developed (Binkley et al., 2012; Lozano et al., 2017; Wiek et al., 2011), calling for systems thinking, future thinking, values thinking, strategic thinking, interpersonal competencies, and implementation skills. Less attention, however, is being given to the power of emotional and spiritual intelligence as a lever of transformation, creating a deeper engagement to action. It seems time to go back to the ancient message carved into stone *at the entrance of Apollo's temple at Delphi in Greece: Know thyself.* Our collective fascination with technology needs to be balanced with a new focus, developing our *humanness.* These paths lead to spiritual intelligence, self-awareness, an understanding of our own and the contemporary world's paradigms, and tap into the profound wisdom of our soul and intuition.

For over two decades, a select group of educators have been interspersing their classes with questions like: Why are you here? Why are you doing what you are doing? What makes you *you*? What is your larger purpose? What difference do you want to make? Where are you on the journey? These questions plant seeds in the minds and hearts of their students and launch them on a provocative journey, seeking and crafting the most authentic version of themselves. The transformational power of these experiments addressing the soul has only started to be documented (Hermes & Rimanoczy, 2018; Yang, 2016). I believe we may have found the most underutilized, pervasive source of transformation. We may be shaping not only a more sustainable future but also a more compassionate, imaginative, and peaceful humanity, and possibly also a happier and more resilient one.

It is easy to doubt this and see it as pollyannish and utopian. Earlier in this chapter, however, I mentioned that barely 20 years ago the most ambitious and courageous goal of business leaders was to do less harm. And this goal was discounted as unrealistic and utopian by boards and leadership teams. But over time they began a vision of something even better, and soon people coalesced around the idea of doing something perhaps crazy, but great.

Today, it is unthinkable that any organization would declare that their most ambitious and courageous goal is to do less harm. In 2024, ambitious goals are to restore ecosystems, create flourishing communities, and develop just and fair societies. Our collective moral standards have shifted. How did this happen? Who led this? It was not a set of regulations, or some centralized plan communicated by a supreme leader. It happened by distributed leadership, individuals empowering one another, including children, seniors, women, and activists of all sorts, and also journalists, artists, the youth, spiritual leaders, poets, philosophers, farmers, and yes, educators. In an impalpable way, these messages pervade our cultures across the globe, multiplying and generating a subtle and collective shift in our narrative. We cannot stop now.

References

30th Anniversary Human Development Report (UNDP 2020). https://hdr.undp. org/system/files/documents/hdr2020overviewenglishpdf_1.pdf. Accessed February 20, 2024.

Anderson, R. C. (2009). Sustainability and the bottom line: The responsible collusion of economics, social responsibility, and the environment. *The Journal of Values-Based Leadership, 2*(1), 2.

Binkley, M., Erstad, O., Herman, J., Raizen, S., Ripley, M., Miller-Ricci, M., et al. (2012). Defining twenty-first century skills. In *Assessment and Teaching of 21st Century Skills.* Springer Netherlands, 17–66. doi:10.1007/978-94-007-2324-5_2

Fuchs-Kittowski, K., & Krüger, P. (1997). The noosphere vision of Pierre Teilhard de Chardin and Vladimir I. Vernadsky in the perspective of information and of world-wide communication. *World Futures: Journal of General Evolution, 50*(1–4), 757–784.

Hermes, J., & Rimanoczy, I. (2018). Deep learning for a sustainability mindset. *The International Journal of Management Education, 16*(3), 460–467.

Irwin, L., Rimanoczy, I., Fritz, M., & Weichert, J. (Eds.). (2023). *Transforming business education for a sustainable future: Stories from pioneers.* Taylor & Francis Group.

Ivanova, E., & Rimanoczy, I. (Eds.). (2021). *Revolutionizing sustainability education: Stories and tools of mindset transformation.* Routledge.

Kassel, K., & Rimanoczy, I. (Eds.). (2018). *Developing a sustainability mindset in management education*. Routledge.

Lozano, R., Merrill, M., Sammalisto, K., Ceulemans, K., & Lozano, F. (2017). Connecting competences and pedagogical approaches for sustainable development in higher education: A literature review and framework proposal. *Sustainability, 9,* 1889. doi:10.3390/su9101889

Meadows, D. (1997). Places to intervene in a system (in increasing order of effectiveness). *Whole Earth, 91*(1), 78.

Mezirow, J. (2008). An overview on transformative learning. *Lifelong Learning*, 40–54.

Rimanoczy, I. (2016). *Stop teaching: Principles and practices for responsible management education*. Business Expert Press.

Rimanoczy, I., & Turner, E. (2012). *Action reflection learning: Solving real business problems by connecting learning with earning*. Hachette UK.

Ritz, A. A., & Rimanoczy, I. (Eds.). (2021). *Sustainability mindset and transformative leadership: a multidisciplinary perspective*. Springer Nature.

Sunley, R., & Leigh, J. (Eds.). (2017). *Educating for responsible management: Putting theory into practice*. Routledge.

Wiek, A., Withycombe, L., & Redman, C. L. (2011). Key competencies in sustainability: A reference framework for academic program development. *Sustainability Science, 6,* 203–218.

Yang, C. (2016). Mindfulness meditation and art appreciation as meaning-making practices. In *Academy of Management Proceedings* (Vol. 2016, No. 1, p. 10393). Briarcliff Manor, NY 10510: Academy of Management.

2

THE POSITIVE IMPACT RATING AS A PLATFORM FOR CHANGE

Katrin Muff and Thomas Dyllick

Abstract

This chapter outlines how business schools can accelerate change by collaborating with their own students. It uses the Positive Impact Rating (PIR) for business schools as an example and tells the story of how a group of PIR schools collaborated at an institutional level for a year to identify and implement change at each of their schools. The PIR Working Groups were launched at the PRME Global Forum in New York in June 2023, and the topics for the different working groups came from the 2023 PIR edition, where students from all over the world were asked to evaluate their own schools – to "STOP doing" and "START doing" to improve positive impact. The Collaboratory methodology, developed in the context of the 50+20 project, offered an ideal framework for the PIR Working Group sessions. The Collaboratory is used here on two levels: on the collective level for the PIR Working Groups and on the individual school level. For the latter, we use a case study from a master's course at the University of St. Gallen and highlight experiences from several PIR schools.

Setting the stage

Our personal mission: transforming business education

This chapter builds on our experience in the field of sustainability management and responsible management education in each of our careers. Katrin, as a highly engaged Dean at a small, privately run international business school in Switzerland, where she transformed business education across the whole school and its faculty and systematically integrated sustainability into

DOI: 10.4324/9781003521839-3

all programs and courses. Thomas, as an equally engaged professor in sustainability management, is Dean of the School of Management and Vice President of the University of St. Gallen, a leading Swiss and European business school. We have both focused on changing the business school landscape not only at own organizations but also on a broader institutional level. Our thinking has been shaped by our work as co-creators of the 50+20 initiative (Muff et al., 2013), which developed a vision for business schools serving people and planet. In parallel, we co-created an executive program in sustainability management which has been running since 2011. And more recently, we co-founded the Positive Impact Rating for Business Schools (https://www. positiveimpactrating.org/home), a radically new and different rating system with students as the focus and main driver, who assess the positive impact of their own school. We consider ourselves incurable thought leaders and change agents in the responsibility and sustainability management fields.

The foundational role of the 50+20 vision

Many conceptual roots for us can be found in the 50+20 vision, which was developed between 2010 and 2013 by a large, interdisciplinary group of academics, business schools, and thought leaders from many walks of life. At the core of this highly collaborative work is a vision of management education that does not aim to guide business schools to become "the best *in* the world" but rather to become "the best *for* the world." It was launched at the PRME Global Forum at the international Rio+20 conference in Rio de Janeiro in 2012 and proposes a new vision for management education. The vision is developed in the book "Management Education for the World" (Muff et al., 2013, as a book and a film).

The 50+20 vision proposes three key roles for business schools: educating and developing globally responsible leaders, enabling business organizations to serve the common good, and engaging in the transformation of business and the economy (see Figure 2.1). At the heart of the vision is the Collaboratory, representing a methodological as well as physical space of co-creation to resolve issues relevant to society, including climate change, biodiversity, hunger, and inequality. The Collaboratory has been defined as "an inclusive learning environment where action learning and action research meet and involves the active collaboration of a diverse group of participants bringing different perspectives to a given issue or topic" (Muff et al., 2013, pp. 64–72; Muff, 2014a). We see the Collaboratory as a core philosophy of management educators whose task is to facilitate collaborative learning and research processes. It builds on the belief that business schools are excellent conveners for resolving wicked societal issues.

A new rating system for business schools: the Positive Impact Rating

We were also among a group of 50 scholars who developed a new rating system for business schools called the Positive Impact Rating (PIR), begun in 2016. Launched in 2019, the PIR is based on the 50+20 vision of the role of business schools. Its purpose is very different from existing rankings and is based on a different set of measurements. As a result, the PIR answers a unique set of questions: Which business schools are true leaders in creating societal impact? Which schools are developing students as change agents? Which schools effectively walk their talk in creating impact, and which schools have processes in place to integrate their students' voice into key decisions (Dyllick, 2023; Dyllick & Muff, 2020)?

We knew that if we wanted to shift the focus toward tangible societal impact, we would need to hear and include stakeholders' voices. In intensive discussions with representatives from student organizations and societal stakeholders such as Global Compact, Oxfam, and the WWF, we tried to understand how to measure positive impact. And here the foundational ideas of the 50+20

Educating
- Transformative learning
- Issue-centered learning
- Reflective practice and fieldwork

Enabling
- Research in service of society
- Supporting companies toward stewardship
- Accompanying leaders in their transformation

Engaging
- Open access between academia and practice
- Faculty as public intellectuals
- Institutions as role models

COLLABORATORY
- The preferred place for stakeholders to meet
- Collaborative action learning and research platforms

FIGURE 2.1   The 50+20 vision.

vision proved invaluable. The PIR methodology comprises three broad attributes that collectively encompass seven dimensions: Energizing (governance and culture), Educating (programs, learning methods, and student support), and Engaging (institution as a role model and public engagement).

The PIR assessment targets a stakeholder group that is usually neglected: the school's own students. To conduct these surveys, PIR works with both schools and local or international student organizations such as oikos International and Net Impact. It seeks to not only measure impact but also enable a closer connection between the school and its students. PIR is designed for this dual purpose: First, as a rating tool to measure, report, and compare the positive impact of different business schools, and second, as a tool for school development as well as a place for sharing learning and co-creating change at and across business schools.

In the first five years of the PIR's existence, we have come to realize that the student voice greatly matters to schools – it is often an important enabler of internal change. Students know their schools from their own experience, they care about their education, they are clear in their criticism, and they are willing to help effect change. Schools that have built a trusting relationship with their students tell amazing stories of accelerated transformation. Examples are EADA in Barcelona, Spain, S.P. Jain Institute of Management and Research in Mumbai, India, CENTRUM PUCP in Santiago de Surco, Peru, and the Antwerp Business School in Belgium.

Overview of the chapter

This chapter outlines how business schools can accelerate change by collaborating with their students. It tells the story of how a group of PIR schools collaborated at an institutional level for a year in five sessions to identify and implement change at each of their schools. The PIR Working Groups were launched at the PRME Global Forum in New York in June 2023. The topics for the different working groups were drawn from the 2023 PIR edition, where students from all over the world were asked to share their expectations toward their own schools to STOP doing and START doing in order to improve the positive impact of their schools. We used the Collaboratory as methodology. The Collaboratory can also be used at the individual school level. The chapter also provides insights and recommendations based on a case study from a master's course at the University of St. Gallen and highlights the experiences of several PIR schools.

Transforming business schools using the PIR

Using the PIR student feedback as starting point for a change process

When we launched the PIR in 2019, we had purposefully focused on students as a single stakeholder perspective. Students, we realized, offer a unique opportunity in the transformation process of a school: They are present at the school, they are recipients of the school's educational offerings, they become the carriers of that education to the business world, and lastly, they are keen and critical participants and observers of what is going on at school. Their appetite for learning and for acquiring new and relevant competencies as well as their sharp sense of concern for what is going in the world are valuable attributes of positive changemakers. Many schools, however, have been reluctant to engage with students, and it has taken courage for them to participate in the PIR. We consider the 100 schools worldwide that have engaged so far in the PIR process as pioneering business schools, and we are keen to help them integrate this valued stakeholder voice into their ongoing change process.

We also quickly realized that the student input collected through the Positive Impact Rating (PIR) was of incredible value. In addition to assessing their school in the three areas, Energize, Educate, and Engage, the two open-ended questions on "What should your school start doing?" and "What should your school stop doing?" have generated a rich source of qualitative data. In the first four years, we have collected between 8,000 and 12,000 responses which we have analyzed and transformed into general recommendations for all schools. Since 2023, thanks to the rapid growth of artificial intelligence, PIR has also provided each participating school with a personalized analysis of the top five items from their student responses.

The seven topics identified by students in the 2023 PIR rating

In preparation of the PIR Report 2023 (www.positiveimpactrating.org), we also worked with two Co-Presidents from oikos International, Darija Miletic and Carolin Lemke, to collate top student concerns. They identified six topics with a further topic added during the PIR Summit, here finalized as the seven topics of the PIR Working Group 2023–2024:

1. Integrate sustainability broadly into the curriculum now (and make it mandatory)
2. Address relevant practical problems and solutions
3. Integrate stakeholders from business and society into the learning process
4. Stop unethical partnerships
5. Make sure the teaching faculty is open-minded and committed to the topic
6. Clean up your act: Stop the waste of resources on campus (plastic, paper, food, energy, etc.)
7. Ensure diversity and inclusion on your campus, among staff, and in your programs

To put the dual purpose of the PIR into practice – as a rating tool and as a transformational tool – we created a one-year Collaboratory process for interested PIR schools to develop new prototype solutions in these selected topics.

An overview of the methodology used for the change process

The Collaboratory process was originally developed in the context of the 50+20 project (50 + 20 project webpage) and offered an ideal outline for the PIR Working Group sessions (Muff et al., 2013, pp. 64–72). It was designed to solve wicked problems by engaging with concerned stakeholders in a collaborative process. And changing a business school may well be considered a wicked problem! The purpose of the PIR Working Group sessions was to offer a carefully curated series of online sessions that would allow the development and testing of prototype ideas at various schools around the world, ideally to be shared with other PIR schools.

The PIR Working Groups were launched at the 2023 PIR Summit in June 2023. A big part of the summit was designed around the identified topics, each facilitated by a PIR school student. The feedback from the deans, directors, and professors at the Summit was phenomenal, as was their appreciation of the value provided by students leading these conversations. After the summit, an invitation was sent to all PIR schools to register for a PIR Working Group session starting in September 2023.

In the meantime, Katrin adapted the Collaboratory process to fit a multi-school online process. A critical element of the design was to have students lead and facilitate the process and to have Deans or Directors act as chairs for the seven topics. To ensure diversity, each school's participation was limited to two representatives covering administration, faculty, or students.

PIR also engaged one of the students who had co-facilitated the 2023 PIR Summit at the PRME Global Forum, Verity Blackburn. Verity was completing her master's degree as well as serving as oikos President at St. Andrews University in Scotland, one of the PIR schools.

Overview of the five two-hour online sessions of the PIR Working Groups, which will be described in more detail in the following section:

- Session 1: Understanding the problem – listening to all stakeholders
- Session 2: Visioning the problem solved – identifying prototype ideas
- Session 3: Developing viable prototypes – selecting courageous school teams
- Session 4: Quick innovation – reporting on quick fails, early wins
- Session 5: Confirming scalable solutions – selecting case studies to share

The Collaboratory process for multiple schools

While our process is designed for multiple schools, we hope that the following inspires institutions to run a Collaboratory at their own school. Alternatively, if a school prefers to experience the multitude of ideas that come from a multi-school process, PIR is happy to welcome interested schools to participate in a collective learning process. Let us now look at the Collaboratory process in more detail.

Session 1: Understanding the problem – listening to all stakeholders

The purpose of the first session is to ensure that all participants as well as their perspectives and insights are welcomed and appreciated. Otto Scharmer calls this the "downloading" phase in his Theory U approach (2009). Our two-hour session is designed so that participants first meet in a plenary representing all seven topics, to set expectations. Prior to the first session, we identify one student for each of the seven topics who is prepared to facilitate a breakout session and at least one admin or faculty member from the participating schools to serve as a topic chair. In the breakout groups which follow the plenary, the students share their insights from the PIR global student survey as well as their own personal experiences. Other participants in the session are then invited to share their perspective on the topic and to collect the participant insights in a nicely designed online board (we use Mural, but any software should work). Returning to the plenary, the students then share the collected insights for each topic, which also allows each participant to learn about the other topics. As many participants have multiple topical interests, they appreciate being brought up to date across all topics.

Session 2: Visioning the problem solved – identifying prototype ideas

The second session is about letting go of known solutions or viewpoints and diving into a world of new ideas and possibilities. For this, we first onboard new additional participants and bring everybody up to speed regarding the essence of session 1. This is to have everybody present and ready. Now comes the tricky part. We embark on a five- to ten-minute shared visioning process, basically a guided meditation, in which the lead facilitator takes everybody into a future world where the identified problems have been resolved. Given that the topics cover many aspects of a business school, I prepare a visual journey that touches on each of the seven topics. It takes a bit of courage and experience to ask participants to close their eyes and to anchor themselves in their body, to focus on their breathing, and to step into a shared consciousness space. I have done this in many settings, small and large; the first one at the RIO+20 conference. With 450 participants it was scary, but since then I have learned that it works (detailed instructions of how to conduct such a visioning process are available in Muff, 2014b, pp. 238–239).

At the end of the shared visioning process, participants choose a breakout session based on their topic where student facilitators are prepared to collect the impressions of the visioning exercise and to collect what they have seen, smelled, heard, and experienced through the prepared online murals board. This is the most vivid experience of the process as each insight builds – pearl after pearl – to a total vision which the participants experience together. Each breakout session then designs a first emerging shared vision of their topic in a short one- or two-sentence description.

Session 3: Developing viable prototypes – selecting courageous school teams

As there are regularly new participants in each session, it is important to onboard them and to ensure their perspectives are welcome and appreciated, as otherwise they may obstruct the process. To achieve this in our 2023 Working Group, Verity, our lead student facilitator, shared the visions developed in session two for each of the topics. All participants were then given space and time to comment and to add to the vision across all topics, which allowed for rich additional input as well as verification of the visions, and also the possibility to contribute to other topics. Session 3 then focuses on imagining new prototype ideas that bridge the current reality of each school present with the future vision that was co-created. Individual school participants then adapt the vision to their particular school and identify first steps they would like to test in reality.

At the end of this session, we had a dozen schools who had committed to hold a first conversation with their Deans and Administration about the possibility of developing a prototype solution in the coming months. For example, two schools were going to explore a cross-disciplinary course, a South American school was considering a safe space for student mental health issues, a UK-based school was considering an interactive learning space for students and faculty, a United States school was going to check out incentives for non-research-related work of faculty, and two European schools were each going explore hosting a roundtable on unethical partnerships.

Session 4: Quick innovation – reporting on quick fails/early wins

In preparation for session 4, Verity reached out to all of the schools that had committed to developing a prototype. She wanted to know how many of them had updates and what the quality of this feedback was. Not surprisingly, a number of schools were unable to implement their ideas as quickly as planned. As a result, we created an additional space for another round of ideation for new prototypes. We also created a template so that schools could plan what it would take to implement their prototype. We wanted them to come up with a set of steps for the next 3–6–9–12 months. At the end of this session, the students focus on obtaining a commitment from the schools to implement the first steps of their prototype in the following two months and to report on whatever result they achieved in the next session.

Session 5: Confirming scalable solutions – selecting case studies to share

In this session, the schools starting to implement their prototype ideas share their insights about challenges, obstacles, and the early wins they have experienced so far. While the prototypes vary depending on the topic and the geographic region, the reasons for a potential failure in implementation are similar. As with any new project, the challenge exists in integrating it into existing activities and ongoing projects. Top-level buy-in is also needed to ensure project support when competing priorities challenge resource allocation. We have found that embedding a project into an existing school process, such as a project space in a curriculum, can be an effective way to ensure its further continuation.

Challenges and insights

As in any change process, going from an initial (great) idea to an implemented successful solution has its challenges. We have seen many schools face difficulties in implementing initial prototype ideas, as these new projects end up competing with the limited resources of the school. The opportunity to share a prototype project as a case study in a global peer community, however, can sometimes also create support at home.

We recommend schools find a way to embed such change projects into their curriculum. Imagine a project to reduce plastic waste at school. The idea may have emerged from a PIR student survey and can be kicked off and worked on in a regular sustainability leadership (or project management) course at the bachelor's or master's level. Students can lead the project, working with relevant stakeholders at the school and reporting on what has been achieved during the course. In the next semester, the project can be further advanced by another group of students. Goa Institute of Management in India has had success with such a format, in its GIVE GOA program which hands over projects from year to year to a next cohort of students. Additional concrete examples are outlined in the next section.

Also, most undergraduate and graduate programs have either a course or a for-credit project space that can serve as a container for such projects, especially as the student energy is often an important resource to advance such labor-intensive project items. Finding a way to give students credit for their work and embedding the project into the curriculum increases the chances of its success. In addition, creating such a space in the curriculum ensures that such student-led initiatives will become an ongoing part of the school, bringing students and the administration closer together.

The Collaboratory process for individual schools

Let us now look at how a school can integrate the PIR student input and the Collaboratory process to accelerate change in their organization. First, a school is welcome to join the annual PIR Working Groups using the methodology outlined in the previous section. A participating school can send two representatives and follow our process as a "user" without having to invest in the process or in the facilitation of events. It serves as a great starting point for schools that would like to explore working with students in developing change. However, for schools with an appetite and the capacity to run such processes by themselves we conclude with examples where an individual faculty or a school has started such actions. We hope that they will demonstrate how to go about it and encourage fellow change agents to launch into action.

I (Thomas) have used the Collaboratory process in one of my master's courses (Strategies for Sustainable Development) at the University of St. Gallen since 2013. Each year, I have picked three current societal issues to work on with my students. In general, I have had 40–50 participants with the students selecting which issue to work on, ensuring a balance of participants across the groups. What follows is one example which also serves as a broader illustration of the process: How to make tap water the most popular drink in Switzerland? (Dyllick & Muff, 2014).

The general outline of the Collaboratory process builds on Otto Scharmer's Theory U (2009). After a first session dedicated to understanding the topic, the students identified with Thomas four relevant stakeholders for Collaboratory 1. They invited the Head of Communications of the Swiss Water Works, the General Secretary of the Swiss Association of the Mineral Water Industry, the Head of Quality Assurance of the St. Gallen Water Works, and the manager and chef of a popular St. Gallen restaurant.

The half-day Collaboratory 1 had three objectives: First, to acknowledge the challenge of listening to and understanding each of the different perspectives presented by the invited stakeholders (downloading phase); second, to develop a collective vision of what the world would look like if the issue was resolved (visioning phase); and third, a first round of ideas for making concrete steps in resolving the issue through back casting from the future to the present (harvesting phase). This was achieved by developing a set of concrete prototype ideas to be worked on in the next session. The students organized the whole session, from inviting the external stakeholders, setting up the room, preparing, and leading the discussion, to reporting on the results and defining the next steps. Thomas served as a guide and coach to the students, not as an all-knowing "sage on the stage."

The half-day Collaboratory 2 built on the ideas harvested in Collaboratory 1. Its objective was to develop specific action plans for the most relevant ideas, and to involve experts that could implement these action plans. Three priority areas were defined for further investigation: the University of St. Gallen, the City of St. Gallen, and restaurants in general. Relevant experts and guests included the Head of Infrastructure, University of St. Gallen; the Director of Public Services, City of St. Gallen; the CEO of Switzerland of an International Water Dispenser company; and the President of the Association of Restaurants, Canton of St. Gallen.

The students split into different groups, each including one external expert, to define core ideas for putting the ideas into practice. Again, the students were responsible for setting up the groups, and for moderating and capturing the discussions. The students then presented the emerging ideas in a plenary with students and experts jointly commenting and selecting the most promising ideas for implementation. Afterward, the small groups reconvened and developed specific action plans, which were again presented in a plenary.

This course has had surprisingly positive results, repeatedly year after year. The engagement of the students and their learning outcomes have been impressive. Their experiences and learnings have been recorded in individual reflection papers and demonstrate how deep an impression the course has made. Throwing the students into cold water by facing real experts addressing real-life issues, while offering a clearly defined process as well as help from the sideline, has proven a magic formula. The ideas and results are creative and often realistic. For example, the students convinced the University St. Gallen to install public water stations, so that they didn't have to refill their bottles in the bathrooms. The students were a part of the internal meetings to implement this change and gained experience in the diverse skills necessary between having an idea and selling it effectively with relevant arguments for the decision maker.

The external stakeholders and experts also left these discussions impressed by the students' great engagement and the relevance of their insights, won in an open, sharing atmosphere. And the students profited greatly from such expert knowledge and experience. As faculty, I (Thomas) was able to switch from my role as a sustainability expert to that of a moderator in this interactive and open learning process. This is a crucial change of roles which often proves as important as challenging because one has to step out of one's traditional comfort zone. In my case, an intensive phase of personal development training during a sabbatical semester was certainly very helpful together with gaining practical experience in participating in Collaboratory processes and using the method myself.

Two secondary outcomes of this course are also worth mentioning. One student decided to write her master's thesis on the particular competencies she obtained from the Collaboratory course she had participated in. Additionally, she developed a responsible leadership typology which was then used by Katrin to create a freely available online tool "Competency Assessment for Responsible Leadership" (www.CARL2030.org). The tool is used to assess varying degrees of competency for students and practitioners, such as assessing a group result before and after a teaching intervention. Separately, another student later applied the methodology at her workplace in the pharmaceutical industry. She conducted a full Collaboratory process with medical researchers about pharmacogenetic tests, helping them to arrive at new perspectives and conclusions in this critical area.

In addition to the University of St. Gallen example, there are many other examples of integrating PIR results in schools. We collect the most relevant ones each year and provide them in an online case study section (www.positiveimpactrating.org/case-studies). These include student–school collaborations from business schools around the world. Here are few examples:

- At **Audencia Business School** in France, the school's CSR Team and student associations cooperated closely to use the results of the previous PIR edition to identify areas of progress and to build a concrete action plan. They worked together to co-create a carbon footprint calculator for digital activities and launched a communication campaign for all new students.
- At **CENTRUM PUCP** its commitment to the Peruvian society has determined its vision and purpose as a "School for Good Business." The school added business training programs for small business owners and entrepreneurs, serving more than 100,000 people. Initially, teachers and administrative staff provided these programs; in a second phase, students from different degree programs have also joined in.
- As a follow-up to the Positive Impact Rating 2020 **Antwerp Management School** in Belgium developed a sustainability strategy together with its stakeholders, expressed in detail in the AMS Sustainability Progress Report.
- At the **Goa Institute of Management** in India the Centre for Social Sensitivity and Action and the Centre for Excellence in Sustainable Development together with student initiatives, created opportunities for students to engage in stakeholder dialogues, sharing and co-creating knowledge.

These case studies are a rich repository of insights for other schools, and how to use the PIR results to co-design and implement impact-related programs at your school. The previous examples are only a small selection and hopefully spark your interest.

Benefits to change makers at business schools

With the launch of the PIR in 2019, two objectives have been achieved with the involvement of students in the transformational efforts of business schools. First, the students can experience firsthand the unexpected challenges of implementing change and develop key competencies in overcoming these. This allows them to develop their strengths and to sharpen their profile. Second, the school can use the constructive energy of an important, but mostly neglected stakeholder – its own students – to create change in challenging new areas. The school's governance and culture will also benefit from the stronger influence of the students. And, as a result schools can become more open and agile, inviting change and developing their societal responsiveness by absorbing the ideas and expectations of a younger generation. This should also help make schools more attractive to new generations of students.

Clearly, any stakeholder can provide insights and ideas for change at a business school. In this chapter, we have focused on the student as a singularly important stakeholder and have explored how a school can work with students as a provider of change ideas. Also, as an intended bonus, the students benefit by acquiring critical changemaker competencies that will serve them in their future careers.

We are using the student survey of the PIR as an empirical starting base to generate ideas for change and development. The PIR measures the societal orientation and focus of a business school from the perspective of its students. It assesses a school's culture and governance, a school's teaching programs, as well as its learning methods and the support students receive in their impact efforts. It also assesses the degree to which a school educates graduates ready to be a positive force in society and to what degree a school is perceived to be a role model in the way it engages with its stakeholders. We have outlined how these ideas have informed the PIR Working Groups, enabling a dozen PIR schools to embrace concrete change projects as a result. By outlining the five sessions, we have sketched how the Collaboratory methodology can be used for guiding change processes. We are also confident that the case studies of these schools will help accelerate the rate of change at other business schools.

Additionally, the Collaboratory process can be used by a single school. We have shared an example of a master's course, which Thomas had developed and run at the University of St. Gallen. In our experience, the availability of a proven methodology such as the Collaboratory can serve as an important enabler for a successful change project. Many change agents have found inspiration and support in Katrin's Collaboratory book (Muff, 2014a).

In conclusion, let us summarize the benefits of using PIR insights and the Collaboratory at a single school:

- Students: Learn how to integrate sustainability at an existing organization in a concrete hands-on way – with all the obstacles and challenges – and acquire important future-relevant competencies,
- Faculty: Have a concrete process and continuous flow of ideas to advance the transformation of their business school,
- Administration and Dean's office: Obtain regular access to the constructive ideas and suggestions of students through the PIR survey, and
- Accreditation agencies/PRME: Receive a quantitative proof of a school's societal impact focus from the student perspective, and potentially a case study of how the school integrates students in its change processes.

For all those interested in working with students in the change process of a business school, we hope that the PIR survey serves as a useful tool to collect empirical insights from the student's perspective. You are invited to join a PIR Working Group which starts every September and can be joined from anywhere around the globe. And of course, if you have any questions or would like to compare experiences and insights, feel free to reach out to both of us.

References

Dyllick, T. (2023, October 24). Rating B-schools for societal impact: Fundamental questions about rankings – and a very different approach. *Poets & Quants.* https://poetsandquants.com/2023/10/24/rating-b-schools-for-societal-impact-fundamental-questions-about-rankings-and-a-very-different-approach/

Dyllick, T., & Muff, K. (2014). Students leading collaboratories: University of St. Gallen. In Muff, K. (ed.), *The Collaboratory.* Greenleaf.

Dyllick, T., & Muff, K. (2020, November 6). A positive impact rating for business schools: Case study. *Sustainability, 12*(22), No. 9551.

Muff, K. (Ed.). (2014a). *The collaboratory. A co-creative stakeholder engagement process for solving complex problems.* Greenleaf.

Muff, K. (2014b). Designing a collaboratory. In Muff, K. (ed.), *The Collaboratory.* Greenleaf, 229–245.

Muff, K., Dyllick, T., Drewell, M., North, J., Shrivastava, P., & Haertle, J. (2013). *Management education for the world. A vision for business schools serving people and planet.* Edward Elgar. Also published in Chinese by Peking University Press.

Scharmer, C. O. (2009). *Theory U. Leading from the future as it emerges.* Berret-Koehler.

Webpages and tools

50 + 20 project webpage. https://www.positiveimpactrating.org/50plus20. Provides access to the 50+20 book, the 50+20 agenda, the award winning 50+20 film, and the Rio + 20 experience with the public launch of the 50 + 20 project.

CARL – The Competency Assessment for Responsible Leadership. www.carl2030.org, a free online tool for measuring student progress in responsible leadership competencies, with supporting methodology and insights.

Positive Impact Rating for Business Schools (PIR). www.positiveimpactrating.org

3

A TEACHING JOURNEY FROM CORPORATE RESPONSIBILITY TO SYSTEMS UNDERSTANDING

Sandra Waddock

Abstract

Since beginning, my teaching has focused on attempting to establish ways for students to develop the capacity to think systemically about the issues and, more recently, crises, facing the world and the roles that businesses (and other institutions) play in creating and potentially dealing more effectively with them. That, of course, means becoming aware of and responsive to socio-ecological systemic issues. My own awareness, insight, and systems thinking capacity, however, needed to develop and evolve along similar lines as I hoped my students would before I could begin to share it at least moderately effectively with them. That process has been a journey of (so far) nearly 40 years. From a stance of fully accepting business as usual, my own thinking has evolved from mostly uncritical acceptance to a critical approach to catalyzing whole systems transformation toward both social and ecological (eco-social) thriving. This chapter shares that journey to a teaching approach that I hope fosters the emergence of systems-based understanding and recognition of the need for tomorrow's leaders to serve as change agents for catalyzing systemic change toward equity, inclusiveness, justice, and fostering life and well-being for all. I will not claim success with all students, but I will share that journey.

Introduction

Starting in the mid-1980s, my teaching (and, not incidentally, scholarship) initially focused on understanding how businesses could become more responsible to a broad set of constituents (stakeholders), initially through articulating how ethics, corporate (social) responsibility, and awareness of the external

DOI: 10.4324/9781003521839-4

environment influenced company behaviors. Over time, with growing understanding and awareness of my own, that stance has evolved to attempting to establish ways for students to develop the capacity to think systemically about and potentially act on the issues and more recently social and ecological (eco-social) crises facing the world, as well as the roles that businesses and other institutions play in creating and potentially dealing more effectively with those crises. I would note here that this journey aligns neatly with what Rimanoczy calls developing a sustainability mindset (Rimanoczy & Laszlo, 2017), though is focused more broadly on whole systems understanding.

The key pedagogical insight here, however, is that my *own* awareness, insight, and systems thinking capacity needed to develop and evolve along the very lines that I hoped my students would. Only then could I begin to find more effective pedagogical strategies for introducing them to systemic awareness – and the broader roles of businesses in our social–ecological systems. That orientation might be termed "sustainability"; however, I believe that the need is broader – for whole system transformation that encompasses all kinds of socio-ecological understandings, relationality, and responsibilities. Personally, over time, I moved from a stance of generally accepting business as usual, though always with some questions, toward a considerably more critical systems-based understanding of the role of context, ecosystems, and values. That also involved identifying the need for systemic change toward how businesses and other institutions are or could be involved in generating just, inclusive, equitable societies in a flourishing natural world, which is my current framing. While, in a sense, that was always the goal, my understanding of the system and what it would and will still take to bring that about has evolved significantly over time, and that is reflected in both my teaching and the content of my course.

This chapter thus shares a few core insights based on my experiences along with some of the approaches that I have used and am currently using in the classroom to bring about these insights and awareness. To wit: (1) Teaching is a journey that involves both our own evolving understandings and how we share those understandings with students and others. (2) We all grow and change over time, shifting our views both about the content of our courses and what we share with students – and how we do that, thus courses necessarily change as circumstances and our own understandings evolve if we approach teaching reflectively and interactively. (3) In that evolution, however, it is important to remember that while we may have been on a lifelong journey to whatever our current understandings are, most of our students are just beginning that journey. Therefore, it is important to try to figure out how to meet them where they are and not dump too much on them at once. Put differently, as a mentor once said to me in my doctoral program, in teaching "less is more": if students take away one core insight from each class session, you have done your job.

Some background

Teaching, like all processes, is for me an ongoing learning journey – and also hopefully for my students. I was truly lucky in my MBA in the late 1970s and doctoral programs at Boston University in the early 1980s to be exposed early on to systemic ways of thinking about the broader roles of businesses in societies – beyond profit maximization and growth, a perspective that has influenced just about everything since. Initially that happened in the MBA program through two courses that would today be called strategic management and business in society courses – in those days management policy courses – that shaped my thinking and my lifelong pedagogical and, not incidentally, scholarly journey.

Strategy and business as usual

The first course was more or less traditional general management/management policy as it was understood at the time. It was the second course, which emphasized the social (ecological was not a consideration in those days) roles of businesses in society, that blew my mind open. It was team taught by Henry Morgan, who later became dean, and Bob Dickie, a business law scholar. The course raised core ethical, social, and responsibility issues that were at the time considered quite marginal. Admittedly I came into the program with some of this orientation in mind, as I recall arguments with another, far more "conservative" student across the room. He argued strenuously that the sole purpose of business was profit maximization and growth, while I equally strenuously argued for a considerably broader set of responsibilities to what would soon become known as stakeholders. That learning and orientation to the role of the general manager and strategic management as understanding the business, social, and ecological roles of companies stuck with me through the doctoral program. There I gravitated toward Jim Post, a leading business in society scholar, as my dissertation chair. Jim had written an influential book with Lee Preston that emphasized a systemic "interpenetrating systems" approach to understanding business's social and political realities (Preston & Post, 2012). A second core influence was L. Dave Brown, an organizational theorist who early on had focused on whole system change with an action learning orientation (Brown, 1980).

Those orientations toward social responsibility and systemic change took root and found themselves in evidence when I joined Boston College's management school in 1986, where, luckily, there were two similar capstone courses in the MBA program, albeit only one undergraduate management policy (now strategic management) course. As a junior faculty member, I found myself teaching that strategy course for undergraduates, a case course with a common set of cases pretty much solely focused on business as usual. There was not a lot of room for innovation initially in that course, although my pedagogical philosophy became immediately clear: involve students in their own learning through active engagement in discussions, case analyses, and, where possible, controversy. Ecological issues, however, were not part of the picture. Remember that the Brundtland Commission Report (Brundtland, 1987), which introduced and defined "sustainable development" was not published until 1987. Further, social/ethical issues were barely considered during those early days, which were also relatively early days for the Social Issues in Management Division of the Academy of Management, which quickly became my academic home – and which, at the time, did include ecological issues to some extent.

So . . . my first teaching experiences focused strongly on fostering a business-as-usual, profit, and growth-driven approach to general/strategic management, with a case analysis orientation. Reasonably soon the strategic management framework introduced by Michael Porter as the five forces framework and other strategy content made their way into the curriculum, providing new analytical frameworks for students to use. Given my orientation toward active learning, during this period, students were asked to analyze cases using these frameworks to understand the industry and competitive contexts in which companies operated and, internally, using SWOT (strengths, weaknesses, opportunities, and threats) analysis. It is my impression today that strategy courses (and the field more broadly) still struggle to incorporate social issues, stakeholders, and, possibly even more so, ecological issues fully.

Business in society

Soon enough, I found myself teaching the second, more socio-politically and, ultimately ecologically oriented MBA capstone strategy course. That course was also taught through strategic/general management lens. There I attempted to convey that company executives needed to understand not just their competitive environment and internal SWOT (strengths, weaknesses, opportunities, and threats). I also broadened out responsibilities to consider how the external environment shaped strategic opportunities and threats, mostly through the lens of cases. In this course, however, I begin introducing various in-class exercises aimed at more fully engaging students in a topic they generally resisted. For example, based on my emerging research understandings from studying, for example, businesses' engagement in public–private partnerships and, a bit later, their corporate responsibility, this course offered students an opportunity to engage in the responsibilities of the firm debate. The focus emphasized questions like "what would Milton Friedman's neoclassical economics position be versus a more 'social' orientation for businesses?" Exercises included ethical analysis of various dilemmas managers might face sometimes drawn from cases and other times from students themselves. In addition, the course, still largely case-based, included broader case analysis that today would likely be termed PESTLE, that is, political, economic, social, technological, legal, and environmental, and hopefully be considered part of good strategic management.

Leadership for change

Around 1990, several schools of management colleagues, with several sociology colleagues, an inspirational graduate student convener, and a number of practitioners got together and designed a program called Leadership for Change (LC), which we co-organized and ran for about 17 years. Not only did this program greatly expand my teaching repertoire, in part because we sat in on each other's sessions, but it also exposed me and participants to ideas and in-class activities not strictly within the management disciplines. Aimed at mid-level managers, the LC program was actively hands-on, work-based learning oriented, and used numerous innovative pedagogical approaches rather than cases that drew on participants' own experiences, insights, and knowledge in developing on-the-job actions and initiatives for their own work-based projects.

Though my orientation was toward the broader social environment of business, that section was taught by a sociology colleague, so I ended up teaching the organizational-level module of the program. The goals of this module involved understanding organizations as both efficient and responsible learning enterprises, drawing here from Peter Senge's work on systems thinking and personal mastery, which was highly influential to my own thinking (Senge, 1994). It also included segments on managing stakeholder and nature-based relationships, using the total responsibility management framework that I had co-developed with Charlie Bodwell of the UN's International Labor Organization, which encompassed an ecological emphasis, and developing participants' leadership and change agency. Note here the inclusion of nature, albeit still not central to companies' strategy. By then I had also published a text called *Leading Corporate Citizens* that firmly placed companies within the context of their economic, political, and civil society stakeholders. Importantly all of that occurs in the broader context of the natural environment that was used to frame the positionality of companies in nature and society. As an illustration of how thinking evolves, today, I would envision what were initially intersecting circles representing the company's three contexts (social/civil society, political/legal, industrial) in the context of the natural environment as nested embedded circles, with the company nested in the center, in nested layers of economic, social/political/legal, and related contexts, all firmly embedded within the broader context of nature (see Figure 3.1).

One core exercise used both in LC and in the MBA classroom during this time was gleaned from a colleague in an attempt to develop students' capacities for futures and systems thinking. It asked students to begin to learn to think systemically by envisioning a potential future "Dark Ages and Renaissance" of an organization. Typically, in the LC program that was one of the participants' organizations to help ground their thinking in the reality of one of their own employers, while in the MBA classroom it might involve a well-known company or one based on a case analysis. Taking this context, learners were asked to identify what practices,

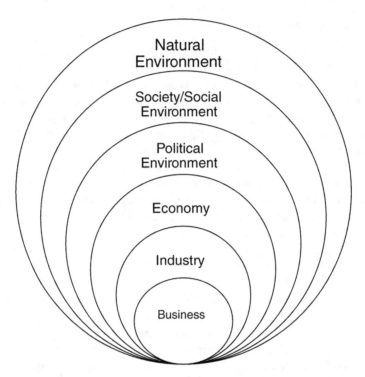

FIGURE 3.1 The nested eco-social context of businesses.

strategies, and activities got the company into the dark ages (or renaissance), what values were expressed in doing so, what stakeholder relationships were involved, and how well did the company manage its stakeholder and ecological responsibilities. Then they were asked how to get out of the dark ages or sustain the company's well-being in the renaissance. Their insights and visions were shared collectively to co-develop a whole-class conversation about these issues.

In another exercise, students in small groups were asked to conceptualize or "imagine" a new paradigm organization – one that takes into account issues of responsibility, accountability, and transparency, values, stakeholder relationships, and ecological sustainability, and is fit for purpose in a complex and difficult future. They drew an image of this organization and shared their conceptualizations by showing and explaining all the different drawings with classmates. In doing so, they identified the steps and actions needed to get to the envisioned future from a change agent perspective, including core drivers of resistance, and how a leader might overcome those obstacles. The sharing typically engendered interesting conversations about similarities and differences in their visions, different sets of values and responsibilities, as well as the issues and obstacles that arise.

University capstone

Some of these exercises have evolved to become part of the course I currently teach, a university "capstone" course that involves seniors reflecting on their journey so far, their values and passions, and their future. That course is offered through the lens of what I call "leadership and mindfulness," which today engages students explicitly in developing their systems thinking and change agency skills. That includes skills related to thinking about organizations in the context of the natural environment, to the extent that is possible in a one-semester course. Note, too, the slowly evolving introduction of "nature" or "environment" into these activities and courses over the years, especially as my own understanding of systemic issues evolved. Further, because this course includes students from across the university with a wide range of majors, an understanding of business cannot be assumed. Thus, the focus has shifted entirely away from cases, toward individual reflective exercises, which is a required aspect of university capstones, during the initial classes moving toward more systemic – and ecological – issues, activities, and understandings that affect enterprises of all sorts toward the end.

The progression of activities moves from a reflective focus on self in the past to the future, toward at least beginning to understand the bigger systemic context of societies today, where ecological issues like climate change, biodiversity loss, inequity, and related "sustainability" or eco-social issues predominate. For example, the course currently begins with a reading from David Korten on the broad ecologically embedded idea of ecological civilization (Korten, 2021). Throughout, there is an emphasis on students' potential agency as change makers and leaders. When systemic socio-ecological issues are emphasized about halfway through the semester, however, it is common for students to feel overwhelmed and discouraged. Note that the same is true of students in the business in society course, too.

To help learners enlarge their understanding of their own potential efficacy as systems-based actors, I use what I hope is an increasingly more systems-understanding-based series of activities oriented toward enhancing understanding of their visioning capacity, efficacy, and systems thinking. These in-class activities are accompanied by a short vision quest in nature and semester-long "do good in the world" project that, for most though probably, not all viscerally demonstrate their own leadership and change agency. The rest of this section briefly explains this series of exercises, which embody my current and long-standing orientation toward active learning via hands-on activities, as a way of illustrating the hoped-for progression.

- *Vision Quest.* This assignment, done outside of class, asks students to spend three hours alone in nature safely and without technology, food, or company. They are to do so with an intention of determining how they will serve the world, what their purpose might be, or some other question of importance to them. The key is, as with Indigenous peoples who seek wisdom and insight from nature, the students are asked to carefully observe nature around them, both living and inorganic beings, and see what they can learn from them. The time frame is limited to three hours because for many students spending time alone in nature is a relatively unusual experience and they are certainly not used to asking nature's beings for insights or lessons for their own life. They are instructed to ask permission, create a sacred circle where they settle, thank the beings who come to them with lessons, and then write up their insights and experience for a formal grade. While not all students allow themselves to sufficiently "let go" into this experience, for many it is in fact profound, with clear connections being made that might not otherwise be made. Most students express that typically they spend very little time in nature and almost none alone, and that they initially resented the assignment because of busyness and time constraints. Then they go on to state that they both learned a lot from nature's beings, whatever they observed, and hope to spend more time in nature in the future because they have already realized benefits.

- *Design Thinking Exercise.* Design thinking (Liedtka et al., 2018) has become an important way to introduce students to both systems thinking and the ways systems are designed – and can be changed – to achieve better socio-ecological outcomes. Prior to class, students read about the elements and processes of design thinking, that is, empathize, define, ideate, prototype, test, and get-together in their learning teams to figure out a local, typically university-based, issue that they think needs to be resolved. A frequent contender here is student mental health services, with food costs or service and housing assignment also common. Over the course of two, two and a half-hours class sessions students go through a series of exercises to diagnose what is currently happening in their chosen system. Steps involve: defining the problem, identifying key stakeholders to the problem, and then undertaking a force field analysis based on Kurt Lewin's ideas (Swanson & Creed, 2014) to assess what holds the system in place as is and what might help it shift. Once these steps are completed, they begin a brainstorming process that explores potential options for changing/redesigning the system and their envisioned outcomes, emphasizing divergent thinking, and then discuss those options to converge on one or more that they think would best resolve the problem holistically. The prototyping phase involves creating a diagram, image, or other type of description/model of their revised system. That is followed by a presentation of their ideas to the rest of the class and related discussion about how effective that solution is likely to be, the systemic implications of it (and what was and was not considered in their design), as well as the issues and unintended consequences, if any, that their solution potentially raises.
- *Systems Thinking/Sustainability World Café.* This exercise, which takes most of a class session and might be accompanied by the *Story of Stuff* and

related videos, was initially developed by colleagues in the Leadership for Change program discussed earlier and has been adapted for college seniors. In small groups, students pick or are assigned an item in popular use. Often items are present in the classroom that raise key systemic issues around social or ecological stability and sustainability. For example, I typically like to pick a non-reusable plastic water bottle because of its ecological and cost implications, a disposable coffee cup, a cell phone through a complex item, or an item of clothing. I also like to choose a banana because it is useful to identify the implications of monocultural crop production, particularly as bananas in current production are predicted to all be affected by a blight and may become unavailable in the not-too-distant future. Items with plastic are important to include, because it turns out that most of my students have no idea where plastic comes from. But just about any item will do to expose the social and ecological complexities and issues associated with producing, using, and disposing of these items in today's systems. The first part of the exercise asks students to address and draw an image of the system that produced and uses their item with respect to four key questions:

- What systems were needed to *create* this item? Where did it come from and how did it become what it is? Have them go to the roots of the production process here, ensuring that if the item is plastic, for example, they determine where plastic comes from and how it is produced, and allow them to look it up if necessary. If coffee or other crops are included, how is that crop grown and processed? Who does that? Under what conditions? All aspects of the item need to be addressed, for example, the ink on a plastic cup, the plastic lid, the paper if it is a paper cup, and so on.
- What systems are required to *supply* this item? How did it get here?
- What systems *use* this item? What does it do? How does it provide value? How long is it in use?
- What systems *dispose* of this item? Where will it go when it leaves here?

- Once the images are drawn, using pictures to the extent possible, which taps right brained, creative thinking and can enhance left-brained oriented analytical processes (McGilchrist, 2019), groups share their drawings and related insights with each other. In doing so, they identify and address the systemic complexity, interconnections, and socio-ecological implications of producing, distributing, using, and disposing of their item. You as an instructor might want to be prepared to address the issue of plastic, including plastic waste, that is, where it comes from, how it is made, its toxicity, how long it lasts in nature. In addition, be prepared to discuss the marketing and branding of some possibly not so useful and very costly products like bottled water in places where water is safe to drink, and similar systemic issues.

- If there is time and such issues haven't already come up, which likely they will have, you can introduce a second set of questions: What is the impact of your item on individuals, for example, cell phone addiction, wastefulness, organizations, society, and the planet as a whole? What does this item mean in the context of "being human" today? And, of course, any questions particularly relevant to your course content or to issues of ecological flourishing.

- *Mindmapping the Future:* The final in-class exercise in my current course involves groups of students "mindmapping" a better future or some aspect of the future, for example, future of leadership, social challenges, a better world for your children, future of organizations, future of nature, future of society, or a question you or students come up with that relates to your course content. The mindmapping process is explained here (https://www.tonybuzan. edu.sg/about/mind-maps/). Note that this exercise is an extension of the one described earlier used in the LC program. Once again, students draw their image of this future, including identifying shifts in core values, leadership actions, skills, and other issues relevant to your course needed to achieve this vision. You can also ask them to identify where and how their own leadership fits into that picture or other course-relevant questions. Though they are typically assigned different questions for each group, many of the visions tend to converge, which can generate an insightful conversation.

- *Do-Good Project.* The culmination of the capstone course as currently designed is students sharing the results and impacts of a semester-long project that they have undertaken with the general instruction "do something good in the world." While I provide ground rules and some ideas for possible projects, the set of instructions is: Use your creativity and leadership skills, including initiative taking, to develop something that does good somehow/ somewhere in the world. Possible focuses include but are not limited to sustainability/environmentalism, ethics in organizations, systems change and transformation, shifting economics/economies, building a better future for all including reducing inequality, inequities of all sorts, or social divisiveness, meeting some real need that has been unmet, offering education, information, hope, or creative new ideas on an issue you are passionate about to a specified audience, or . . . you tell me what your interest/passion is.

  - The project is oriented toward initiating a leadership activity and some sort of typically small systemic change, with impact measured to the extent feasible. Importantly, the idea is student generated and hopefully builds on a passion or something of clear interest to the student. Over the course of the semester, students have a 15-minute individual meeting with me to discuss ideas and submit two short written updates on actions taken so far. In addition, we have several in-class discussions of progress where they can request inputs or help from others.

- Deliverables are a formal written report and an in-class project presentation that demonstrates their leadership and what "good" or impact was achieved.
- This project serves to demonstrate in a quite visceral way that despite all the problems in the world, frequently discussed in class, it is possible for anyone, anywhere to have agency to make a difference. The outcomes of most of these projects demonstrate that agency to the individual undertaking and, collectively, to the class as a whole. As a note, project topics vary widely, ranging from developing social media guidelines for a new initiative on campus oriented toward disadvantaged youth, to fundraising for good causes, to developing mentoring programs within university clubs, to one that created a collaboration between the student newspaper and local news outlets and developed an ongoing internship with the local outlet. I do stress to students that their project must be doable within the context of a semester, so scope tends to be limited. With respect to nature, one student created an initiative explicitly oriented toward reducing "nature-deficit disorder."

Takeaways, personal insights, and conclusions

Over time, with experience and learning, my teaching has involved a long-term struggle to shift student thinking away from narrowly conceived ideas about the roles and purposes of businesses – and other organizations and institutions – in society toward a broader sense: that we are all responsible for generating the common good and civic well-being. Sharing this perspective has also involved efforts to help learners begin to "see" the system in which they are embedded and view it with a somewhat more critical lens than most typically have at the start of the course. That seeing includes recognition that human enterprises of all sorts exist within and are dependent on the natural environment. This approach also has involved different attempts over many years to help learners recognize that they too can take action to make change, however stuck the system might seem to be and however many crises abound ecologically and socially. That is not easy because wherever they are, most of the students I have met at least initially are firmly embedded in the existing system and seldom "see" any ways to change it. Nor do they necessarily assume they have much agency around change processes.

A personal journey shared with learners

Most importantly, though, this struggle has involved my own evolution along much the same lines as hoped for the folks whose learning I try to facilitate, because before I could begin to think about teaching in these ways and with these ideas, I too needed to understand and adopt them. While I have always advocated and implemented various forms of active learning to engage students in their own learning, the evolution has been toward finding ways for students to find their own interests and passions and take responsibility for their own agency as change makers who understand whole systems – socially, politically, and, importantly, ecologically. One thing that bears mentioning is that over the years I have learned and, sometimes, practice a variety of mindfulness techniques and approaches, which also appear prominently in the course to offer students multiple ways to induce their own mindfulness practices. Starting that journey involved reading systems theory and systems thinking, with Peter Senge's pathbreaking *The Fifth Discipline* (Senge, 1994), which advocates personal mastery – a mindfulness practice. Then, I moved through numerous of Fritjof Capra's books (Capra, 1983, 2005, 2015; Capra & Luisi, 2014), to studying popular press versions of complexity, chaos, and physics theories, and a wide range of other readings outside my field, which is where the interesting things are, as a mentor once put it.

Over time, and as my own thinking evolved toward more of a systems understanding embedded with an ethics, values-based, responsibility and ecologically oriented ethos that sought to ask companies to behave better for people, societies, and nature, I have been able to incorporate those ideas into teaching, too. That shift meant an evolution away from standardized case studies toward in-class activities that are more frequently these days student-defined. Cases, of course, have the advantage of exposing students to management practice and the business context, but they also have the disadvantage of limiting analysis to the information presented in the case and problem definition envisioned by the case's author. Activities based on students' own observations, experiences, and issue identification are less structured and therefore less amenable to teaching current business practice. Such approaches, however, involve students in topics that can be of more personal interest and engage them more fully in their own learning, fostering what I hope is active rather than passive learning. It also makes each class experience unique and unpredictable – and because of the interactive nature of this approach, makes learning more time-consuming than would be, say, a lecture or even a case, but potentially more impactful as learning theory suggests people remember best what they "do."

Takeaways and personal insights

My syllabus is constantly evolving and changes as I learn and incorporate new things. The "do good in the world" project, for example, is as of this writing in its third iteration. I have been surprised by the impact it seems to have had on students. This year in particular in the reflections that followed the set of presentations, students pointed out that they were impressed with their classmates' projects, which to them demonstrated that their classmates – and they themselves – could actually begin to make a systemic difference in some part of their worlds. That, to me, was incredibly gratifying as it signified that despite their earlier discomfort with systems thinking and the complexity of issues they face as future leaders, they recognized their own potential agency in ways that were not present at the start of the course.

There are other takeaways that I would tentatively offer bulleted as follows:

- The evolution of teaching, and understanding of how to do it, is a journey. Nothing stays the same for long, and periodically refreshing the course is necessary to cope with the evolving world as well as to ensure that I, as an instructor, am fully engaged. We evolve as teachers, as learners ourselves, and thus in what we can offer to our students as our own understandings and, presumably, insights grow.
- Since teaching, for me, involves constant learning, I have found it important to use and adapt good pedagogical ideas from wherever they arise and try them out. Then keep what works and move on from the rest.
- Students differ at different levels of their education and as the times have changed. Hence, it is important to consider where they are coming from, what their experiences have been and are, and attempt to meet them where they are. For example, at the undergraduate level where my current course is situated, that means orienting exercises not to managers and leaders in organizations but to their own institution (the university in this case) and personal contexts where feasible.
- Most students struggle to think systemically. They have not generally been taught to do so in their other courses. Despite their education, they can be largely unaware of critical socio-ecological or other systemic issues and need to be introduced to those things incrementally so they are not overwhelmed or too discouraged to feel like action is possible.

One important point: I have absolutely no idea how successful these interventions and exercises are in the long run. Feedback from learners at the end of semesters suggests that they have learned something and possibly have grown a bit, that particularly after the "do-good" projects, they might even have more trust in their own capacities. But that is for them, not me, to decide and only time and experience will tell.

References

Brown, L. D. (1980). Planned change in underorganized systems. In Cummings, T.G. (ed.), *Systems Theory for Organization Development*. Wiley, 181–208.

Brundtland, G. H. (1987). *Report of the world commission on environment and development: "Our common future."* United Nations.

Capra, F. (1983). *The turning point: Science, society, and the rising culture.* Bantam.

Capra, F. (2005). Complexity and life. *Theory, Culture & Society,* 22(5), 33–44.

Capra, F. (2015). The systems view of life: A unifying conception of mind, matter, and life. *Cosmos and History: The Journal of Natural and Social Philosophy*, *11*(2), 242–249.

Capra, F., & Luisi, P. L. (2014). *The systems view of life: A unifying vision*. Cambridge University Press.

Korten, D. (2021). *Ecological civilization: From emergency to emergence*. Club of Rome. https://www.clubofrome.org/publication/ecological-civilization-from-emergency-to-emergence/

Liedtka, J., Salzman, R., & Azer, D. (2018). Design thinking for the greater good: Innovation in the social sector. In *Design Thinking for the Greater Good*. Columbia University Press. https://doi.org/10.7312/lied17952

McGilchrist, I. (2019). *The master and his emissary*. Yale University Press.

Preston, L. E., & Post, J. E. (2012). *Private management and public policy: The principle of public responsibility*. Stanford University Press.

Rimanoczy, I., & Laszlo, E. (2017). *Big bang being: Developing the sustainability mindset*. Routledge.

Senge, P. M. (1994). *The fifth discipline fieldbook: Strategies for building a learning organization*. Currency.

Swanson, D. J., & Creed, A. S. (2014). Sharpening the focus of force field analysis. *Journal of Change Management*, *14*(1), 28–47. https://doi.org/10.1080/14697 017.2013.788052

4

TRANSFORMING BUSINESS EDUCATION TO CREATE REGENERATIVE VALUE AT SCALE

L. Hunter Lovins, Michael Pirson, and Walter Link

Abstract

"Life on planet Earth is under siege," say the world's leading climate scientists (Ripple et al., 2023). The Secretary General of the United Nations directly challenges business: "If you cannot set a credible course for net-zero, with 2025 and 2030 targets covering all your operations, you should not be in business" (Guterres, 2023). Business education needs to answer this imperative. It has to evolve beyond business as usual to support the full integration of business success and regional economic development with the regeneration of people and societies, nature, and the climate. We call this new DNA of the necessary economy "Regenerative Value Creation" (Now Partners, 2023).

Regenerative business

Unlike business as usual, regenerative business solutions serve all stakeholders in mutually reinforcing ways. They attract, for example, talent especially from younger generations who want to combine promising careers with serving the world. Consulting firm BCG reported that millennials have a strong preference to work for more sustainable companies (Hutchinson et al., 2023). Companies that engage employees in implementing more regenerative practices as part of their day job deliver increased productivity of up to 24% and a 21% higher profitability (Gallup, 2024). Similar numbers apply to other stakeholder groups such as investors (Versace & Abssy, 2022), consumers (Am et al., 2023), and business clients who increasingly see Regenerative Value Creation as a key element of performance.

DOI: 10.4324/9781003521839-5

This growing recognition that Regenerative Value Creation is becoming the business of the future has led us three principals of NOW Partners Foundation, to create the NOW ACADEMY. We previously helped found the United States' first accredited MBA in Sustainable Management in which sustainability and leadership were not electives but baked into every class (Presidio, 2007). Additional MBAs and hundreds of corporate programs followed in which we supported innovation leaders and many of the world's leading brands to chart their course into a promising future that builds economic success on positive impact for people and planet (Sroufe et al., 2023). We also helped to create a new management and leadership discipline that integrates knowing, doing, and being to activate purpose, passion, and capacities needed to succeed in Regenerative Value Creation (Hancock, 2022).

All of this was good. But none of it is enough. Our latest programs, co-created with many global partners from academia, the private and the public sectors aim to significantly grow the number of leaders who can successfully implement Regenerative Value Creation. Fortunately, across continents and industries, concrete solutions already demonstrate that Regenerative Value Creation is already the key to building sustainable economies and future fit business success. Companies and other stakeholders can learn from these pragmatic alternatives to business as usual and find the inspiration to act.

This chapter describes what is wrong with much of today's business education and outlines what we are doing about it. MBAs were, for many, a coveted terminal degree, especially if granted by prestigious institutions. Or so asserts the Director of MBA Admissions at New York University's Stern School of Business (*MBA – still a coveted degree*, 2010). But in 2023 applications for admission to schools of business globally fell by almost 5%. This followed a 3.4% drop in 2022 (Yahoo, 2023), leading the London Business School to declare that we are past "Peak MBA." To which the Financial Times columnist Pilita Clark declared, "Thank Goodness" (Clark, 2024).

Clark's article repeated a litany of complaints leveled at business education, most importantly the assessment, shared by many business leaders: MBAs are typically not sufficiently connected to the real world and evolving business needs. Leaders who don't understand the challenges to the current mainstream of business and who have not mastered Regenerative Value Creation are increasingly becoming a menace to their companies and the well-being of economies, societies, and nature. Increasingly financial markets are recognizing this trend. When Bayer, one of the world's largest chemical and pharmaceutical groups decided to buy Monsanto, a leader in GMOs and agrotoxins, it created the largest destruction of corporate value in the history of the German stock exchange. After paying 64 billion euros for Monsanto, Bayer's value collapsed to 57 billion euros (France 24, 2019).

Financial markets recognized that chemical agriculture, which systematically harms the climate, biodiversity, soil, water, and human health, is the land-use equivalent of energy generated by coal power plants and transport propelled by diesel fuel. Both are still with us, as we transition into the future, but savvy business leaders and investors know that these are dying technologies. They diminish not only natural and human capital but eventually also financial capital. At the recent UN Global Climate Summit COP28, even the major oil producers declared that they would phase out fossil energy systems in the foreseeable future. The U.A.E. is already one of the world's largest investors in renewable energy better business. This makes good business sense because renewable energy is now cheaper everywhere on earth than fossil technologies and is outcompeting polluting alternatives (Takemura, 2023). Now, Bayer has badged itself as "regenerative," with its head of Bayer's Crop Science unit saying, "Regenerative agriculture is the future of this industry" (Freitas, 2023).

Regenerative agriculture is where renewable energy was 20 years ago. Forward-looking leaders should learn about this now. In India, one million smallholder farmers in Andhra Pradesh are transitioning from chemical to true regenerative "Community-managed Natural Farming" or APCNF (Vijay Kumar, 2024). Within the first year of leaving chemicals behind, their profitability increases. By year 2, farmer income outperforms chemical agriculture on average by 50–80%. Many farmers earn far more. This innovative organic agriculture approach also strengthens food and water security, human health, and biodiversity and sequesters massive amounts of carbon. A banana farmer we met produces 50–100% more bananas, as well as 17 other crops that grow among the banana plants and mature before the bananas, providing the farmer with healthy food to eat and sell throughout the year. Under a chemical farming regime, this farmer needed to water his plants 6 hours a day. Now it requires only one hour every two days.

With such results, it is not surprising that APCNF grew from 40,000 farmers to 1 million in only seven years. Now it is being scaled, with the full support of India's Prime Minister, to many more of India's 120 million smallholder farmers. NOW Partners Foundation is working closely with APCNF to scale this innovative agriculture to the many other countries that want to adapt and implement it.

Among our masterclasses in Industry, Finance, and Leadership, NOW ACADEMY is also offering a class in Regenerative Agriculture in collaboration with the European Union's Innovation and Technology Institute. This covers APCNF and other farming and ranching approaches that are based on Regenerative Value Creation. For example, Native in Brazil, which produces one-third of the world's organic cane sugar on 50,000 hectares, strongly outperforms Brazil's sophisticated GMO and chemical agriculture. Its co-leader, Leontino Balbo, is asked by other farmers owning hundreds of thousands of hectares to optimize their performance in a wide variety of crops (Link, 2023).

The opportunity of great business education is to learn about the groundbreaking innovations that will become the mainstream solutions of the future. The leaders of the American, German, and Japanese car industry failed to take Tesla's innovations seriously, until Tesla's market value outpaced that of these countries' entire car industries. Now all car companies are playing catch up, struggling to transform their fleets from gasoline and diesel combustion to electric motors. Chemical agriculture will likewise go the way of the internal combustion engine; Regenerative forms of agriculture will be the new Tesla. This is predictable because technologies that are bad for people and nature will sooner or later be replaced by those that implement Regenerative Value Creation. The time to learn about these is now.

Yet too many business schools still teach business as usual. They socialize students to prioritize short-term profits, heedless that many corporate practices contradict natural laws, exceed planetary boundaries, and put life on earth at risk (Willcock et al., 2023). They forget that ultimately business can only make healthy profits in healthy societies and sustainable environments. While doing business in ways that moves us toward environmental and societal collapse may still be profitable in the short run, it is already bad economics. Using the International Disaster Database, researchers writing in Nature Communications calculated that global warming is already costing the global economy $16 million every hour (Newman & Noy, 2023).

Top leaders are waking up to these numbers and their implications. The World Economic Forum's annual survey asks global CEOs what they see as the top risks facing their companies. The 2024 edition listed extreme weather events as the second most serious risk, followed by social polarization (Global Risks Report, 2024). Global warming was seen as the top risk over the next decade, joined by critical change to earth's systems, biodiversity loss, ecosystem collapse, and resource shortages. Yet few business leaders are yet trained to recognize and manage such risks and how to turn resulting opportunities into profitable solutions that grow companies and economies into a sustainable future.

Paul Polman, former CEO of Unilever, in "Countering a Crisis of Greed" (Buckholtz, 2022) a piece written for the International Finance Corporation, argued,

> We cannot solve these issues of climate change or food security, of poverty, of inequality, just by optimizing our current systems. If the system itself isn't designed to work for us, we need to start working on broader systems changes, like making the financial market again subservient to the real economy, valuing next to financial capital also natural or environmental and social capital.

In other words, we need to learn how to activate Regenerative Value Creation.

Yet systems thinking and tools for systems change are not part of traditional business education. Reductionist thinking and siloed curricula that divide business activities and education into disconnected siloes are taught in discrete courses. Typically, sustainability and leadership are taught as separate and often elective classes that are not fully integrated with the financial and business aspects of curricula. This leaves graduates ill-equipped to find profitable, systemic solutions to resolve the interactive polycrisis of climate change, loss of biodiversity, worsening inequality and poverty, food insecurity, and loss of social cohesion, among a growing number of other crises. It feels overwhelming.

In a recent conversation, a next-generation business owner of a successful U.A.E. construction company said, "Everyone tells us that we have to become more sustainable, but no one tells us how we can do this profitably?" It's a question conventional business education does not answer in enough depth to equip learners to succeed. Recognizing opportunities to profitably solve challenges requires a deep, hands-on understanding of Regenerative Value Creation. Entrepreneurs and managers become more and more successful when they integrate such knowledge to make thinking and acting from this perspective second nature. Regenerative Value Creation has to become the core of business education to enable leaders to integrate it into strategy, corporate culture, and every aspect of operations.

Innovation for Regenerative Value Creation also benefits from timeless insights about human development. Human formation was traditionally seen as a holistic endeavor, best couched in the approaches to leadership development of the whole person. This leadership aims to elevate personal and societal flourishing that delivers economic success. We therefore integrate humanistic management theory and praxis that raises self-awareness and elevates human consciousness about intrinsic values and value creation into our masterclasses. These basic building blocks for ongoing personal and interpersonal growth instill lifelong learning and adaptive action in the unpredictable contexts of the polycrisis. They help unlock new opportunities for Regenerative Value Creation.

To meet the need for ongoing leadership development for Regenerative Value Creation, NOW ACADEMY developed a suite of programs aimed at professionals at all levels of career. Our customized programs enable learners to gain basic regenerative literacy rapidly and virtually. This can be delivered to all employees in a company, through hybrid courses to management and through learning journeys tailored for the C-Suite. All of the in-person and online programs take learners through a process of "Knowing, Doing and Being," to allow them to "Become" more successful leaders for Regenerative Value Creation. We support learners to recognize and create value that sustains economic success because it supports the flourishing of life on earth. This enables those in all sectors of the economy to meet the polycrisis with understanding, agility, creativity, and rigor.

"Knowing" focuses on the fundamentals of Regenerative Value Creation and basic sustainable business literacy. The business case for implementing more regenerative practices in your company details how caring for people and nature drives better business decisions and sustainable business results. It covers the challenges now facing companies and how to overcome them. The material goes beyond the traditional business case, engaging students in reflections and discussions of how to succeed in a world in crisis.

The "Doing" component introduces learners to a suite of tools to manage effectively in uncertain times. These include Integrated Bottom Line Accounting, Scenario Planning, systems thinking, and others. It challenges learners to apply the knowing portions of the curriculum to their own operations in ways that deliver increased economic performance and greater sustainability. At the same time, we provide in-depth case studies of leading organizations that already put in place regenerative practices, such as SEKEM, Natura, Philips, Unilever, and others.

"Being" introduces learners to the world's leading regenerative leaders. What is it that makes them so innovative and successful? From where do they, and we, draw their courage and purpose? How do they and we translate inspiration into concrete behaviors and actions that inspires our team members to become the best they can be as we co-create Regenerative Value?

To complement virtual learning, we organize in-person learning journeys that include in-depth meetings with the leadership teams of companies such as SEKEM in Egypt and Natura in Sao Paolo and the Amazon (Link et al., 2024).

Helmy Abouleish, CEO of the SEKEM Group, the Middle East's leading regenerative corporation, is another such leader. SEKEM includes companies in six industries producing a variety of products sourced from organic, biodynamic agriculture. This has already lifted thousands of farmers from poverty. Its Heliopolis University is with 3,000 students the region's largest sustainability development university. Its Whole Systems Carbon Credits scheme sequesters carbon while increasing biodiversity, health and food security, and social entrepreneurship (*Economy of Love*, 2024).

João Paulo Ferreira, the CEO of Natura, as well as Natura's Co-founders are regenerative leaders. Founded decades ago in Brazil as a purpose-driven start-up, Natura grew into one of the world's largest beauty companies that supports all levels of outer and inner beauty.

Natura's products are distributed across Latin America via direct sales by over 2.5 million "consultants," mostly women, often from marginalized communities. Natura provides them with sustainable products, business training, leadership mentoring, microfinance, high-tech supply chain management capability, and a mutually supportive community of business practice. Since decades, this has driven female empowerment in very concrete ways that also help societies evolve. With the purchase of Avon, the number of consultants across Latin America grew to 4.5 million.

Natura also helps build a sustainable bioeconomy in the Amazon where it empowers sustainable sourcing practices, collaborating with diverse local communities that include 5,500 families. Natura helps them develop production facilities that transform native plants into oils and products. As a result, these family earn several times the income they made from cutting trees, increasing the economic value retained in these communities.

Through economic ups and downs, Natura has maintained its deep human and environmental values and challenged the status quo. It demonstrates how to successfully integrate positive economic, social, and environmental impacts. For example, having achieved carbon neutrality already in 2007, it now showcases how climate solutions can support rather than hinder business success, even in large industrial companies. Natura's public "Integrated P&L" measures the societal impact of all of its activities. It shows that its social programs generate on average 1.5 dollars of benefit for society for each dollar of revenue. Each dollar invested in carbon reduction generates 20 dollars for society and nature. Each dollar invested in education generates even 30 dollars of positive impact. This demonstrates that economic prosperity is not the problem. Business programs should address this question of what kind of growth enhances business success as well as sustainability.

Becoming a Regenerative Leader begins with the person developing into their full human potential. We can't succeed in business and life as imitations. NOW ACADEMY enables leaders to develop their authentic path to excellence in Knowing, Doing, and Being to fulfilling lives and success in Regenerative Value Creation.

Higher education as now practiced is inadequate to the challenges of an earth under siege (Carrington, 2024). The transformation we propose is not to create yet another academy but to create the curriculum that all business schools will need to incorporate into their programs. Blending the best of what is now known about how to leadership to elicit people's highest potential, with the fundamentals of regenerative value creation, NOW ACADEMY will provide schools everywhere with the tools that they need to deliver graduates able to craft humanity's future.

References

Am, J. B., Doshi, V., Noble, S., & Malik, A. (2023, February 6). *Consumers care about sustainability-and back it up with their wallets.* McKinsey & Company. https://www.mckinsey.com/industries/consumer-packaged-goods/our-insights/consumers-care-about-sustainability-and-back-it-up-with-their-wallets

Buckholtz, A. (2022, February 15). *Countering "a crisis of Greed".* IFC. https://www.ifc.org/en/stories/2022/making-the-case-for-net-positive-companies

Carrington, D. (2024, May 8). *"hopeless and broken": Why the world's top climate scientists are in despair.* The Guardian. https://www.theguardian.com/environment/ng-interactive/2024/may/08/hopeless-and-broken-why-the-worlds-top-climate-scientists-are-in-despair

Clark, P. (2024, February 3). Thank goodness we've reached Peak Mba. https://www.ft.com/content/7608a866-c4f6-4b7b-bda3-6e9d8b115c00

Economy of love – economy of love. Economy of Love. (2024). https://economyoflove.net/

France 24. (2019, April 26). *Bayer shareholders vote against Board over Monsanto merger.* https://www.france24.com/en/20190427-bayer-shareholders-vote-against-board-over-monsanto-merger

Freitas, G. (2023, June 20). *Bayer sees 100 billion opportunity in cleaner-farming shift.* Bloomberg.com. https://www.bloomberg.com/news/articles/2023-06-20/bayer-sees-100-billion-opportunity-in-shift-to-regenerative-agriculture

Gallup, Inc. (2024, March 29). *Building a high-development culture through your employee engagement strategy.* Gallup.com. https://www.gallup.com/workplace/267512/development-culture-engagement-paper-2019.aspx

Global risks report 2024. World Economic Forum. (2024, January 10). https://www.weforum.org/publications/global-risks-report-2024/

Guterres, A. (2023). *Secretary-general's briefing to the General Assembly on priorities for 2023.* United Nations. https://www.un.org/sg/en/content/sg/statement/2023-02-06/secretary-generals-briefing-the-general-assembly-priorities-for-2023

Hancock, J. (2022, August 21). *Teaching teachers to teach values.* International Humanistic Management Association. https://humanisticmanagement.international/teaching-teachers-to-teach-values/

Hutchinson, R., Novacek, G., Chin, V., & Falco, G. (2023, May 25). *Socially transformative business is SMART business.* BCG Global. https://www.bcg.com/publications/2023/socially-transformative-business-is-smart-business

Link, W. (2023). Interview with Leontino Balbo. other.

Link, W., Eguiguren Huerta, M., Osgood, D., Cummings, T., Lovins, H., & zu Eltz, M. (2024, May 1). *Regenerative value creation in the regenerative market economy.* NOW Partners. https://now.partners/regenerative-value-creation-in-the-regenerative-market-economy-2/

MBA – still a coveted degree?. EducationTimes.com. (2010, February 24). https://www.educationtimes.com/article/editors-pick/69558785/mba-still-a-coveted-degree

Newman, R., & Noy, I. (2023, September 29). *The global costs of extreme weather that are attributable to climate change.* Nature News. https://www.nature.com/articles/s41467-023-41888-1

Presidio. (2007, January 17). *[node:title].* CSRWire. https://www.csrwire.com/press_releases/21379-presidio-school-of-management-ranks-among-top-bay-area-mba-programs

Regenerative value creation. NOW Partners. (2023, May 22). https://now.partners/regenerative-value-creation

Ripple, W. J., Wolf, C., Gregg, J. W., Rockström, J., Newsome, T. M., Law, B. E., Marques, L., Lenton, T. M., Xu, C., Huq, S., Simons, L., & King, S. D. A. (2023, October 24). *The 2023 state of the climate report: Entering uncharted territory.* OUP Academic. https://academic.oup.com/bioscience/article/73/12/841/7319571

Sroufe, R., Hart, S. L., & Lovins, H. (2023, September 13). *Transforming business education: 21st century sustainable MBA programs.* Archīum Ateneo. https://archium.ateneo.edu/jmgs/vol9/iss1/3/

Takemura, A. F. (2023, September 1). *Chart: Renewables are on track to keep getting cheaper and cheaper.* Canary Media. https://www.canarymedia.com/articles/clean-energy/charts-renewables-are-on-track-to-keep-getting-cheaper-and-cheaper

Versace, C., & Abssy, M. (2022, September 23). *How millennials and gen Z are driving growth behind ESG.* Nasdaq. https://www.nasdaq.com/articles/how-millennials-and-gen-z-are-driving-growth-behind-esg

Vijay Kumar, the founder of APCNF, to Walter Link, Andhra Pradesh. (2024, January). personal.

Willcock, S., Cooper, G. S., Addy, J., & Dearing, J. A. (2023, June 22). *Earlier collapse of Anthropocene Ecosystems driven by multiple faster and noisier drivers.* Nature News. https://www.nature.com/articles/s41893-023-01157-x

Yahoo! (2023, October 27). *GMAC survey: Global B-school applications dropped 5% in 2023.* Yahoo! Finance. https://finance.yahoo.com/news/gmac-survey-global-b-school-171657004.html

5

CLIMATE SAVVY GRADUATES

Because it is time, and we must

Kristin Kusanovich

Abstract

The discourse around transforming the business curriculum to address environmental sustainability, without simply conflating sustainability with financial viability, is now decades long. The climate and ecological emergencies are visceral, and the scientific consensus that the situation is perilous is undeniable. Some business schools are stepping up to develop compelling, program-wide, sustainability, or climate goals, but many are still teaching as if business as usual has not and will not stoke runaway global warming and ecological collapse, to name a few predicted tipping points. In response to understandably slow-moving processes of curricular overhaul, business school culture shifts, and resetting faculty mindset, or in the presence of resistance to larger changes, can immediately achieve robust learning outcomes about the climate crisis in any course they teach while the program they work in catches up to our climate reality.

The tUrn climate action model has inspired course-level transformations in and out of business schools for five years. This chapter suggests five action ideas for ensuring more climate savvy business graduates – ideas that are not dependent on curriculum overhaul, but ultimately support it. The five concepts include:

- converging toward a baseline understanding of the climate crisis,
- diversifying the sources and voices comprising the course content,
- personalizing the climate crisis for today's learners,
- fostering critique of business practices that perpetuate the climate crisis, and
- leading structured, effective reflections.

DOI: 10.4324/9781003521839-6

This framework has succeeded in transforming student, faculty, and staff wisdom and capacity to be involved in solutions. This chapter shares steps to take, followed by notes from a proverbial student lounge, and strategic and systematic tips for effecting successful climate crisis education one class at a time. It includes critiques of businesses and business schools that have not conceded their net effect on Earth.

Background

Many business schools are beginning to own up to the greatest failure of business since industrialization: the failure to address the climate crisis.

> In the past, extreme heating of 5°C above pre-industrial average temps was thought necessary to pass global tipping points, setting off a cascading and catastrophic series of scenarios, but the latest evidence suggests that this could happen between 1C and 2C. According to NOAA data, 2023 was the hottest year on record ever, with average temps 2.12 °F above the 20th-century average, meaning, we are now +1.18 °C above average with certain cities already at +2 °C.
>
> *(NCEI, 2024)*

> It is an excruciating experience . . . to watch the planet fall apart piece by piece in the face of persistent and pathological denial.
>
> *(Gelbspan, 1998).*

We cannot fashion a more just, humane, and sustainable world if there is no world to fashion. Climate action needs to be everyone's business and everyone's part-time side hustle.

Many business schools are beginning to own up to the greatest failure of business since industrialization: the failure to address the climate crisis, the failure to be honest about it with the public, to adjust harmful behaviors, and to minimize or prevent the worst effects. Virtually all commercial activities of medium and large-scale businesses have proceeded in a profit-driven, ethical vacuum, a system that tells itself that we have the right to maximize profits maximally and keep climate impacts off the spreadsheet.

I am a professional theater director, choreographer, and producer, whose professions require that I perform close observations of people's speech and movement patterns, character traits, and analyze verbal discourse. It is the job of a theater artist to unearth a person's or group's or community's motivations. How else can a convincing performance be built? I teach and publish in the fields of child studies, creativity, leadership, and critical arts-based research. I have taught in the business school and have observed the business school culture for several years by facilitating course discussions, attending lectures, interacting closely with business majors, and partnering with colleagues on a climate initiative called tUrn. I have experienced how climate conversations are embraced by a handful of informed members of the faculty and staff but avoided or mildly dismissed by most. I have observed how b-school culture performs itself in order to persist in forwarding a hegemony of ideas and power relationships, through its established, conformation-based codes of dress, speech, conduct, and thought for decades. This hegemony does not avow the connection between core principles of business and core reasons for a faltering world.

I also direct tUrn Climate Crisis Awareness and Action (Santa Clara University, 2024), an invitation to lean into the climate crisis, because it is time, and we must. There are tUrn faculty and staff partners in every school and college at this university, and six amazing folks with whom I regularly collaborate and who teach sustainability in various business fields. But the undergraduate business major is the least likely attendee of tUrn week. What is the story there?

In my profession, we analyze performance and performativity. Theater artists know you have an objective (what you want, an obstacle, what is getting in the way of obtaining that) and an action (the thing you will do to try to get your objective). Business school seems to be its own obstacle when it comes to the objective of getting sustainability going full steam ahead, but the action it keeps taking is a self-referential one, thinking it can use its own tactics to solve a problem it has largely caused.

For reasons that span from unwitting to nefarious, the displacement and destruction of cultures, customs, languages, livelihoods, resources, and natural phenomena, and the human and creaturely lives lost due to climate and ecological disasters are mostly due to business at large. In the name of business or commerce, the worst activities of imperialism, colonialism, white supremacy, and religious persecution have amplified the worst traits in our humanity and created the worst outcomes for those who are oppressed, including our Earth. Due to some innovations in the name of business, some beautiful things have happened too. But none of that matters when your island is disappearing, or your children are sick due to the global north's prosperity.

Activities that do not properly account for the real costs of global warming, for example, are leading to Earth's faltering as a decent home for all humans and most other living beings. Nothing is stopping global temperature rise at present. Nothing. *Business as usual is detrimental to life. So why are we so adamant about keeping the curriculum that sets it all into motion "as is"?*

I began tUrn at my university with no budget, no office, no staff, and no directive. It required all of my creativity, boldness, professional experience producing large-scale events, and almost every one of my interdisciplinary and transdisciplinary research and teaching connections. It involved producing and curating talks on different facets of business and climate, and all other disciplines typically found at a liberal arts university. We talked about sustainability for decades, but I felt we needed to share and actually teach the urgency of the situation, how to make a u-turn, to drawdown the curve of global warming justly, how to use the "U" or the university as a site to promote and motivate that, and how "u" as in you and I, all needed to be involved. Hence, the name tUrn.

The tUrn conference occurs every October and April for five days, 12 hours a day, and has three main components: partners, headliners in the form of sessions/workshops/performances, and resources. Information can be found at the University of Santa Clara website, slash tUrn (https://www.scu.edu/turn/). tUrn has grown to be the largest regularly produced conference the university hosts. It is interdisciplinary, intercultural, international, inter-faith, and intergenerational, and in 2024 it surpassed 10,000 attendees, 50% of whom report never attending a talk or workshop on the climate crisis before tUrn.

We included voices of climate leaders representing groups that tended to be less than centered in our predominantly white institutions and in some predominantly white-led climate organizations. In my vision, we did not need wealthy venture capitalists touting dangerously insular ideas or technological solutions to the climate crisis with implications for human and planetary health that they did not fully understand. Instead, we should have Indigenous water protectors explain the dynamics of illegal pipelines and how our addiction to the fossil fuel economy was ruining their, and our, and everyone's water, and literally undermining livelihoods, security, and culture. We should get to the bottom of the climate crisis, not try to skim off the top.

Some of my colleagues in business schools throughout the United States say that talks and articles with the title of "sustainability" sound more palatable than "climate crisis." Being "palatable" may be what makes business schools feel so pleasantly closed off from actual crises happening in and to the world. The word "sustainability" may allow us to avoid hard truths about the climate crisis, but we need to ask, the sustainability of *what?* The field of environmental justice springs from this question of "sustainability of what – by whom – for whom – and at what ultimate cost?" We must approach the dazzlingly dismal climate crisis without blinking and learn how to easily teach about the difficult topic of the climate crisis.

The climate crisis requires that we face the unpalatable with extraordinary courage and tenacity

A diagram is needed to give us a picture of why business school discourse generally fails to change business student's awareness of the climate crisis. We have to look at business and non-business knowledge as separate for just a moment, even though there are overlaps, of course.

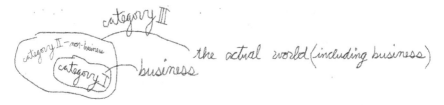

FIGURE 5.1 Categories of knowledge.

In this chapter, we will refer to traditional business education subject matter as category I. Think of it as an island, populated with all the different business activities and business education programs put together. All other non-business disciplinary knowledge and all else in the world that happens, the damages that business does not account for, will be category II. This area could be thought of like the ocean, here shown as surrounding, and larger than, category I. The sum total of both of those, business and non-business added together, will be called category III.

My experience with category I culture is that most purveyors and professors who set the tone and agendas of things that happen under the auspices of a business school do not easily, readily, or freely admit there is a climate crisis, or that mitigation could be vital. The Association to Advance Colleges and Schools of Business (AACSB) accredits over 1,600 business schools, almost all of which teach what has been called the "greed is good" capitalism (Collier, 2019) that envisions endless economic growth. Ironically, the flipside of endless growth is endless decay and endless misery that is growing as temperatures rise.

We are seeing devastating results all around in the rough waters of category II. Business (category I) assumes that globalization, using standard business practices to pry open new markets, is given, and endless growth on a planet we are already overusing is possible. Thankfully, a large number of business schools are signing onto compacts to follow better guidelines, like the UN's sustainable development goals, and other frameworks that question unchecked and unregulated capitalism and globalization.

The actual world here on Earth (category II) with its rapidly accelerating warming and climate destabilization has been damaged by business programs that tend to promote business (category I) belief systems. Those systems promote a fundamentally incomplete knowledge of the processes of life that are harmed by our actions in the name of business. The financial viability of an idea tends to trump the *value* an idea has in relation to the ethics of protecting life itself. To be clear, a business class might talk about something meaningful and heartfelt in the world, but the underlying point is to master business knowledge to create a market for something, somewhere, and succeed in the business venture, to succeed financially. People can tell themselves they are helping others, creating happy employees, and outdoing the competition, but they are not conducting business unless they are helping themselves financially and that is often done at any cost to the category II world. Seeing the climate crisis as a business opportunity, or the teaching of greed, seems to be as close as some curricular adjustments have gotten to admitting there is a climate crisis.

It is our spiritual responsibility (Trudell, 2001) to focus beyond this dangerously and enticingly closed system in which profiting off of climate misery, rather than working to cause less climate misery, becomes the only possible business learning objective regarding the climate crisis. Through tUrn, we invite all business faculty to admit more category II knowledge and wisdom into their classrooms, knowledge that does not necessarily loop back and fortify business as usual.

Category I business discourse is a subset of reality that poses as category III at times. Many a guest speaker in the business school have begun their talks or seminars with the phrase "let me tell you all how *it really is.*" The "*it*" here seems to refer to all of reality but usually only indicates that stories will be told that lead to category I success, that is, financial success in the business world. The blurring is instructive and makes people think category I is more like category III or "everything." The reason it is hard to teach about sustainability is that category I knowledge is presented as if it is the full map of reality on which all other aspects of life play out, as if sustainability is a subset or facet of business. For a professional businessperson, it may feel like this is the case. Everything can be seen and described as business, as transactional.

Most departments and disciplines across universities still do not really get the climate crisis and why we all need to lean into it. Unfurling the facts about our climate's dismal reality in business school contexts remains a special challenge. Even when business schools adopt sustainability as a goal, they often cannot get away from the language of – and ultimate adherence to – extractive capitalism.

Luckily, with the support of over 100 partners who stepped in to fill the science communication gap about the climate crisis, I developed a workaround in the form of five ideas that are swifter than whole curricular overhaul for getting beyond business education as usual and fostering climate savvy business students.

Five ideas framework

I have used this tUrn 5-step framework as a guest lecturer in business school classes and covered these subjects during tUrn week headliners and at national and international conferences including at COP27. Business schools can use these ideas to open the floodgates of category II knowledge. If they do not, sea level rise and other environmental calamities will flood us all. I hope they offer some inspiration and give people permission to be fully creative and brilliant. Because it is time. And we must.

TABLE 5.1 tUrn five ideas framework

*tUrn climate crisis awareness and action | five ideas to foster
Climate savvy business students*

	Ideas	Notes from the student lounge	Tips
1	CONVERGE: Create a common baseline by hosting comprehensive, non-business, climate talks in one class session	*Students are already thinking about the climate crisis. Tap into that. Dedicate class time to this looming subject*	1.1 Host climate experts or assign overviews of the climate crisis 1.2 Listen to student responses and co-learn with students 1.3 Inquire about their exposure to the science and the solutions 1.4 Share your insights later, affirm their reasonable insights 1.5 Reflect on Idea #1; See Idea #5, guide to reflection
2	DIVERSIFY: Send students to two unique sessions at any virtual, recorded, or live climate conference outside of class	*Assign out-of-class climate crisis events for credit, because they (and anyone) can be especially avoidant about climate learning*	2.1 Students RSVP and attend free online or in-person conferences, like tUrn, during a particular month of the course 2.2 Students present their findings with a three-slide method 2.3 Give credit for learning from diversely situated speakers 2.4 Faculty model learning as a world/mind-expanding endeavor 2.5 Reflect on Idea #2; See Idea #5, guide to reflection
3	PERSONALIZE: Analyze personal, non-business interests, and connect them to the climate crisis	*Students will be challenged by realizing – and then articulating – the climate impacts of some of their favorite activities*	3.1 Students explore environmental impacts of a hobby, etc. 3.2 Students present their findings, drawing initial conclusions 3.3 Students might understand how easy it has been for people older than them to do nothing when they see themselves similarly 3.4 Faculty share struggles/ successes you have had in making the best personal choices for environmental and climate outcomes 3.5 Reflect on Idea #3; See Idea #5, guide to reflection

(Continued)

TABLE 5.1 (Continued)

tUrn climate crisis awareness and action | five ideas to foster Climate savvy business students

Ideas	Notes from the student lounge	Tips
4 CRITIQUE: Question devious business practices like greenwashing, and promoting climate denialism	*Students are aware that misinformation and disinformation surround them and should learn to critique these business practices*	4.1 Students find sources that debunk climate disinformation 4.2 Introduce students to the prevalence of greenwashing 4.3 Students can learn from Indigenous Forest protectors and other climate leaders of color, about what business failings are 4.4 Faculty help students account for the actual costs of doing business 4.5 Reflect on Idea #4; See Idea #5, guide to reflection
5 REFLECT: Broaden the impact of all of the above through powerful reflection practices. Help students stay open, curious, and fearless	*Students need and deserve time to process their thoughts, feelings, and understanding, and encouragement to pursue further studies*	5.1 Circle up and follow serial testimony guidelines 5.2 Then have a student facilitate an open discussion 5.3 Clarify misunderstandings, affirm their understanding without qualifying it as good/bad/cool, right/wrong. Ask for facts when statements are clearly "off" 5.4 Encourage larger business projects, thesis topics, capstones, internships through your additional advising of students in and out of class. 5.5 Instructor reflects on whole process after the course, notes what to change or keep the same for next time. Stays curious

After two decades of observing business school culture in higher education from both inside and outside the classroom, I am now witnessing how these five simple but uncommon ideas can help business schools become prime sites for learning about climate solutions. The first four ideas are the most efficient way to ensure a paradigmatic shift, a worldview overturned, in our students. Idea #5 is applicable to all of the previous ideas, because it is about reflection. Reflection seals the deal on learning and is the conclusion to any time you spend on climate learning with students. This is tough stuff and can be depressing. Human connection while learning about and leaning into the climate crisis is really important.

The ideas of *notes from the student lounge* are composites of very important sentiments I heard students express on multiple occasions. I wrote the student lounge comments from their point of view and they represent the average student. When students get involved in the climate movement and receive mentorship, their observations become even more sophisticated, subtle, complex, and focused. The *tips* provide guidance and a possible sequence for planning and structuring the activities of Ideas #1–4. The tips in Idea #5 are about how to structure a reflection.

Getting started: You need an hour

If you can only dedicate a single class session to any of the ideas later, try Idea #1, followed by a short reflection from Idea #5. That baseline knowledge is the story we need to hang new information on in the future. Two days of this topic can allow you to cover Idea #1 on day 1, and Ideas #2, #3, or #4 on day 2. Building in time for reflection, even if it is just the last ten minutes of a session, as shown in Idea #5, is critical to allow new ideas to sink in.

Make it a unit

A longer, more comprehensive two-week thematic unit on the climate crisis can be produced by assigning one class period to each of the ideas – for a total of five classes – or two for a total of ten meetings on this subject.

What is NOT needed?

Eventually, business schools, and all of higher education, will require entire courses on the climate and ecological crisis and environmental justice. In the meantime, we have the tUrn approach to climate crisis education in *any* business school course starting when your next teaching term starts. Many things are **not** required to enact this: you do not necessarily need expertise, a long history of climate awareness, a budget, faculty meetings, committees, outside validation, permission, social group approval, family and friends backing you, and you certainly will need to set fear and doubt aside to proceed.

Idea #1 converge

FIGURE 5.2   Idea #1 converge.

Idea #1: Convergent experiences – gathering together and studying the climate crisis

> Focusing on one or two common sources for comprehensive climate crisis education, such as a Climate Reality talk, summarizes the problem and solutions at hand without you having to be an expert in environmental or climate science, and brings you and your students onto a level playing field.

Many faculty members believe they cannot bring the climate topic into their classroom because a direct connection to the course subject they are teaching does not appear to exist. Who wants to depress their students if they do not have to? But therein lies the rub. Few people in positions to educate have owned this problem in higher education because of the lack of ability to imagine it could be justifiable to include this content. Someone else would be better suited to teach it, right? To make things worse, most of us believe we have too much content to pare down already.

This is business as usual for all of academia, and it is producing graduates who are not, on the whole, climate aware, let alone climate savvy. They will have a degree, but they will have little idea regarding what is predicted to be disastrous in the next ten years. They have no idea that the time is now for a U-turn. Students need educational leaders in every program to create the space, time, and social permission to talk about it. Students are themselves often rich resources about the climate crisis, because they have lived in fire zones, flooded areas, experienced environmental racism, or born with the weight of toxicity, pollution, inequitable resource distribution, and corporate greed. When resources are needed on just about any subject, the tUrn resources page can provide baseline articles and videos to foster lively discussions and debates about the best course going forward.

Once you try Idea #1 and it proves to be enriching, include this experience every time you teach the course. If you do not let comprehensive climate crisis materials and speakers in the door, it will be harder to discover the connections and uncover amazingly relevant, subject-centered resources for your students.

Notes on Idea #1 from the student lounge

Hi Profs. Finally. We are already thinking about and dwelling on the climate crisis. We already know almost everything is headed in the wrong direction. We do not feel like we have the space and time for climate conversations. Half of us do not understand the urgency of the climate crisis and 90% of us do not know anything about social change, civic engagement, issue campaigns, legislation and policy, the real world of work, and how anything new and good can happen to change any of this. Everything seems broken or corrupt or both. Many of us believe that we are all going to die in the coming heat and in climatic emergencies as nature's systems break down.

We mostly feel like victims in this situation, like there is nothing we can do. We notice the profound silence of most school leaders on this issue. We need you to say this is actually real. It feels surreal sometimes, especially on a nice weather day and with no adults ever mentioning it. We need to see you doing something about it; it helps. We really do not like it when you say you have hope in our generation to fix this, and you who are out of school and have jobs and some stability in your lives are not fixing it.

Tip 1.1: Bring great speakers in

Two speakers representing different worldviews and experiences are better than one. While aiming for enrichment, and perhaps departing from your area of expertise, try to diversify the role models you provide for students. Work to include diverse voices and people. People who represent frontline communities who are most affected by the climate crisis (Indigenous, Black, and Brown communities and other vulnerable or historically marginalized groups) should be heard.

Tip 1.2: Curate the experience, then focus on student response

Take notes and capture immediate responses. Listen. See Idea #5 on how to lead a more in-depth reflection.

Tip 1.3: Ask them about their previous exposure to any of what they learned and if they wish they had learned about this before

We cannot predict what will be meaningful for students and cannot ensure the relevance of any of our course content to their lives (because meaning and relevance depend on positionality and are constructed in the learner's imagination). It often happens that people are upset when encountering a thorough explanation of the climate crisis, because they did not know how bad things really were. They can feel angry about climate disinformation led by corporate interests or governments or powerful individuals. Let them express how they feel.

Tip 1.4: Give yourself time to reflect on the experience before lecturing, and maybe forego lecturing

Encourage students to lean into their issues or topics starting with small solutions and building from there. Withhold your views until you have had time to consider the most succinct way to share them, and if they are based on science. This will give you time to ponder. You do not have to knit it all together. You can say, this is just a very important issue and I wanted to learn more about it and share it with you. You can thank your students for being a part of this important discussion and encourage them to seek out more opportunities to learn about the climate crisis and it's just solutions.

FIGURE 5.3   Idea #2 diversify.

Idea #2: Divergent experiences – learning from multiple facets of the climate crisis

> *Meaningful climate crisis education can take place outside of your classroom, then students can come together to discuss the divergent topics they encountered.*

Think outside the business school education formula and syllabus rectangle and embrace category II (non-business centered) learning. Learning about the climate crisis can happen through in-person climate talks, symposia, workshops, teach-ins, and conferences in your area. There are online climate conferences everywhere, every week. And there are millions of recordings of these conference talks on all social media platforms. There are also great articles on the subject, and excellent, reputable journalism.

Idea #2 does not require that you devote a full class to a climate lecture. To make the learning experience matter, part of a class can be given over to reflection. See Idea #5 for reflection guidance.

Notes on Idea #2 from the student lounge

We may need you to assign this because some of us live in denial (as a coping mechanism), or are misinformed, or are suffering from apathy, or are sincerely experiencing eco-anxiety/numbness and may be avoidant. When you, the faculty and staff, hide your feelings and pretend everything is ok, this wrongly makes us students think things must be ok, but we have cognitive dissonance knowing things are not ok.

*Our brains are wired to avoid the uncomfortable and to reject the scary. We have all sorts of built-in protections to help us cocoon away from reality, and those are very helpful in acute trauma situations. But they are not helpful when we need to step up to solve a massive problem. Hard as it is to face the climate crisis head on, it is probably more anxiety producing to **not** talk about it, than to talk about it. Not expressing things leads to bad health outcomes, both bodily and mentally, for people.*

Tip 2.1: Students' choice

Students attend free conferences or campus talks in person or online about the climate crisis, and they seek out climate news from any country or region. If you want to control options and concepts, students can consult tUrn's curated resource pages and dive into a theme of their choosing from a very full but finite set of offerings.

Tip 2.2: Assess their presentations and have standards

A professor can assess short presentations by students on their chosen talk based on a few criteria that do not require subject matter expertise:

- Did the students effectively communicate the main points of the talk or article?
- Did the students demonstrate their comprehension of the topic and their own insights?
- Did the students have some discussion questions prepared?
- Did the students demonstrate thoughtfulness and take it seriously? Or did they laugh their way through it? (90% of the time when people laugh it is out of nervousness or insecurity. If they fall down a bit on this last point, it is from fear of looking vulnerable.)

Tip 2.3: Support finding diverse voices in climate leadership

Give some credit for attending, reading, viewing, or reflecting so that the students see you value it. This may help motivate them past the understandable, justifiable, and appropriate fears about the situation. Give credit when they locate and learn from speakers who have diverse viewpoints.

Tip 2.4: Model learning as a world-broadening and mind-expanding endeavor

Let students observe you absorbing new concepts. Make sure to reflect on this with your students, perhaps following the reflection tips in Idea #5.

FIGURE 5.4   Idea #3 personalize.

Idea #3: Personal experiences – relating daily life to the climate crisis

> *Effective climate crisis education can be connected to lifestyles, and related to students' personal, everyday choices, or customs.*

Students can explore environmental and climate positives and negatives associated with topics they care about on a day-to-day basis. Here, we take up category II (non-business-centered) everyday topics like streaming movies, using Instagram, or AI, eating fast food, having a pet, decorating for birthday parties, eating chocolate, wearing sweatshirts or make-up, putting some money in bank accounts or the market, serving meat at family get-togethers, doing theater, or traveling for athletics. Ask them to make a short list of a few favorite activities.

Next, allow them to study and sort out the climate impacts of one of these possibly normative activities. Most students will successfully connect any non-business interest they have listed to the harms it is causing the world on a larger scale and to the overall ecological and climate crises after they search up the connection. Ask them to discover something they did not know and present it. The point of Idea #3 is that students are bringing new resources forward about the climate crisis that are led by their interests.

Notes on Idea #3 from the student lounge

We want to be pushed, but we want to be met where we are at before that happens. Doing this provides us with the mental architecture on which to hang a new story or new information. Do we love thrifting? Some of us have probably decreased our climate impact by participating in that reused clothing economy. But do we fly to different cities and countries to enact this hobby? Well, then it is a different story. No one is guiding us here.

When we realize our daily actions are contributing to the harms experienced by others, especially in the global south, this is a life-changing experience for us. We feel guilt and shame, we feel like bad people, especially if we were generally unaware. Our love of meat and dairy is killing the rainforest, using up all the land, water, food and accelerating the warming of the planet? We are surprised we did not know about all this and wonder why all of our years in school did not teach any of this to us, except for recycling. Many of us had no clue that recycling better wouldn't solve the climate crisis, we were led to believe it would. We had no idea the classic food pyramid and recycling were diversions.

Tip 3.1: Ask students to investigate one hobby or behavior they love in their personal life, as a solo or group exploration

Usually, people do not know the environmental impacts of their daily actions. Find reputable journalism on the subject, or consumer protection groups to research. Students will report on positive and negative effects on human, animals, insects, water/soil/air, ecosystems, and natural phenomena from their activities.

Tip 3.2: Students present their findings in written or as a report with slides

Ask for three slides from each student to be added to a shared slide deck. This builds an efficient presentation and virtually eliminates transition time between speakers. One slide can introduce words and images that establish the behavior they will focus on, with pictures of themselves if they wish. The second slide can summarize the research showing the problem with that action, when scaled up, and the third can show how they could modify their behavior to have less of a negative climate impact.

Tip 3.3: Consider developing two-way intergenerational empathy

If students see that their habits and enculturated, that their socialized rituals are impacting people and beings outside of their immediate awareness, they might understand how we have come to this point with all these educated adults going along with our business as usual, for the most part. You may have to point out what enculturation is. It is the social process by which an individual learns from others, in verbal and non-verbal ways, the traditional content of a culture and starts to embody its practices and values. If the culture at large is causing the climate crisis, enculturation will teach others to do the same.

Tip 3.4: Share struggles or successes in being environmentally aware

Be able to share that you/we are imperfect. How has your own environmental or climate-driven thinking, advocacy, or behavior shifted as you have learned about the climate crisis recently? What are you doing well? What could you be doing better? This will resonate with your students. They will feel more connected to you.

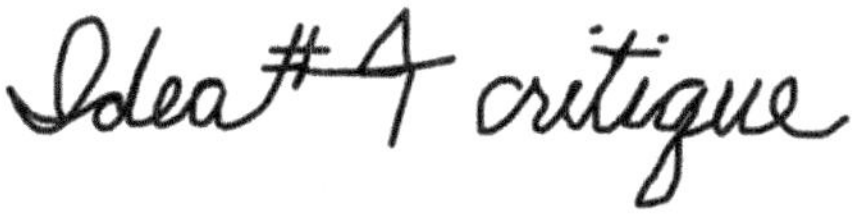

Idea #4 critique

FIGURE 5.5 Idea #4 critique.

Idea #4: Critique greenwashing experiences – understanding business' role in accelerating the climate crisis

Understand how business as usual contributes to and promotes climate denial and the ecological and climate crises we are burdened with through deliberate marketing of disinformation, through virtue-signaling, and through greenwashing.

Climate denialism is big business and enables business to dodge scrutiny. Introduce concepts of climate-denial propaganda financed by companies and corporations, and explain the depth of disinformation in climate-denial campaigns, the marketing of falsehoods through greenwashing, and efforts made by corporations, some elected officials, and powerful individuals, with business interests, to undermine climate progress.

Students can compare and contrast a company's statements about sustainability and their actual behaviors. Independent journalism is a good source for watching corporate greenwashing and other virtue signaling. Idea #4 requires business professors to introduce the topic of the faults and complicity of business in harmful business practices. Business journals, existing for the most part in the self-preserving category I space, will not implicate business. Therefore, go beyond business trade journals to reputable journalism in category II where the real reporting on the detrimental harms of category I actions is found.

Notes on Idea #4 from the student lounge

We are aware that misinformation and disinformation surrounds us, and can scrutinize climate disinformation, greenwashing, corporate greed, etc. if we are taught that it is valuable to do so. But we have no idea about decades-long campaigns to undermine our progress on climate action. Normally we are only exposed to hopeful, positivist, green business strategies, and hear a lot about sustainable business practices, in the context of category I business success. None of that should stop. But we need to see examples of greenwashing as well, taught by our business professors. We do not want to work for these companies, and they target us with promises of being environmentally friendly even when they are not, but we fall for it because their social media videos and job fair materials appeal to our sensibilities.

Tip 4.1: Look for the climate disinformation debunkers

Ask students to find sources, groups, and science journalists, whose job it is to debunk climate disinformation. This will be fascinating to them because they may never have understood that false notions from propaganda, marketed by marketers, can be dissolved with knowledge.

Tip 4.2: Discover greenwashing through imagery by studying the marketing of grocery store products versus reality

In this activity, students share one climate myth, who is promoting it, why, and the actual reality. Another idea is to have students compare and contrast a company's verbal or non-verbal (imagistic) sustainability claims against its actual behaviors. Greenwashing requires a complicit, interwoven set of business actions, and independent (category II) journalism is needed to unearth it. If students recognize the behavior within their own organization, they may suggest how to improve what they now see as a problematic business practice.

Tip 4.3: Delve into the Amazon rainforest protectors and all indigenous-stewarded zones of biodiversity (80% of all that is biodiverse on the earth is in the hands of Indigenous people)

Students can learn incredible things from leaders of the climate movement who identify as frontlines, global South, and people of color. Indigenous forest protectors have long articulated how corporations and the addiction to hamburgers in the global north is destroying their lives and traditional homes, and the lungs of the planet (one-sixth of our oxygen is from the Amazon rainforest, that is, one of every six breaths we take).

What abuses are happening in the name of business? The class can crowdsource the longest list possible of all the businesses who are directly benefiting from the undermining of the forest and Indigenous people who have called it home for millennia. They can list the top five fossil fuel invested banks. They can also look in the neighborhoods and districts of their city where structural and intentional environmental racism and the destruction of the ecological balance are being committed, and how business participates in minimizing public knowledge of those harms. The global picture can be a catalyst for local advocacy, and vice versa.

Tip 4.4: Explain how businesses might participate on the right side of history and finally generate spreadsheets that account for the real costs of doing business

What would that spreadsheet look like? If net worth is redefined as the net good a company has done, what is the net worth of the average company considering the state the world is in? Branding can deceive. Business reputation can be scrubbed. Character cannot. What is the real character of most businesses? Who are the anomalies? The environmental, sustainable, climate champions? Let students support their assertions with evidence.

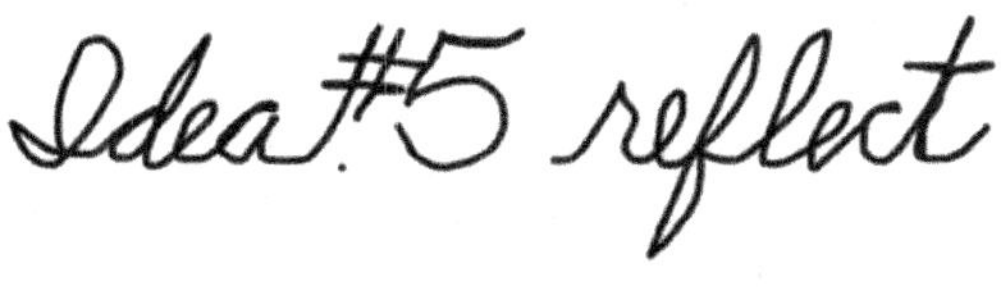

Idea #5 reflect

FIGURE 5.6 Idea #5 reflect.

Idea #5: Reflection and the arc and spiral of learning

> *Broadening Experiences: Deepening the impact of the learning through reflection completes the arc and building up a student's identity as a person with the potential to conduct further research and enact viable, grounded climate solutions gives them an upward spiral of opportunity and hope.*

Employ a research-based, practically tested, structured process of reflection. Learning is an iterative process, and by looping back, encouraging further research, and being open to good questions, you help students feel this issue is important for them as business students, you help them express themselves, and you help them stay curious. In business school culture, conversations about the climate and environmental justice are generally absent. Reflection will remind them this problem is real and business has not taken responsibility for the damages it has caused.

Notes on Idea #5 from the student lounge

We need and deserve time to process our thoughts, feelings, and new realizations that hit hard. Do not bring this up once and drop it forever. Summarize our climate day or unit at the end of the term, let us reflect again, or we may forget it because of the protective nature of our brains when faced with potentially depressing information. We might retreat to an avoidant or anxious stance until the experience of talking about the climate crisis is normalized in our culture. It will never be easy for us to talk about this. We will be repeatedly bummed by all of this. We need help recovering from the sense of loss, accepting what we can, and responding thoughtfully and from an informed place, not an ignorant one. We need to express ourselves.

Tip 5.1: Serial testimony

To effectively retain the lessons inherent in an experience, reflection is critical. Serial testimony, or a talking circle, is a method of reflection that many leaders and members of communal cultures use to conduct a discussion.

Structure: This is an Indigenous practice that has sprung from many collectivist cultures in various continents around the world. A prompt is given from the facilitator, such as, how did this video make you feel? Or what new information are you now thinking about? Or how is business itself contributing to the climate crisis? Each person in a circle speaks from the heart, in their own words, without referring to what anyone else has said. There is no commenting by the facilitator or by the participants, until conversation is opened up at the end. A maximum time can be given per speaker, such as 1 minute or 2 minutes. The facilitator holds up a pencil when the time has been reached. Whomever is speaking wraps up, and it moves to the next person. People can "pass" if the topic is overwhelming them or too personal. People can sometimes hand an object to the next speaker, an eraser, a piece of paper, a rock, to symbolize that the time to speak is held only by the person holding the object. This democratizes the classroom and brings quieter voices forward. The facilitator needs to participate as well and hold themselves to the same time limit: there are no bystanders in a talking circle, not even the so-called authority figure.

If you conduct serial testimony with students sitting in rows and columns, the energy will lag. If you do it in a circle, the energy will be palpable. Everyone's face and body language can be seen this way. It is worth circling up if you are in a flexible room that allows for that. It is worth booking a room for this day, with moveable chairs and desks, just for the reflection portion alone.

Tip 5.2: Open discussion, facilitated, or not

Following short or longer serial testimony, open it up for an organic discussion with people talking in any order, with you or a student moderator calling on people, or just in a free flow state where no one calls on people, but all agree not to interrupt. Your goal is to listen and try to understand. Affirm what you are hearing from each person who speaks and ask clarifying questions when needed.

Tip 5.3: Affirm their mixed emotions

Allow especially for some moments of quiet heaviness. Bring it back to something hopeful and affirming. Always bring it back to our power to make change. Individual and collective changes need to be encouraged. Encourage your students to join a climate or environmental group on campus or in their city. They will feel less alone when they learn that climate work is being done at every level of society and almost everywhere by millions of people around the world, but success requires their participation to the best of their capacities.

Tip 5.4: Model caring about the issues and being involved

Follow up with students in groups, or individually. Offer extra credit for students doing additional research and encourage their theses and senior capstone projects to take on the climate crisis as a subject.

Tip 5.5: Teachers need to reflect on what they have just experienced when teaching

In solitude following the class, write out the highlights and challenges of this experience, keep your notes, and build on them. Keep a list of great resources and a sample presentation or paper.

Take your tUrn

The five ideas of the tUrn framework for improving an individual college course and tUrn's resources are available at scu.edu/tUrn. tUrn is the ultimate partner in business school change management for building out curricular supports for climate crisis learning and in transforming how business graduates move through the world. Business professors working with these five ideas, experimenting, staying curious about them, will be more climate savvy themselves, gracefully stepping in to fulfill new, necessary visions of a curriculum, already having experienced success in teaching about the climate crisis and relating it to their area of expertise. If your school or institution would like to start its own tUrn week, you can regularly send your students to climate action talks. Schools adopting or partnering with the tUrn model of hosting a biannual week-long climate crisis awareness and action conference have the built-in consistency for their syllabi.

A few final points:

Do not start to offer solutions. Students may think they want you to give them a list of climates "to-dos." Effective climate education and social support about the climate crisis will only have a profound and lasting impact if it affects what is experienced by a person. As with all social justice work, once your heart is broken over an issue, you are not the same. Replacing what we thought we knew with what we now know is not always easy. Offer student care and let their newfound curiosity lead them to seek solutions.

Unless students have what Pope Francis describes as an "eco-conversion," or what is referred to as a "paradigm shift," and connect to these facts and stories on a visceral, emotional, and intellectual level, until they understand how they may have contributed to it, how it got so bad, and why it is still not fixed, and what their life will mean if they do not do anything about it, a slick bullet-point list of climate solutions will not stick.

Until they know their objective, understand the obstacles, and commit to getting the training they need to enact the needed actions, they will feel like powerless victims. We can do as the great theater of the oppressed theorist Augusto Boal did and take people from being mere spectators in life to being spect-*actors*, influencing the action, influencing the story (Boal et al., 2019).

We are in the middle of it, and the future is unknown. But not trying is not an option, and, as Greta Thunberg said, "humanity has not yet failed" (Toraya & Scott, 2021). With these five ideas for a climate savvy business classroom, we can be a part of a genuine culture shift for the good, while our business schools are in the process of making larger, perhaps slower, curricular, and structural changes.

We can help the university business program make a U-turn for the good of all of our shared futures in our one shared home. What will we be able to tell our children and grandchildren we accomplished to avert these disasters? Let it not be our excuse that we did not know we could change our syllabus.

References

Boal, A., Charles, A., Mcbride, M.-O. L., & Fryer, E. (2019). *Theatre of the oppressed.* Pluto Press. (Original work published 1979)

Collier, P. (2019). *The Future of Capitalism.* Penguin Books Ltd.

Gelbspan, R. (1998). *The heat is on: The climate crisis, the cover-up, the prescription.* Perseus Books.

NCEI.Monitoring.Info@noaa.gov. (2024, January). *January 2024 global climate report.* January 2024 Global Climate Report | National Centers for Environmental Information (NCEI). https://www.ncei.noaa.gov/access/monitoring/monthly-report/global/202401

Toraya, N. V., & Scott, J. P. (2021). *Humanity has not yet failed.* https://www.humanityhasnotyetfailed.com/

Trudell, J. (2001, March 15). *What it means to be a human being.* https://ratical.org/many_worlds/JohnTrudell/HumanBeing.html

University, S. C. (2024). *Welcome to tUrn.* Santa Clara University. https://www.scu.edu/turn/

6

EMOTIONS, AI, AND COACHING PEDAGOGY FOR THE EVOLUTION OF SUSTAINABILITY EDUCATION

Ayako Huang

Abstract

The future of education is undergoing a profound transformation that emphasizes personalized learning to cater to individual student needs and addresses complex global issues related to ecosystems, climate, and human flourishing. In sustainable management education, this creates an opportunity for collaboration between artificial intelligence (AI) applications and coaching. The integration of AI and coaching works to connect theoretical knowledge with hands-on application in sustainable business practices. This educational shift is further emphasized by the introduction of the 3 E model (Engagement, Empowerment, and Enthusiasm) and the application of the 5 C's coaching model (Connect, Contract, Collect, Collaborate, and Challenge). The 3 E model acts as a strategic framework, illustrating the dynamic interplay between self-development and AI in the pursuit of sustainable management education. Simultaneously, the 5 C's coaching model, rooted in professional coaching principles, guides course design and fosters a transformative and student-centered learning environment.

Introduction

In starting this chapter, I reflected on a recent event that has given me much to ponder. After being away from my home country, Taiwan, for seven years, returning was not what I expected. What I encountered left me with a sense that I no longer knew the place. Restaurants now prominently feature QR codes, the farmers' market has embraced digital payments through Apple Pay, and traditional forms of currency or credit cards are less accepted anywhere. The integration of artificial intelligence poses a question: Is this the essence of sustainability?

DOI: 10.4324/9781003521839-7

My experience during this recent trip unfolded against a world that has transformed from familiar surroundings. As we navigate the ever-changing landscape of AI applications and online learning platforms, traditional teaching approaches undergo a transformation. This chapter explores an innovative method that recognizes the interplay of emotions and AI, coupled with a coaching-based pedagogical process. Together, these elements foster connections on a human-centric level, paving the way for the future of sustainable management education.

Sustainability management education teaches students to balance environmental, economic, and social needs effectively. It provides skills for strategic resource management, preventing resource depletion and reducing environmental harm. This education translates sustainability principles into practical strategies that improve resource efficiency and lessen organizational impacts. AI enhances this education with personalized learning paths, scenario simulations, and data-driven insights, equipping students to address future sustainability challenges with a mix of emotional intelligence and technological advancements.

Departure from traditional lecture-centric classrooms

In the domain of education, the traditional pedagogical approach has been for lecture-style teaching, with educators as conveyors of information. Fortunately, new educational practices are departing from this conventional model. Educators are increasingly becoming learning facilitators guiding students through interactive and participatory learning experiences, particularly in the context of sustainable management education. This paradigm shift acknowledges the efficacy of active engagement and collaborative learning over the passive reception of information (Cottafava et al., 2019).

The integration of coaching tools has emerged as a powerful and innovative facilitation methodology (Dallakyan et al., 2022). Coaching creates a shift toward a collaborative learning atmosphere and leverages diverse strengths and perspectives among students. Consequently, this fosters an enriched educational environment characterized by heightened dynamics and inclusivity (Jones et al., 2012).

Acting as a learning facilitator

The contemporary educator's role extends beyond being a disseminator of information; we are now integral to the learning process itself. As learning facilitators, we can guide students in exploring and comprehending concepts, moving beyond rote memorization. This shift is grounded in the belief that authentic learning occurs when students actively engage with the material, question assumptions, and apply knowledge in real-world scenarios (Van Poeck et al., 2017). It also supports examination of topics that are complex or where answers and solutions are evolving.

Educators, in their dual capacity as facilitators and coaches, create opportunities that inspire students to actively participate in critical thinking and problem-solving. Research indicates that active engagement in such cognitive processes significantly contributes to deepening understanding and skill development (McCombs & Marzano, 1990; Alismail & McGuire, 2015).

This novel instructional approach involves the deliberate use of powerful questions, a strategy acknowledged in educational literature for its efficacy in stimulating critical thinking (Nappi, 2017). Additionally, wearing a "coaching hat" fosters a rapport with students that facilitates effective learning environments, promoting student engagement, and cognitive immersion (Bizami et al., 2023).

In their role as coaches within the learning facilitation framework, educators enhance the positive impact of scenario-based learning and developing problem-solving skills. As students and educators face a world with urgent, complex, and fast-changing crisis, this pedagogical approach enhances critical thinking and fosters personal growth and development, aligning with the broader goals of education.

Empowering unique learning journeys

To accommodate individual student needs and unique learning preferences, strengths, and challenges, personalized education tailors instructional strategies, content, and assessments to meet their diverse needs. Biggs (1979) emphasized that personalization enhances educational outcomes by meeting students at their unique developmental points. Zimmerman (2013) advocated for differentiated instruction to accommodate diverse learning styles and promote academic success. Vygotsky (2011) highlighted that learning is a socio-culturally mediated process, and personalization facilitates effective knowledge transmission. By adopting personalized approaches, educators empower students on their unique learning journeys, providing tools and resources that resonate with their abilities and interests. Combining these theories underscores the multifaceted nature of personalized learning. This holistic approach ensures that teaching strategies are aligned with not only educational standards but also the personal growth and development of each student.

I implemented coaching techniques and personalized learning in a classroom exploration of the circular economy. Each student chooses a topic related to the circular economy that genuinely sparked their interest. From sustainable fashion to composting systems, their chosen subjects were as diverse as they were intriguing. With the aid of several dynamic coaching sessions to set the direction, the students then proceeded to create their own websites to address their chosen topic. These platforms were not just ordinary sites but vibrant showcases where they could cultivate their ideas, allowing them to blossom into impactful projects. This creative process not only deepened their understanding but also sharpened their skills, preparing them to integrate sustainability into practical, real-world applications.

The impact of this project reached far beyond the classroom, setting a foundation for future potential business endeavors in sustainability. As an example, two students secured job placements before graduation, a testament to the practical value and relevance of their work. One student excelled in devising sustainable marketing strategies, while another focused on sustainable business analytics. Their websites demonstrated their ability to address complex and critical problems while serving as both portfolio and platform that demonstrated their skills, knowledge, and commitment to sustainability.

Shaping the future of education through AI applications and coaching

The emphasis on personalization in education is a fundamental shift that is shaping the future of the educational landscape. Personalized learning recognizes that students are more likely to thrive when their educational experiences align with their individual needs and preferences. Educators significantly drive this shift by adopting innovative teaching methods and using technology to personalize educational experiences.

In sustainable management education, Abulibdeh, et al. (2024) and Di Vaio et al. (2020) provide a comprehensive overview of the existing literature on the intersection of artificial intelligence and business models within the context of sustainable development goals. The role of AI-driven simulations that dynamically adapt to individual learning styles and offer synergistic sustainable business practices bridges theory and real-world application.

I found that integrating coaching principles significantly enhances the pedagogical impact by infusing a humanistic dimension into the learning experience. This holds particular significance in sustainable management education where sole reliance on theoretical knowledge proves inadequate to address emerging problems. As Ox (2015) elucidates, the coaching process nurtures and empowers students to incorporate practical skills and sustainable business practices into both their personal and professional spheres.

My first application of the shared leadership coaching principle was in 2021 during the pandemic. I felt there was a need for more emotional support for the students. I began with a check-in connection session from the coaching principles that helped build trust and created a psychologically safe environment. Immediately, I could feel the increased engagement from the students.

Integrating these principles of emotional support and trust-building into education aligns with the UN PRME Sustainable Development Goals (SDGs) by promoting inclusive and equitable quality education. Creating a supportive and trusting environment helps students to engage more deeply with the material, encourages innovative thinking, and fosters a collaborative spirit. This not only enhances their academic performance but also provides them with the social and emotional skills necessary to address complex global challenges. As students learn to navigate and implement sustainable practices, they are better prepared to contribute to sustainable development initiatives in meaningful ways.

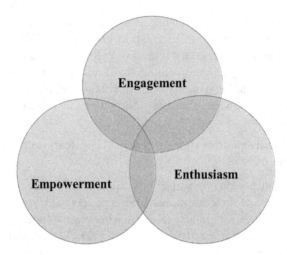

FIGURE 6.1 3 E model.

In exploring this innovative approach, I developed my "3 E model": Engagement, Empowerment, and Enthusiasm. This model emerged from practical experiences and ongoing refinements. I developed this model a year ago after two years of applying coaching principles and one year of teaching students how to use Chat GPT to create stories for reflecting on their reading assignments or develop games for their midterm assessments. I observed how students are more engaged in doing their homework when they create their own learning assessments, and the process has fostered enthusiasm and a desire to learn.

The model illuminates the dynamic interplay between self-development and AI in the pursuit of sustainable management education while fostering a coaching-based pedagogical process. The insights presented draw on academic literature and empirical evidence that establishes a scholarly foundation for the 3 E sustainable educational framework.

Engagement

To facilitate a comprehensive learning experience in sustainable management education, active participation from students is imperative. Supported by academic research, AI applications play a significant role in enhancing student engagement. They provide personalized learning experiences and integrate interactive elements such as simulations and gamification (Koravuna & Surepally, 2020; Santos-Villalba et al., 2020). This pedagogical approach not only adds an enjoyable aspect to the learning process but also equips students with practical skills essential for addressing real-world sustainability challenges (Ahmed & Sutton, 2017).

Empowerment

Grounded in transformative pedagogy, specifically through coaching, there is substantial academic evidence supporting the impact of empowering students to autonomously discover solutions (Kidman et al., 2001). Beyond fostering academic growth, numerous studies highlight the impact on personal development that acknowledges the holistic nature of the learning experience (Jones & Turner, 2006). By empowering students, we promote their skills for self-directed learning and self-reliant living.

Enthusiasm

Academic literature underscores the transformative impact of enthusiasm on sustainable management education, particularly in driving positive environmental and social impact (Karatzoglou, 2013). The synergy between AI applications and coaching strategies need still to be academically recognized as facilitating knowledge acquisition and cultivating an intrinsic passion for sustainable education. However, students are increasingly vocal about their desire to ensure that a regenerative and flourishing world is achieved. When students lead their own learning journey, a genuine connection is forged with the subject matter that can foster a deep commitment to contribute meaningfully to a sustainable future (Diduck, 1999; Shapiro et al., 2021).

The coaching approach moves beyond mere transfer of knowledge and creates a dynamic and interactive educational experience. When students take charge of their learning, they develop critical thinking skills, become more engaged, and are better prepared to tackle real-world challenges. This empowerment aligns well with modern educational frameworks that emphasize collaboration, creativity, and critical reflection. One effective framework that embodies this student-centered approach is the 5 C's coaching model.

5 C's coaching model

In my course design, shared in this chapter, I followed the 5 C's principles outlined by professional coaches Ernie Turner and Tan Swee Heng in their 2023 book, *Share Leadership Disciplines*: Connect, Contract, Collect, Collaborate, and Challenge.

Connect phase

The Connect phase highlights the significance of building rapport and open communication within the class setting. The purpose is to recognize individual connections to the broader academic and social context. This involves starting class with a brief, lighthearted sharing session before the main agenda. For example, as I conducted a recent lesson on waste management business practices, I began with the check-in question: "Please list one recycling habit you have practiced today and share how you are feeling tonight." Here is the one student's response from this check-in session.

Recycling Habit Practiced Today: Today, I made sure to separate my paper and plastic waste into their respective recycling bins. I also reused a glass jar to store leftovers instead of using a disposable plastic container.

How I Am Feeling Tonight: Tonight, I am feeling quite content and relaxed. It's been a productive day, and I feel good about the small steps I've taken toward being more environmentally conscious.

The Connect phase aligns with the *Engagement* aspect of my 3 E model, emphasizing the importance of building strong relationships and fostering open communication between faculty and students.

Contract phase

The primary goal of the Contract phase is to ensure alignment and commitment between faculty and students. Successful classrooms depend on clearly outlined expectations, resulting in explicit commitments mutually agreed upon by both parties. It is crucial to acknowledge that faculty members are not the sole contributors to establishing class learning objectives; students actively participate in defining class expectations and articulating their contributions.

This collaborative effort contributes to the establishment of class norms and ground rules.

Contracting is an ongoing practice involving the definition, alignment, design, refinement, and assignment of expectations among all parties involved (Turner & Tan, 2023). This aligns with the *Empowerment* aspect of the 3 E model, fostering shared responsibility in shaping the learning environment and reinforcing the input of both faculty and students in achieving class goals.

Collect phase

The Collect phase involves gathering diverse perspectives and insights to enrich decision-making processes among student peers. It emphasizes maintaining an open mindset and curiosity, and encourages exploration beyond the confines of the existing mental models to learn and co-create new insights and ideas. The act of collecting is linked with curiosity (Turner & Tan, 2023). A popular shared leadership coaching technique, "Stop-Reflect-Write-Report," encourages students to pause, reflect on a question, write down their thoughts, and share their reflections. Widely used in group discussions and decision making, this process reinforces the principles of the 3 E model – specifically, *engagement* and *enthusiasm*. Another tool would be to employ a survey/poll on a specific topic to enhance inclusivity and participation in a decision-making process.

Collaboration phase

This phase proactively aligns facts, thoughts, feelings, and collective wisdom and intelligence from student peers and external sources. Open dialogues and widespread brainstorming explore diverse perspectives in the collaboration phase. Peer learning involves students drawing on each other's experiences beyond traditional instruction in a structured and supportive way to achieve effective communication and mutual understanding among students. During the collaboration phase, class participation involves active communication with students that aligns with the 3 E model's *Enthusiasm* principles by promoting collective pursuit, recognizing diverse perspectives, and nurturing an environment that fosters openness.

Challenge phase

The challenge phase cultivates a growth-oriented mindset, pushing students beyond their comfort zones and highlighting the importance of continuous improvement and innovation. Through open discussions, students explore diverse perspectives, scrutinize assumptions, and actively seek ongoing enhancement by questioning one's own and others' thoughts and contributions. By embracing challenges in ways that require receptivity to feedback, students become open to inventive solutions and elevated standards with a perpetual learner mindset.

The notion of sustainable management education is an act of challenging established norms and it aligns with intellectual and personal development. *Challenging the status quo is crucial but involves persistent effort to expand boundaries and remain effective.* When we used Chat GPT to address a circular economy scenario, we also used either a forum or group discussion to foster innovation and encourage critical examination of norms among students. We discussed alternative approaches, decision rationales, and underlying assumptions.

By incorporating the 5 C's principles (Connect, Contract, Collect, Collaborate, Challenge) within the framework of the 3 E model (Engagement, Empowerment, Enthusiasm), I attempted to cultivate student's personal resilience as they learn the complexities of sustainable business practices (see Figure 6.2). This pedagogical integration aims to prepare students to confront the multifaceted challenges inherent in sustainable business, by fostering academic proficiency and personal growth and development.

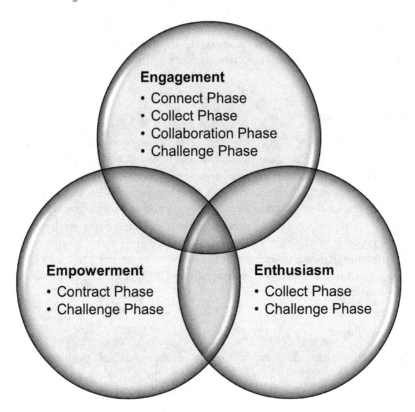

FIGURE 6.2   3 E model with 5 C's principles.

I implemented this approach by reducing traditional lectures and adopting active learning methods to foster a deeper connection with the class material and a genuine commitment to sustainable practices. To make the course content more relevant and engaging, I linked it to students' personal lives and interests. I held several coaching sessions with each student to explore their experiences and consider how sustainability principles apply to their future careers and daily routines to help them realize the importance of sustainability and adopt sustainable practices. These engagements foster a mindset shift that extends beyond the classroom, encouraging them to take meaningful action in their professional and personal lives.

I can see the results of engagement during group discussions as well as in their projects. Students tell me they continue to carry these practices into their personal and professional lives after the class ends. They continue to share their sustainable projects with both personal and professional colleagues.

Context

I applied principles of the 3 E and 5 C's models, emphasizing a personalized and empowering approach to sustainability learning, in a graduate Leadership for Sustainability course for MBA students at a small US Midwestern university. The course meets three times per week on Tuesday and Thursday from 7:30 pm to 9:00 pm (US Central Time) and on Saturday from 10:00 am to 12:00 pm, spanning eight weeks and earning a total of four credits. The course format is hybrid, with the majority of students participating in live Zoom meetings, along with a few asynchronous students. A total of 27 students were enrolled from different time zones and ranging in age from their thirties to forties and engaged in various full-time professions.

The course content focused on circular economic business practices. In the first week, the course introduced the GROW coaching model (Goal, Reality, Options, Will), which serves as a guide for conversations and facilitates problem-solving at the personal and professional levels. Later in the semester, several major assignments were introduced to apply and deepen this foundational knowledge.

One such assignment was the "Circular Economy in Self-Coaching Forum," where students wrote a 250–500-word reflection on applying the GROW model for self-coaching to attain a sustainable practice goal. The students were required to read circular economy articles and watch related videos prior to the class. Following this, each student provided 250-word constructive feedback to two peers, to promote collaborative learning.

Students engaged in two sustainable coaching sessions, each lasting 40–60 minutes. Subsequently, they submitted a three-page reflection paper, delving into session specifics, personal growth, and the impact of coaching on sustainable practices. The reflection incorporated an analysis of successes and challenges, drawing insights from course readings and concluded by outlining future goals for sustainable practice.

In addition to these reflective assignments, students created a Sustainability Showcase Website to demonstrate their understanding of sustainability, utilizing skills developed through their coaching and consulting projects. The website provided a platform for ongoing updates after each sustainability-themed course. For reference, a sample student website is available at https://sucha-kss.notion.site/sucha-kss/Sucha-Portfolio-Sustainability-Data-Driven-Strategist-f5b5547438364f01a64dac0e93e355b7.

Daily dialogue and group discussion sessions were led by students and local business "clients." Client participation was incorporated into this course to provide contextual and experiential learning about local sustainability.

Course structure

This section illustrates the course structure and how it incorporates the 3 E and 5 C's models.

Course Structure	Time	3 E Model	5 C's Model
Check-In	5 min	Engagement	Connect
Class Expectation and Measurement	10 min	Empower	Contrast
Research Phase	30 min	Enthusiasm	Collection
Scenario Host for Class Discussion	30 min	Empower	Collaboration
Reflection on Assessment of Lesson and Team Effectiveness	15 min	Engagement	Challenge

The check-in session

Students are tasked with dedicating 20 minutes daily to immerse themselves in nature, capturing the moment with a photo as their homework assignment. Whether in a local park, garden, or simply by opening a window for fresh air, the goal is to briefly disconnect from daily obligations, allowing nature to be a canvas for self-reflection. The course instructor selects one photo and asks the student photographer to share feelings within the first three minutes of each lesson. Students share their captured moments at the beginning of each class or on the online forum as the warm-up exercise, fostering a sense of camaraderie and personal connection among class peers.

An example from one student's check-in session:

> The gentle touch of a butterfly fills me with delight, amazement, and curiosity, creating a magical moment infused with wonder and happiness.

Class expectation and measurement

Following the check-in session, as an initial coaching strategy, students are encouraged to articulate their expectations for the lesson and suggest methods to measure their success. The instructor provides the syllabus and theme chart to the students first, and then facilitates the process by dividing the students into groups and asking them how they intend to achieve the objectives for each lesson and how they plan to measure their success in reaching the goals of each lesson. The group and the entire class will collectively express their agreement with the learning objectives and measurement methods using a voting method. This approach empowers students to take ownership of their learning outcomes and establishes a collaborative partnership between the instructor and the learners.

Example for one group's student engagement measurement session:

Lesson 10 Circularity in Waste Management
What do you want to accomplish in today's class and why does it matter to you?

In today's class, we would like to learn how circular practices can revolutionize waste management, highlighting the crucial roles of recycling, reusing, and reducing waste in a sustainable loop. This topic is vital as it provides us with the know-how to actively contribute to environmental conservation. Understanding circularity not only improves our grasp of responsible waste management but also teaches habits that positively influence our environment, paving the way for a more sustainable and eco-friendly future.

How do you determine whether you've successfully achieved the objectives of a lesson?

Develop two scenario-based questions for another group to assess their understanding of the fundamental concepts from Lesson 10. Furthermore, be prepared to evaluate and offer constructive feedback on the strategies or action plans proposed by our group.

Research phase

Students were given 20 minutes to research waste management within their groups. The emphasis was on knowledge exchange and collaboration. The facilitator encouraged students to use AI applications to aid the research process, but they had to manually verify citations and references. In addition to their research, students were encouraged to use ChatGPT to formulate two scenario-based questions. These questions aimed to assess another group's understanding of key concepts and principles in waste management. This step not only reinforced their own learning but also promoted a deeper understanding of the subject matter by creating thoughtful queries.

If time permitted on Saturday morning, students played a Kahoot©, a fun, gamified assessment tool that allowed each group to showcase their comprehension of the material. The questions covered various aspects of waste management that were discussed during the research phase and included scenario-based questions.

Scenario host for class discussion (collaborate/enthusiasm)

To apply the acquired knowledge, the instructor begins a scenario-based discussion using the Chat GPT tool. Later, I share one of the circular economic principles, waste management, as an illustration.

Prompting a question to Chat GPT tool. Key Instruction for Waste Management Scenario:

Prompt Question

> *Create a detailed and innovative waste management scenario for a city aiming to achieve the highest level of sustainability by 2050.*

In more detail prompt question.

> *Describe an integrated waste management system that minimizes landfill use and maximizes recycling and resource recovery. Include advanced technologies, community engagement strategies, and government policies that contribute to reducing waste generation and promoting a circular economy. Highlight how the scenario addresses various types of waste, including plastic, organic, and electronic waste, with a focus on environmental conservation, efficiency, and community well-being.*

The case study scenario created by Chat GPT

> *Portland, Oregon, stands as a beacon of sustainability with its pioneering Integrated Waste Management System. This model incorporates advanced sorting technologies in recycling facilities, a city-wide smart bin network providing real-time feedback to citizens, and community recycling hubs for responsible disposal of diverse items. Government policies, including Extended Producer Responsibility programs, foster eco-friendly design, while circular economy initiatives encourage businesses to use recycled materials. Waste-to-energy facilities contribute to renewable energy, plastic reduction campaigns combat single-use plastics, and organic waste composting initiatives enhance local agriculture. Regular e-waste collection events further prevent hazardous materials from entering landfills, making Portland a global leader in environmental conservation, efficiency, and community well-being.*

Key instruction for case study discussion question:

Prompt Question

> *Create discussion questions based on the above case study in Portland related to the circular economy, both on a personal and professional level*

The group discussion questions created by Chat GPT

> - *How can Portland residents actively participate in and contribute to the city's circular economy initiatives on an individual level, considering the specific waste reduction and recycling practices mentioned in the case study?*
> - *What personal lifestyle changes can individuals adopt to align with Portland's plastic reduction campaigns and organic waste composting initiatives, and how might these changes promote a more circular way of living?*

- *In what ways does Portland's waste management scenario encourage citizens to rethink their consumption patterns and make environmentally conscious choices in their daily lives?*
- *How might the use of technology, such as the smart bin network and mobile apps, influence individual behavior in waste management and contribute to a circular economy mindset?*
- *How can businesses in Portland, inspired by the city's circular economy initiatives, adopt similar principles in their operations, including product design, waste reduction, and resource recovery?*
- *How do Portland's government policies, such as Extended Producer Responsibility programs, influence business practices and promote eco-friendly design? What challenges and opportunities might businesses face in complying with these policies?*
- *In what ways can Portland businesses collaborate to create a more circular supply chain, considering the city's emphasis on recycling, waste reduction, and circular economy initiatives?*

Students choose the most interesting top two questions for group or peer discussions. Total discussion time for these three questions is 30 minutes. For asynchronous students, responses are limited to approximately 250 words per question, and they reply to two peers from their online group. Students are encouraged to use any AI search engines for answering their questions, followed by citation verification.

The scenario simulates a classroom challenge where diverse teaching methods can be employed. Students collaborate to devise innovative solutions, promoting critical thinking and the application of pedagogical principles in a practical context.

Reflection on assessment of lesson and team effectiveness

After the scenario discussion session, a reflective session took place to assess and enhance team effectiveness and collaborative dynamics.

This reflection fosters a psychologically safe environment and encourages students to share their insights, learnings, and challenges. By acknowledging the importance of mutual respect and open communication, the class solidifies their ability to function cohesively in team activities.

At the end of each class, students evaluate what they have learned and how they plan to apply it. They identify potential obstacles to their application and assess their commitment levels, in their both personal and professional lives. This comprehensive reflection aims to deepen the integration of acquired knowledge, emphasizing the practical application of pedagogical principles beyond the classroom setting.

Sample list of reflection questions

- How are you feeling by the end of lesson? List one thing you enjoyed most about today's lesson and suggest ways we can continue to improve it for the next lesson?
- In your opinion, did we meet the class expectations? Why or why not?
- In what ways did the class environment contribute to or hinder the sharing of insights, learnings, and challenges during the group discussion or peer review forum?
- Evaluate your personal learning outcomes from the lesson. What specific concepts or methodologies did you find most valuable for your future practices?
- Assess your commitment levels to implementing these principles in your both personal and professional lives. What tangible steps can you take to ensure a high level of commitment?

Student learning feedback

Amid ongoing advancements in educational technology, comprehending the impact of these changes on the student experience is crucial. Student course feedback offers insights into the effectiveness of innovative teaching methods. It becomes evident that the dynamic interplay between technology and teaching methodologies influences not only how we teach but also how students learn and engage with the material.

The following are excerpts from students' feedback on this example course:

Student	Student Quotes
# 1	*This course [gave the opportunity] for students to enhance the professional content and coaching skill, as well as expand awareness with the self-reflection.*
# 2	*This course was great, challenging, and provide many opportunities for reflection. Building the website is nice.*
# 3	*The one aspect of the course I'd definitely keep is the permanent group structure. Dividing us into stable teams of four created a supportive environment that allowed for more effective collaboration and deeper understanding of each other's work styles. It also increased accountability; we couldn't afford to let our team down. Overall, the teams enriched our learning experience and contributed to our individual growth, making it an invaluable part of the course.*
# 4	*Your class structure is really great! Just an idea I had: As a task, one could ask the students to connect a current concept (just learned in class) to any already learned concept.*
# 5	*Of course, the group activities were my favorite experience and an incredible opportunity to apply concepts whilst learning them and gain valuable sustainable learning experience.*

Student	Student Quotes
# 6	*Group discussion was overall helpful to the integration and development of knowledge and information covered in the course. I would keep everything about the course.*
# 7	*Overall everything. Professor did a great job of navigating the material, student's questions and development, as well as stressing the importance of the topic and growth taken over the class. Much appreciated.*
# 8	*The most significant contribution Ayako made to my learning was her unmistakable dedication to our intellectual and personal growth. It was evident that teaching isn't just a job for her – it's her calling, her dharma. Her investment in our success went far beyond what one might typically expect from a professor. This level of passion is a rarity and stood out as a defining quality that not only motivated me but elevated the entire educational experience.*
# 9	*Ayako was an excellent teacher who always pushed me to perform at my best. The atmosphere in her class was both challenging and motivating, making it impossible for me to give anything less than my all. I gained significant knowledge and skills, and even managed to step out of my comfort zone. Overall, it was a valuable learning experience for which I'm very thankful.*
# 10	*The ability to work collaboratively with students as a consulting team. I really liked Ayako's feedback for the assignments. The Nature pic exercise made it fun. Her ability to care so deeply for her students and make a change.*
# 11	*I really enjoyed Dr. Huang's presence and the way she taught the class! Nature Pic Class Break-outs videos.*
# 12	*Games, projects, website, being open and vulnerable.*

Conclusion

Examining the synergy between coaching and AI underscores their transformative potential in enhancing the learning experience and in shaping sustainable education. Technological innovations have revolutionized traditional classroom practices and paved the way for personalized and adaptive learning experiences. Artificial intelligence plays a pivotal role in automating routine tasks (Chen et al., 2020), and it enables educators to focus on fostering critical thinking, creativity, and problem-solving skills among students.

The collaboration between coaching and AI holds promises for the future of sustainable management education. Personalized learning systems can cater to individual needs, promoting a more inclusive (Shemshack and Spector, 2020) and effective sustainable educational environment. It is essential to assess whether students have gained a better understanding of sustainability practices in business as part of this educational evolution.

Incorporating regular assessments and evaluations into the curriculum will help determine the effectiveness of these innovative teaching approaches to ensure that integration of AI and coaching effectively translates into practical knowledge that students can apply in real-world business scenarios. Utilizing the sustainable website demonstrates how students have conveyed their learning and defined sustainability, serving as a portfolio that prepares them for impactful careers in sustainable business.

It is essential to approach the integration of AI and coaching with careful consideration of ethical, privacy, and equity concerns (Hagendorff, 2020). Striking a balance between technological advancements and human-centric approaches ensures that the benefits of AI and coaching are accessible to all learners. In doing so, educators and policymakers must collaborate to establish robust frameworks that safeguard individual rights and promote fairness in the deployment of these technologies. These transformative forces pave the way for a more resilient, inclusive, and sustainable educational future.

AI and coaching can contribute to a holistic approach in addressing the emotional aspects of sustainable management education. Incorporating emotional intelligence into the educational framework leads to improved student engagement, motivation, and overall well-being. This integrated approach ensures a dynamic and adaptive learning environment that prepares students for challenges and opportunities in an ever-evolving sustainable world.

References

Abulibdeh, A., Zaidan, E., & Abulibdeh, R. (2024). Navigating the confluence of artificial intelligence and education for sustainable development in the era of industry 4.0: Challenges, opportunities, and ethical dimensions. *Journal of Cleaner Production*, 140527.

Ahmed, A., & Sutton, M. J. D. (2017). Gamification, serious games, simulations, and immersive learning environments in knowledge management initiatives. University of Sussex. *Journal Contribution*. https://hdl.handle.net/10779/uos.23444615.v1

Alismail, H. A., & McGuire, P. (2015). 21st century standards and curriculum: Current research and practice. *Journal of Education and Practice*, 6(6), 150–154.

Biggs, J. (1979). Individual differences in study processes and the quality of learning outcomes. *Higher Education*, 8(4), 381–394.

Bizami, N. A., Tasir, Z., & Kew, S. N. (2023). Innovative pedagogical principles and technological tools capabilities for immersive blended learning: a systematic literature review. *Education and Information Technologies*, 28(2), 1373–1425.

Chen, L., Chen, P., & Lin, Z. (2020). Artificial intelligence in education: A review. *Ieee Access*, 8, 75264–75278.

Cottafava, D., Cavaglià, G., & Corazza, L. (2019). Education of sustainable development goals through students' active engagement: A transformative learning experience. *Sustainability Accounting, Management and Policy Journal*, 10(3), 521–544.

Dallakyan, A., Martirosyan, N., & Shakarian, K. (2022). Coaching activity and its practical significance in pedagogical process. *Main Issues of Pedagogy and Psychology*, 9(2), 56–65.

Diduck, A. (1999). Critical education in resource and environmental management: Learning and empowerment for a sustainable future. *Journal of Environmental Management*, 57(2), 85–97.

Di Vaio, A., Palladino, R., Hassan, R., & Escobar, O. (2020). Artificial intelligence and business models in the sustainable development goals perspective: A systematic literature review. *Journal of Business Research, 121,* 283–314.

Hagendorff, T. (2020). The ethics of AI ethics: An evaluation of guidelines. *Minds and Machines, 30*(1), 99–120.

Jones, R., Morgan, K., & Harris, K. (2012). Developing coaching pedagogy: Seeking a better integration of theory and practice. *Sport, Education and Society, 17*(3), 313–329.

Jones, R. L., & Turner, P. (2006). Teaching coaches to coach holistically: Can problem-based learning (PBL) help? *Physical Education and Sport Pedagogy, 11*(2), 181–202.

Karatzoglou, B. (2013). An in-depth literature review of the evolving roles and contributions of universities to education for sustainable development. *Journal of Cleaner Production, 49,* 44–53.

Kidman, L., Thorpe, R., Jones, R. L., & Lewis, C. (2001). *Developing decision makers: An empowerment approach to coaching.* IPC Print Resources.

Koravuna, S., & Surepally, U. K. (2020, September). Educational gamification and artificial intelligence for promoting digital literacy. In *Proceedings of the 2nd International Conference on Intelligent and Innovative Computing Applications,* 1–6.

McCombs, B. L., & Marzano, R. J. (1990). Putting the self in self-regulated learning: The self as agent in integrating will and skill. *Educational Psychologist, 25*(1), 51–69.

Nappi, J. S. (2017). The importance of questioning in developing critical thinking skills. *Delta Kappa Gamma Bulletin, 84*(1), 30.

Santos-Villalba, M. J., Leiva Olivencia, J. J., Navas-Parejo, M. R., & Benítez-Márquez, M. D. (2020). Higher education students' assessments towards gamification and sustainability: A case study. *Sustainability, 12*(20), 8513. DOI: 10.3390/su12208513

Shapiro, S., Beninger, S., Domegan, C., Reppel, A., Stanton, J., & Watson, F. (2021). Macromarketing pedagogy: Empowering students to achieve a sustainable world. *Journal of Macromarketing, 41*(1), 104–115.

Shemshack, A., & Spector, J. M. (2020). A systematic literature review of personalized learning terms. *Smart Learning Environments, 7*(1), 1–20.

Turner, E., & Tan, S. H. (2023). *Share leadership disciplines: A better way to lead & coach* (T. Person, Ed.). Candid Creation Publishing.

Van Poeck, K., Læssøe, J., & Block, T. (2017). An exploration of sustainability change agents as facilitators of nonformal learning: Mapping a moving and intertwined landscape. *Ecology and Society, 22*(2).

Vygotsky, L. (2011). *Interaction between learning and development.* Linköpings universitet.

Zimmerman, B. J. (2013). Theories of self-regulated learning and academic achievement: An overview and analysis. *Self-Regulated Learning and Academic Achievement,* 1–36.

7

UNIVERSITY CAMPUSES

Living laboratories for transformational programs

Robert Sroufe and Brad Clauss

Abstract

This chapter delves into why stakeholders were drawn to Chatham University's Eden Hall Campus in Pittsburgh, PA. It explores the campus's history, stakeholders involved in its design, and ongoing development efforts. The industry experience and academic background of the authors converge within a campus used as a living laboratory. Developed as part of this campus, a school of sustainability and sustainability principles are integrated into business education. This chapter highlights interdisciplinary programs at the Falk School of Sustainability & Environment and the role of stakeholders in campus development. It discusses dual-degree programs intertwining business management with sustainability, emphasizing experiential learning. Additionally, it outlines resources driving transformative thinking, including strategic planning and collaboration. Overall, this chapter sets the stage for how Eden Hall serves as a catalyst for integrating sustainability into education and campus operations, fostering environmental stewardship and transformational learning experiences for both students and faculty.

Introduction – the attraction of a transformational campus

This chapter starts with the backstory of the authors and what compelled us to come to a small liberal arts school, Chatham University, and its Eden Hall Campus in Pittsburgh, PA. The campus itself is a living laboratory, a draw for faculty, students, and the community, and we will discuss why it is attractive and provide some storytelling about the stakeholders involved in its delivery of experiential learning. Its attraction is at the center of transformational education with sustainability in its design from the ground up and dual degrees

DOI: 10.4324/9781003521839-8

in sustainability and business administration. A campus can draw people from industry and other academic institutions to come to a unique place where sustainability is embraced.

Brad's Story: His industry (as a water systems consultant, and environmental engineer at Johnson & Johnson) and NGO experience (working with The Phipps Conservatory and living building challenge (ILFI, 2024)) put Brad on a path to becoming more involved in higher education, board governance, and operations. This background and all his prior experience were perfectly aligned to come to Chatham University's Eden Hall campus.

His prior work at the NGO was where he could be in touch with the entire campus, drop into education programs, learn from them, and work directly with leadership on projects aligned with the mission of education broadly. The Eden Hall campus is a similar landscape, yet it's an institution of higher education. He was doing similar work at The Phipps and hosted hundreds of educational groups, internationally and nationally, sharing his experiences with living buildings. Living near Chatham University and seeing the vision and design of a new campus focused on living sustainability, a model for sustainable design, and net-zero emissions amplified Brad's interest in working on this campus. The campus was to be one of the first of its kind, a living laboratory – the transformation of a farm to a sustainable college campus.

Robert's Story: His interests involve the question "How can I design and deliver a unique learning experience students will remember years after the course or degree program" (Sroufe, 2021). Robert's work in this area spanned MBA program development, integrated management as a way to see how sustainability is part of every business function (Sroufe, 2018), experiential learning courses, design competitions, and live project courses (Sroufe & Ramos, 2015). The desire to deliver meaningful course experiences provided several opportunities to develop new courses. Robert developed new graduate courses (spanning strategic sustainability and models, applied sustainability for new projects, supply chain management, a sequence of live project consulting courses, and international study abroad experiences within what became one of the top-ranked MBA sustainability programs in the country. He has also developed undergraduate cornerstone experiential courses and an honors course on imagining a sustainable world, and he collaborated across colleges within a university to deliver courses.

When designing courses and reinventing the delivery of learning modules for students, Robert focuses on project-based courses with teams of students and project partners. These project partners can be external businesses, internal facilities people, or faculty. With the help of a business partner, he developed the first business school with a performance dashboard using energy data, indoor air quality, and a CO_2 price embedded in performance data. This prior work has enabled his interest in utilizing the buildings students spend time inside as a learning laboratory (Sroufe, 2020). Expand this interest to a campus as a living laboratory, and the stage is set for why and how both Brad and Robert were attracted to Chatham's Eden Hall.

Robert came to Chatham with a dual appointment in the Falk School of Sustainability & Environment while working with the Business Department in the School of Liberal Arts. A primary draw to come to Eden Hall was to work across disciplines with sustainability faculty and a campus designed as a living laboratory. This is a place where students, faculty, and business partners learn together, where food is grown, buildings provide inspiration and data, and where water sheds and systems are not just part of the landscape but also part of a learning opportunity to see how all decisions we make have environmental and social impacts.

The remaining sections of this chapter explore the campus's history, stakeholders involved in its design, and continued development. Subsequent sections will discuss stakeholder engagement, the campus as a resource for transformative courses, what we have learned, and outcomes and recommendations for others to create and visit campuses like this.

Intent of a campus as curriculum – living the integration of sustainability

The 388-acre Eden Hall campus is a model for sustainable design and net zero emissions. The vision started with this: a school and campus that is not just a place where you talk about sustainability or read about it; it's something that is experienced. It was a working farm from 1938 up until 2008. Today, it has educational buildings with classrooms, farm buildings, and student housing while monitoring its energy, water, and waste systems (see Figure 7.1). The creation of a campus was so that we could experience it as a living and learning environment where we (students and faculty) are living sustainably; we generate data and monitor the buildings and the results of the technologies employed. It was designed to have a virtual environment monitoring water, energy, bioswales, mini-hydro, solar photovoltaics, solar hot water, heat recovery from composting, and geothermal heat pumps, set up to interface with the academic community and community outside of the campus (BNIM + Andropogon, 2011).

We have a main university campus at Shadyside. It has been a historic learning laboratory that started as a women's college and an arboretum in 1869. The main campus has carbon neutrality goals, and this second newer laboratory, Eden Hall, is separate from the main campus. As an investment, a risk, and an experiment, Eden Hall interfaces with a broader community over 20 miles north of the main Shadyside campus, and makes it a more dynamic environment, experimenting with keeping 100-year-old buildings on site juxta positioned with new designs, new construction, new energy management techniques, new ways of living and learning so we are comprehensively attempting to maximize the benefits of the campus as a "transformational experience." This experience is a purposeful part of placing a multidisciplinary sustainability school on site.

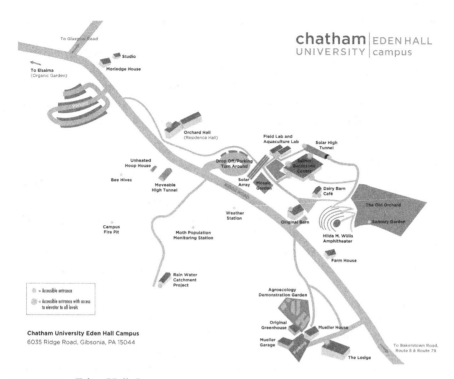

FIGURE 7.1 Eden Hall Campus.

One of the earliest schools of its kind in the country, the Falk School is a wellspring for leadership and education to overcome current and future sustainability challenges. The Falk School is inspired by the work of Chatham alumna Rachel Carson '29 (author of Silent Spring, activist, and inspiration for the proto-environmental movement of the 1960s and 1970s), whose knowledge about the environment and passion for preserving it are traits that drive the school's mission. The academic programs in the Falk School's Eden Hall campus are dedicated to producing professional sustainability leaders and the purposeful intersection of sustainability, business management, and food study students.

Chatham University's Falk School of Sustainability & Environment is distinctive in integrating core sustainability principles and the living laboratory campus at Eden Hall into undergraduate and graduate programs in Sustainability, the MBA program, and the Master of Arts in Food Studies. Recognizing the imperative for sustainability in contemporary business practices, the programs incorporate specialized courses focused on sustainable business practices, energy systems, conservation, sustainable supply chains, and capstone experiential real-world projects courses. By intertwining these topics with the foundational elements of a MBA, and experiential learning on campus, students gain an integrated understanding of how sustainability permeates business functions and management opportunities. This holistic approach ensures that graduates are not only well versed in standard business management but also equipped to address the complex challenges posed by environmental and social considerations in today's global business landscape.

We are continuously maintaining and updating the campus and its goals. This is an ongoing campaign for the continued integration of sustainability, investment in this campus, people, and transformational learning.

Stakeholders engaged in this campus

The Eden Hall Campus is located on land with a rich and deep history. What is now known as the Pittsburgh region was called Dionde:gâ in the Seneca language and stewarded for millennia by Native American nations indigenous to this place, including the Osage, the Shawnee, the Lenape, and the Haudenosaunee Confederacy. We recognize, continue to benefit from, and aspire to learn more about and better honor this history of stewardship at Eden Hall.

The creation of Eden Hall Campus epitomizes a comprehensive approach to sustainability in both design and construction, establishing itself as a dynamic living laboratory for academic exploration. Undergraduate and graduate students can access and interact with campus operations staff and faculty to observe how sustainability is implemented into campus operations, creating a bridge between curricular and experiential learning. Students and their research with faculty act as building blocks for continuous measurement, management, and improvement of campus agricultural, energy, water, and waste systems.

We have three committees made up of Falk School leadership, faculty, and students that meet every month to review land stewardship, buildings, and community sustainability initiatives. Brad and Robert sit on two of these three committees. We have also designed a curriculum so undergraduate and graduate students can do thesis projects that help improve curriculum and course offerings. Students are currently working on the design and delivery of greenhouse gas (GHG) accounting courses that utilize building data. They are also researching decarbonization master plans for the campus and its buildings. Other research involves the feasibility of programs in urban planning and construction management so we can enable more interaction with construction industry businesses and economic development.

Every semester there are efforts to coordinate dual-degree programs and their delivery for the MBA, master's in Sustainability, and Master of Arts in Food Studies. The Program Directors and faculty work to review programs, schedule the delivery of courses across campuses, and advise students on how they can align course offerings with sustainability interests. These courses and the utilization of the campus as a sustainability laboratory are some of the ways we attempt to build on the design of the campus to purposefully connect business practices to sustainability within courses.

Connecting current business practices to sustainable business management

Here, we attempt to describe the ways we utilize best practices in operations as we connect practitioners and facilities professionals who work with faculty to deliver courses. We know we are biased, but we believe these are the ways courses and entire programs should be delivered in the future on any campus and with any school. A recent conversation with Brad included some good advice for the readers of this chapter. "Academics need to come out of our offices."

Pulling from a historical context, facilities professionals wanted to do a walking tour of the campus to review buildings, water systems, bioswales, geothermal fields, and renewable energy generation, and no faculty showed up. In any environment, when learning about sustainability and data is made available to these important stakeholders, faculty participation needs to be a top priority. Getting everyone to show up doesn't work organically, "it's part of a campaign for learning about and integrating information into courses and research."

Next, we will highlight how the design and delivery of dual-degree programs connect business practices to sustainable business management. The MSUS, MBA, and Food Studies dual-degree programs leverage the strengths of Chatham's programs to develop and deliver learning about sustainability leadership in business management. The programs put students across degree programs in the same classrooms and in direct contact with the campus. This purposeful integration positions graduates for leadership positions in sustainability across industry sectors, including business, government, and NGOs. The programs include foundational coursework in business and sustainability as well as advanced work in various aspects of sustainability.

MSUS Sustainability Degree (*Concentrations)	MSUS + MBA Dual Degree	MBA Degree (*Concentrations)	Food Studies Degree
SUS Applied Ecology	FST Sustainable Nonprofit Management	BUS Global Business	FST Food Systems
SUS Political Economy of Sustainability	SUS Pursuing Sustainability Through Governance	BUS Sustainable Human Capital	FST Food Access
SUS Sustainable Cities	SUS Building Sustainable and Resilient Cities	BUS Information Systems Analytics	FST Agroecology
SUS Sustainability Ethics and Equity	BUS Global Business	BUS Economics for Managers	FST Agroecology Lab

(Continued)

(Continued)

MSUS Sustainability Degree (*Concentrations)	MSUS + MBA Dual Degree	MBA Degree (*Concentrations)	Food Studies Degree
SUS Foundations of Sustainability	SUS Applied Methods	BUS Managerial Accounting	FST Food Culture & History
SUS Using the Scientific Method to Craft Research	SUS Research Methods	BUS Marketing Management	FST Research Methods
SUS Research Methods	SUS Thesis Proposal Development	BUS Corporate Finance	FST Elective
SUS Research Proposal	SUS Independent Study	BUS Strategy and Entrepreneurship	BUS Corporate Finance
SUS Concentration Electives: four courses in Urban and Energy Systems, Ecology and Resource Management, *Business and Innovation, or Food Systems	SUS Sustainable Decision Analysis	BUS Business Consulting Capstone	BUS Sustainable Human Capital
*BUS Sustainability Assessment & Reporting	BUS Sustainability Assessment and Reporting	BUS Electives for Concentrations, three courses in: Accounting, Entrepreneurship, Healthcare Management, Project Management, *Sustainability	FST Elective(s)
*SUS Sustainable Decision Analysis	BUS Marketing Management	*SUS Sustainability and Assessment Reporting	BUS Information System & Analytics
*SUS Green and Social Innovation	SUS Internship	*SUS Sustainable Supply Chain Management	BUS Global Business
SUS Solution-Based Experiential Learning	BUS Sustainable Human Capital		BUS Economics for Managers
SUS Solution-Based Experiential Learning II	BUS Sustainable Supply Chain Management		BUS Managerial Accounting

(*Continued*)

(Continued)

MSUS Sustainability Degree (*Concentrations)	MSUS + MBA Dual Degree	MBA Degree (*Concentrations)	Food Studies Degree
SUS Leadership for Transition to Sustainability	BUS Corporate Finance		FST Business of Food & Agriculture
SUS Methods Elective	SUS Sustainable Behavior Change, or Social Innovation		BUS Marketing Management
SUS Internship	SUS Leadership for Transitions to Sustainability		BUS Strategy and Entrepreneurship
SUS Thesis Project	SUS Applied Ecology		FST Thesis
COM Environmental Communications	BUS Information Systems Analytics or Environmental Statistics BUS Managerial Accounting BUS Strategy and Entrepreneurship BUS Business Consulting Capstone or Master's Thesis		

Leveraging a campus as a living laboratory and integrating a dual-degree master's program in Sustainability, an MBA, and Food Studies offers a transformative approach to changing the traditional learning landscape, all puns intended, of business practices. By immersing students in a comprehensive curriculum that intertwines business management with sustainability principles, you create a dynamic learning environment beyond theoretical discussions. Through experiential learning from the campus, students gain hands-on experience in implementing sustainable initiatives, such as energy-efficient technologies, waste reduction strategies, and sustainable supply chain management. This direct application of knowledge allows students to see the impact of sustainable practices on business operations and a return on investment that can also value environmental impacts and social sustainability.

The dual-degree program serves as a catalyst for cultivating change agents in the business world. Graduates not only emerge with a solid foundation in business management but also equip with the skills and mindset needed to drive sustainability initiatives within organizations. MBAs must work with Sustainability Students, Environmental Science, and Food Study students in an environment of collaboration. As they enter the workforce, these individuals become ambassadors of change, influencing corporate strategies and fostering a culture of sustainability. By demonstrating the success of this dual-degree approach in producing professionals who can connect current business practices to necessary sustainable business management, you contribute to a paradigm shift in the business world, where sustainability is not just an add-on but an integral part of strategic decision making.

We also offer an undergraduate curriculum with several tracks, including Sustainability, Sustainability and Society, Natural Resource Management, Sustainable Energy and Urban Systems, and Sustainable Business Studies. Some unique aspects of the undergraduate or graduate curriculum are the ways we can deliver learning. For example, we have decision analysis, statistics, and analytics classes taught by experts with backgrounds in corporate environmental goal setting using climate and carbon emissions data in their classes. Faculty delivering sustainable human capital along with behavioral change can speak to the campus as an agent of change. Faculty delivering content on energy management systems, energy conservation, and urban planning can use our buildings in courses and projects.

As noted from a Performance Excellence in Electricity Renewal (PEER) certification and Anna Grace Mbow, program manager for strategic partnerships at the United States Green Building Council (USGBC), "it was a really collaborative, real-world, hands-on experience for the students." These same buildings can be learning laboratories on any campus utilizing best practices in more sustainable business management, and design competitions for improving the health and productivity of occupants while decarbonizing (see Sroufe, 2022, net-zero module for MBA courses).

Experiential elements of one faculty member in undergraduate classes in Sustainability and Technology, Renewable Energy and Society, and Sustainable Energy Applications course utilizing the Eden Hall campus include, but are not limited to, tours of energy systems, visiting electrified kitchens that do not use fossil fuels, energy audits of buildings or individual systems, identifying and presenting data on energy production and consumption with Automated Logic, semester-long projects examining energy systems for additions or modifications, photovoltaic electricity production estimates using NREL tools, impacts of sub-metering older buildings, recommendations for future buildings for student housing, and retrofitting analysis of 50-year-old buildings.

Energy and GHG information used in classes can be pulled from campus buildings. In 2022, Green Business Certification Inc. recognized a faculty member's work for PEER certification for utilizing student teams to chase down data during the pandemic to document the campus's energy infrastructure and earn certification points (Hennick, 2022). While university officials were confident in the sustainable features of the campus's energy infrastructure, designed so the buildings at the campus achieve LEED Platinum certification, the PEER certification process (Guide to LEED Certification, 2024) helped students gather and organize information on multiple systems.

This level of detail helped to document the whole microgrid in detail. This level of detail included the local power generation capacity of 341 kW, with multiple solar installations, two natural gas cogeneration turbines, a geothermal energy loop, and a mobile battery storage system. Eden Hall also has a 2.5 kW microgrid, featuring solar panels and a wind turbine. These systems provide a different kind of classroom experience, a deep dive into data collection; they get some non-sustainability students interested in sustainability; and experience managing projects that make them more attractive job candidates.

We also use the university as an example of what corporations need to do when pulling together an annual Global Reporting Initiative (GRI – Home (2024)) based sustainability report. To this end, we have students in the Solutions-Based Learning courses, thesis courses, and independent studies to help with obtaining the necessary data for the Association for the Advancement of Sustainability in Higher Education (AASHE) Sustainability Tracking, Assessment & Rating System (*STARS*, 2023). Much the same as what corporations must do, STARS allows students to help measure our sustainability performance, create a baseline for continuous improvement, and integrate sustainability into planning and development efforts.

Here, we engage students and staff in the reporting process and build a culture of sustainability on campus. During the pandemic, while a student team was looking at a particular STARS credit, they worked with a data analytic professor to develop a contract tracing program so we would know if a student got sick, what classes they came into contact with others, and even what shuttle they were utilizing for transportation, and then use these data to help keep other students healthy. Students involved in these STARS data collection efforts in the past have gone on to do sustainability reporting work for consulting companies and corporations.

GHG auditing using campus data is part of independent studies; and thesis classes and can be part of work-study jobs for students annually. Thesis projects also utilize agricultural food plots on campus which include certified organic farms, demonstration garden, and multiple greenhouses. These projects are at the intersection of food studies, entrepreneurship, and the business of the food industry. Environmental science, urban planning, and food studies faculty know how to leverage the campus in classrooms, can find examples of best practices from our own systems, and provide a classroom experience for students that is not theoretical, but instead practical and grounded in the campus and its infrastructure.

Business students from the marketing program have helped with international recognition among over 300 colleges and universities as leaders in campus waste reduction. Business faculty and students participated in what was called Recycle Mania and is now called the Campus Race to Zero Waste. Developing the marketing plan for this on campus helps to promote measurable waste and energy reduction. The goal is to promote waste reduction and encourage students to think about where the products they use every day are going. For eight weeks, progress is measured by the Chatham University Office of Sustainability and is part of hands-on projects in marketing classes. Business faculty and students have also helped to develop a student green fund. This started as a suggestion to have food services locations on campus round up at the cash register. The program is utilized by Café Rachel, a coffee shop and in dining halls to have students donate money equivalent to rounding up the receipt to an even dollar amount so that the money donated helps fund campus sustainability projects.

With ongoing efforts toward continuous improvement, last semester, we developed a new Sustainable Business Practices required course in the dual-degree and MSUS programs as a first-semester introduction to business management with a focus on how sustainability is part of every business function, that is, Integrated Management (Sroufe, 2018), materiality, and industry best practices. We continue to build on experiential courses such as the Business Consulting Capstone and Solutions-Based Learning courses, where teams of students work with external business partners to solve real problems, benchmark industry best practices, and apply learning to on-campus opportunities for improvement. We are developing more integrated capstone experiential learning classes across programs in the terminal semester for sustainability and dual-degree students. With the foundation of a learning laboratory campus and options for students to take classes and work with business and the school of sustainability faculty, we can develop and deliver courses with a unique campus experience at the center of learning.

Resources used in transformative thinking

We help students envision more sustainable and responsible business practices and apply these concepts as part of the collegiate experience at Chatham University and Eden Hall's campus. Campus as a living laboratory gets traditional MBA students onto a campus where each building, the connected systems, and the campus provide opportunities to learn from and interact with its best practices companies embrace, that is, decarbonization, goals of net zero energy, high-performance buildings, and sustainable agriculture practices as the food grown on campus goes to the kitchens and then to students for consumption, with a much shorter food to table value chain.

Resources to help enable strategic planning for the university, the campus, and the curriculum include working with external partners to create digital twins of the campus infrastructure, GIS mapping, and decarbonization plans. This planning will help inform research and capital planning for the maintenance and next phase of development for Eden Hall. With this plan, we will be better at connecting building and system data to measure and manage progress toward goals of net zero energy and a lower carbon footprint. We will be able to put a price on CO_2 emissions and use this information in business and sustainability classes to see how it will impact decision making, accounting, finance, reporting, and strategic planning. The available data and modeling are all available tools for our use in developing curriculum, lowering operations costs, and including students and faculty as important stakeholders. This type of planning can help secure funding for improving the campus and differentiate us in the marketplace.

Chatham is benchmarking with AASHE staff on their Sustainability Change Leadership Program and teams from Swarthmore and Stanford who have already participated and implemented living-learning laboratory models based on these principles into their university programs. Chatham is evaluating the participation of various faculty, staff, and students in the AASHE Sustainability Change Leadership Program to expand its capacity in this area by acting as change facilitators.

Other connections to AASHE include but are not limited to a team of students who help collect data for over 100 environmental, social, and governance (ESG) performance metrics for the university and this campus. In this way, students collect and disseminate the same information found in corporate sustainability reports and real-world sustainability reporting initiatives aligned with the GRI as corporations collect similar data for corporate reporting. This is recognized externally by employers who hire the students on this team to help companies manage their reporting processes. By connecting existing campus operational resources and needs with learning activities, students are able to contribute to measuring and managing the changes needed to transform sustainability at the campus, within academic programs, and after graduation within enterprises.

What have we learned

As a living and learning community, Eden Hall Campus will encourage students and faculty to immerse themselves in a setting that promotes the study and advancement of sustainable development based on restorative principles. This is a dynamic, exciting place – a living laboratory in which to explore fundamentally different approaches to how we manage resources, both physical and intellectual. It will inspire us to model development and behavior, changing how we occupy the land, design buildings, interact with our communities, fuel our economies, and design systems for energy, waste, water, transportation, and food.

Students learn the skills, tools, and frameworks to confidently design, propose/present, and implement/execute changes that advance sustainability in their organizations. Regular interaction between staff, faculty, and students breaks down the barriers of understanding and allows for broader collaboration in overcoming common challenges that exist in the implementation of sustainability in operations (resource constraints, data, expertise, training/education). For example, if a problem develops with a rainwater harvesting system, one of the three committees, that is, land stewardship, buildings, or community sustainability initiatives, can identify the problem and connect with faculty on the committee along with facilities to see what work needs to be done. This potential problem can easily become material to discuss in a class such as Applied Ecology, a Solutions-based Experiential class, or a thesis project for an individual student.

In the past, there was a big push to get and spend money and build things as fast as possible. Some rainwater harvesting systems and a wind turbine were installed without the necessary expertise to connect all the systems. This example stressed the need for a budget planning process and not ending up in a place where some systems must be reengineered to work at less than full capacity. Better enabling planning and understanding "handoffs" between acquiring, installing, maintaining, and someday replacing new technology can payoff in learning and lower costs in the future.

We have learned there is a leadership void and pushback from faculty in many places that will need to be more collaborative to make more campuses and change agents, such as faculty and facilities professionals, a reality in the future. Prior experience has shown us the importance and enabling power of strong leadership that gets it. The importance of knowing and working with leadership should not be overlooked. We have been fortunate to be part of conversations around strategy and how a school or a campus is much more than a cost center. Facilities professionals need to be as elevated as possible to be part of the processes and capital planning to make an entire campus a reality. It's a campaign; no one will do this because you expect them to or because it's the right thing to do. We have to actively campaign for it all the time.

While writing this chapter, there is a business management pushback with a focus on cutting costs in universities and the business world. The financial reality of the university environment, that is, with many small universities experiencing financial issues, is that facilities are among the first stakeholders to feel the fiscal pain of budget cuts. Isolation makes everything difficult, from developing a non-core-required course to a campus that is separate from the main campus. Strategic, long-term planning can help weather these periods of time. Whether developing a program or a campus building, good planning goes beyond the need just to build the building.

Leadership should think about building capacity, hiring people with experience with sustainability, learning curves, and knowledge management so that parts of campus are not put on the deferred maintenance chopping block. Another important point to make here is that we need to find the right people. Hire those willing to learn and grow and think about how to spend time and resources to recruit the right people to move a strategic plan for a campus, maintenance of the campus, curriculum, and individual course in the right direction. In a post-pandemic world, we have seen turnover in key positions hinder progress on sustainability initiatives and hiring the right people becoming even more important.

Other examples of pushback can be found in:

- A Dean once said sustainability and environmental management have no place in a business school.
- Pushback from business faculty in accounting took the form of spending 18 months researching the feasibility of sustainability as part of the curriculum and concluded it wasn't possible. They then held their ground after being shown textbooks, case studies, and accounting professional associations along with academic research with tools and training on integrating this into their classes.
- Some administrators and faculty miss the opportunity that understanding sustainability provides by saying it means "sustainable profits." This myopic view misses a larger value proposition.
- This brings about another cautionary note. Do not underestimate the resistance some will have to change when that change involves sustainability. We find it interesting how entrenched neoliberal economic perspectives are within accounting, finance, economics, and entire business schools.

Instead of pushing a "sustainability" initiative, position change as "innovation," best practices in the industry. There is an opportunity to tell better stories of leading corporations doing these same things, that is, high-performance buildings, less waste, and GHGs are a measure of waste, better health, and regenerative agriculture as good business, and parts of innovative pedagogy. It is not easy to change 50-year-old memes, yet we do know that change is possible, and to borrow a cliché "if you build it, they will come." Those who resist this change by saying it's not possible can be shown innovative courses, curricula, and entire campuses as proof it is not only possible but already happening.

Designing a university campus with a dedicated focus on sustainability, akin to Chatham University's Eden Hall Campus, can have far-reaching effects on students, colleagues, and community partners. At the heart of this impact is the educational environment that such a campus fosters. Students immersed in a sustainable campus setting are not merely recipients of knowledge; they become active participants in a living laboratory where ecological principles are integrated into daily life. This transformational learning enhances their understanding of sustainable practices, instilling a sense of responsibility and environmental stewardship that transcends the classroom. It can attract people from industry and academics, that is, the authors and, when the timing is right, a new university president. Dr. Rhonda Phillips came to Chatham within the last year because of this campus and its strong ties to sustainability. With leadership support and collaboration across schools, we now have new efforts underway to integrate sustainability into learning outcomes for all business management courses while starting a new School of Business & Enterprise with sustainability integrated within the curriculum.

Colleagues within this sustainable campus environment find themselves part of a collaborative community that values interdisciplinary approaches to problem-solving. The design encourages open spaces, shared facilities, and the incorporation of renewable energy sources, fostering a culture of innovation and cooperation. This interconnectedness is essential for addressing complex sustainability challenges, as professionals from diverse fields collaborate seamlessly to develop holistic solutions. The campus itself becomes a testament to the integrated management of sustainability into the fabric of academic and professional pursuits, attracting and inspiring faculty to incorporate these principles into their research and teaching methodologies.

Externally, the impact of a sustainably designed university campus extends beyond its borders. Community partners witness the tangible benefits of sustainable practices, ranging from reduced ecological footprint to enhanced quality of life. The campus serves as a hub for community engagement, offering resources, expertise, and shared spaces that contribute to the broader region's sustainable development. Committing to environmental responsibility, the university becomes a catalyst for positive change, influencing local businesses, government entities, and residents to adopt more sustainable practices. In this way, a thoughtfully designed sustainable campus becomes a beacon of inspiration, fostering a ripple effect that extends far beyond the university gates.

Outcomes – recommendations

It's easy for many people to not envision what the future of university education can look like. Faculty are told to keep their heads down, publish, and not have a chance to design systems for long-term resilience. They can be among the first to tell you what is *not* possible. To change the arc of the future of business education, we can structure opportunities to change a campus, a curriculum, or a course in a way that accommodates interactions and sustainability early in the design phase. With over 20 years of combined experience in designing and integrating experiential learning into traditional business education, the authors are actively campaigning for more sustainability at the intersection of experiential learning and campus infrastructure. We find University buildings, energy systems, and an entire campus built with sustainability in mind from the ground up as one example of the transitions necessary for business education. It's a heavy lift, yet we know that when someone can see an example of a campus as a living laboratory, and see that they exist, then we know "it is possible."

Within this type of school and campus, sustainability is an integrated part of dual-degree programs, food studies, business education, and environmental science. We can leverage experiential learning in agriculture, water systems, energy systems, food systems, supply chains, renewable energy, and high-performance buildings in new ways traditional business programs have not been able to in the past. With transitions to more sustainable business programs, these types of living laboratory campuses will someday be commonplace. Since the first phase of this campus started ten years ago, the Falk School's graduate programs reached the top ten nationally for degrees conferred in their field; and Chatham University has been consistently recognized at the top of the list of green colleges in the nation and ranked #4 by the Princeton Review.

Although not large in absolute terms, the Falk School has added undergraduate degrees in sustainability to complement its graduate programs and enrollment is on a growth trajectory with the University's largest undergraduate majors. There is a strong interest by many to figure this out and to just do it. But another word of caution here, don't do 50 small things unless they map into the overall vision. Think BIG, that is, if we can't do it at a megawatt scale, maybe we should rethink what we are doing and how it aligns with a strategic plan. Ask big questions, like what will it take to have a net zero campus? We literally would be generating all our power only on campus and learning about the infrastructure and planning to run a campus and a business in this way.

As a professor specializing in sustainable business practices situated at Chatham University's Eden Hall Campus, Robert has a unique opportunity to promote transformative learning experiences while working with colleagues like Brad and faculty across a school of sustainability and a school of business. The campus itself, with its emphasis on sustainability, serves as an immersive learning environment. Encourage students to engage in hands-on projects integrating sustainable principles into business practices. Field studies, collaborative projects with local businesses, and internships emphasizing sustainable supply chains and energy systems can provide students with practical insights and skills extending beyond traditional classroom learning.

What we hope readers can take away from this chapter is optimism in knowing these same spaces in which we live, and work provide dynamic opportunities for sustainability aligned with transformative education in core-required courses across degree programs. By taking a deeper dive into understanding buildings such as our homes, offices, cafeterias, and businesses, along with how we get to and from those spaces, we can personally walk the talk of sustainability. We should challenge our environmental science, business, engineering, health sciences, and other colleagues to be more innovative. There is not enough space in this chapter to take on all the limitations or the 50 years of entrenched business-as-usual attitude resisting the sustainability paradigm. To our business management colleagues in the academy, what are you waiting for? We need your help in measuring, valuing, and managing emerging, more sustainable business practices as together we can have an impact at scale.

Consider organizing workshops and seminars to inspire more faculty members to transition to sustainable business education and become change agents. Share success stories from your own experiences, demonstrating the positive impact of integrating sustainability into your teaching and research. Emphasize the relevance of sustainable business practices across various disciplines, illustrating how these principles can enhance not only environmental outcomes but also economic and social well-being. Foster a sense of community among faculty by creating interdisciplinary platforms for knowledge exchange and collaboration. Provide resources and support to those interested in incorporating sustainability into campuses, programs, and courses, making the transformation more accessible and rewarding.

Furthermore, develop places and academic programs promoting educators as change agents. Signal the importance of promoting those who have taken the risk to be different and focus on sustainability, which integrates it into teaching. University teachers/scholars are catalysts for broader societal change. Advocate for the importance of producing graduates who are not only well versed in traditional environmental science, urban planning, food science, or business concepts but also equipped with the knowledge and mindset to address global challenges through collaborative, sustainable practices. Foster a culture of mentorship, where experienced faculty members guide their colleagues in navigating the evolving landscape of sustainable business education. By building a strong community of change educators and an entire campus, the impact can extend far beyond individual classrooms, creating a collective force for positive transformation in business education.

It's a campaign. No one will do this because you expect them to or because it's the right thing to do. We must actively campaign for the integrated management of sustainability where we work, for an entire campus as a learning laboratory, and for where we live, and push for positive change all the time.

References

BNIM + Andropogon. (2011). A Splendid Vision, Chatham University//Eden Hall Campus Master Plan.

GRI – Home. (2024). *The global leader for impact reporting.* https://www.globalreporting.org/

Guide to LEED certification. Guide to LEED Certification | U.S. Green Building Council. (2024). https://www.usgbc.org/guide-LEED-certification

Hennick, C. (2022). PEER certification final: College students gather energy data during a pandemic. https://www.usgbc.org/articles/peer-certification-final-college-students-gather-energy-data-during-pandemic. Accessed February 24, 2024.

ILFI. (2024, April 5). *What is the living building challenge?*. International Living Future Institute. https://living-future.org/lbc/

Sroufe, R. (2018). *Integrated management: How sustainability creates value for any business.* Emerald Publishing Limited.

Sroufe, R. (2020). Business schools as living labs: Advancing sustainability in management education. *Journal of Management Education, 44*(6), 726–765.

Sroufe, R. (2021). *3. Design for the experience: A more sustainable future.* Personal Sustainability Practices: Faculty Approaches to Walking the Sustainability Talk and Living the UN SDGs, 23.

Sroufe, R. (2022). Net Zero Energy Module, Page Prize Honorable Mention, University of South Carolina. As part of the Dr. Alfred N. and Lynn Manos Page Prize. For Sustainability Issues in Business Curricula; supporting efforts to introduce or substantially upgrade sustainability courses and associated coursework into the curriculum of business schools. https://sc.edu/study/colleges_schools/moore/documents/page_prize/2022/module_net_zero_energy.pdf. Accessed February 24, 2024.

Sroufe, R., & Ramos, D. P. (2015). Leveraging collaborative, thematic problem-based learning to integrate curricula. *Decision Sciences Journal of Innovative Education, 13*(2), 151–176.

Stars, Sustainability Tracking Assessment & Rating System. The Sustainability Tracking, Assessment & Rating System. (2023, July 17). https://stars.aashe.org/

8

WOXSEN UNIVERSITY AS A MODEL FOR SUSTAINABLE BUSINESS SCHOOL TRANSFORMATION

James Weichert, Pavana Kiranmai Chepuri, and Chahat Mishra

Abstract

Woxsen University in Hyderabad, India, has an innovative approach to business education, including sustainability, experiential learning, and a global perspective. Its holistic learning environment and integration of social, environmental, and ethical considerations prepare students for the challenges of the modern business landscape. In 2023 Global Movement Initiative (GMI), an initiative created to transform business education had the opportunity to support Woxsen in the transformation of their curriculum for a sustainable future. Visiting Woxsen and discovering firsthand their vision – led by young professionals fluent in sustainability and prepared to create a better world – has led to the conclusion that Woxsen University may serve as a model for others seeking to renovate their own curricula.

Introduction

Transforming business education from the neoliberal narrative currently taught in the majority of business schools to a curriculum that includes sustainability, especially in the introductory and core courses is imperative if we are to become the kind of people who can live on this planet without destroying it (Stoner, 2021). Business schools are the best lever to create this change – they train future business leaders, currently 70 million annually across the globe – and business is recognized as both contributing to our current global unsustainability and holding potential solutions to heal our broken planet (*PRME Principles Refresh – Final Report*, 2023).

This is not an isolated view and should come as no surprise. In 2021, UNESCO published *Reimagining Our Futures Together – A New Social Contract*

DOI: 10.4324/9781003521839-9

For Education, finding that the 20th-century rationale for education – to provide an informed citizenry and support economic development – was insufficient to address today's challenges, including climate change, resource use that exceeds planetary boundaries, and widening social and economic inequality. It held education to account and proposed a fundamental realignment of our teaching practices.

> Currently, education attainment and completion correlate with unsustainable practices. The world's most educated countries and people are the ones most accelerating climate change. While we expect education to provide pathways to peace, justice, and human rights, we are only now beginning to expect and indeed demand that it opens pathways and builds capacities for sustainability. This work needs to intensify. If being educated means living unsustainably, we need to recalibrate our notions of what education should do and what it means to be educated.
>
> *(International Commission on the Futures of Education, 2021)*

Business schools are an excellent lever to address these challenges because they possess the intellectual and financial resources, the missions, and the global reach (Global Movement Initiative). Also, business schools are generally seen to be responsive to the needs of industry which is increasingly demanding that 20th-century capitalism be revisited. The Business Leadership Roundtable, the World Economic Forum (*Davos Manifesto*, 2020), and the NY Stock Exchange are each addressing the financial risk associated with a failure to integrate stakeholders and the environment. This is a paradigm shift, promoting a broader understanding of business success that incorporates both financial performance and societal well-being (Laszlo et al., 2017).

However, it remains unclear what business schools should look like in this changed world. Teaching sustainability remains a challenge that few schools have adequately addressed, with outliers still viewed as pioneers (Irwin et al., 2024). Industry is demanding leaders who can thrive in a world of VUCA (volatility, uncertainty, complexity, ambiguity) which demands both critical thinking and a "different operating system" (Scharmer, 2018).

One such system that meets all of these challenges is the Sustainable Development Goals (SDGs), created and agreed to by the member states of the United Nations in 2015. The SDGs clearly demonstrate a pathway that balances people, planet, and prosperity (*Transforming Our World: The 2030 Agenda for Sustainable Development | Department of Economic and Social Affairs*). Since 1987 when Gro Harlem Brundtland was tasked with creating a set of actionable steps to preserve *Our Common Future,* the United Nations has been the strongest voice of a shared responsibility for life on this planet. The SDGs build on that responsibility and provide a common language for educators and their students.

Woxsen University – a model

One case that demonstrates how business school curriculum might address sustainability is Woxsen University outside Hyderabad in Telangana State, India. In late 2023, I, James Weichert had the opportunity to visit them on behalf of GMI and to conduct research on their sustainable curriculum transformation. Woxsen is a private university, being built as we speak – both the curriculum and the campus – and is an example of an institution currently updating its curriculum to meet the needs of a sustainable future. The brainchild of Praveen K. Pula, it was started in 2014 to "create socially responsible global citizens" (*Chancellor's Message – Woxsen University*). Based on a disruptive set of educational concepts, Woxsen curriculum is constructed on experiential learning in a global context paired with academic excellence, inclusivity, as well as Ethics, Responsibility, and Sustainability, or ERS.

Woxsen University aims "to develop an outstanding cadre of international business leaders with a high level of performance orientation and human sensitivity" (Woxsen University), underscoring the overarching ethos of the institution. Embedded within this vision is ERS, and a foundational commitment to effecting societal change, highlighting the centrality of ERS principles within the institutional framework of Woxsen. To embed these concepts, the university has created a steering committee with members from each of the seven schools coordinated by an ERS project officer. What follows are examples from the university that reflect this vision.

Coursework at Woxsen University's business school is similar to that found elsewhere with a four-year undergraduate program and a two-year MBA; however, ERS accounts for 20% of content at the MBA level and 10% elsewhere (Rodriguez, 2023). For example, students are required to complete a social internship project (SIP), of six credits, in their first summer and to take core courses dedicated to ERS. Also, following the SIP, which is 4–6 weeks long, students are required to deliver a comprehensive report encapsulating their endeavors and acquired insights. This report serves as a platform for reflective analysis, prioritizing the cultivation of human sensitivity within the experiential learning process. Further, to foster sustainability consciousness among students, the institution is currently launching an award recognizing exemplary performance in SIP projects to incentivize and catalyze student engagement with sustainability-focused endeavors. Finally, coursework at Woxsen is based on the Principles of Responsible Management Education or PRME (Woxsen University).

Students are also exposed to ERS at Woxsen through experiential learning, predominantly through sustainability projects and programs led by each of the steering committee members. Examples include Elevate project, Sustainability Week, the Rural Entrepreneurship Initiative, and multiple projects and non-compulsory workshops benefiting the local rural community.

Each of these elements is built around specific SDGs, predominantly *1. No Poverty, 4. Quality Education, 8. Decent Work and Economic Growth, and 12.*

Responsible Consumption and Production. The individual schools – business, technology, architecture and planning, arts and design, liberal arts and humanities, law, and sciences – each target SDGs relevant to their individual coursework. The School of Business focuses on SDG 4 – Quality Education, SDG 5 – Gender Equality and SDG 7 – Affordable and Clean Energy. Individual professors, their research projects, and their extracurricular activities highlight how the SDGs are inculcated on campus.

Woxsen professors

Speaking with Centre of Excellence – Diversity Equity and Inclusion (DEI) Leader and Dean of the School of Business, Dr. Kakoli Sen, she explains, "We respect each of our students," which may explain the high percentage of young women on campus. Dean Kakoli is committed to supporting all of her students including minority and LGBTQ – she coordinated a symposium on LGBTQ awareness that took place in 2023 on campus – which is a progressive view in much of India. It does, however, put her squarely in line with the SDGs for quality education and gender equality.

As with each of the 17 SDGs, *4. Quality Education* has multiple specific targets. As an umbrella for inclusive and equitable quality education, the SDG promotes safe, inclusive, and effective learning environments. It also seeks to eliminate gender disparities and to ensure that all learners acquire the knowledge and skills needed to promote sustainable development (SDG Knowledge Hub).

Dean Sen recently spearheaded the *Woxsen Inclusion Conference* with a Woxsen professor, Dr. Anindo Bhattacharjee to "revisit the existing narratives around Diversity, Equality, and Inclusion" – bringing together both industry and academia – to improve existing paradigms and organizational practices centered around sustainable development. Another initiative, *Project Aspiration*, has focused on empowering girls in the surrounding villages and providing career development and confidence-building through a training program run by Woxsen students. The students working on this project develop capabilities in project management, leadership, graphic design, photography, social media, and content development as well as reinforcing social responsibility.

Dr. Bhattacharjee, professor of entrepreneurship and organizational behavior, is a part of the *SDG 8. Decent Work and Economic Growth Initiative* launched in 2019 by the International Association of Universities to support the role of higher education in achieving the United Nation's Agenda 2030 Sustainable Development Goals. Representing India in this initiative, Woxsen is part of a global network of universities driving sustainable economic growth, employment, and decent work through applied action research and policy interaction, and Dr. Bhattacharjee recently attended a conference in Gothenburg, Sweden to collaborate with 30 other educators. On campus, he regularly organizes projects in aid of the local public schools and coordinates programs on rural entrepreneurship for the surrounding communities.

Another educator, Dr. Shilpi Agarwal, Professor of International Finance, is personally committed to bettering the lives of the local community with financial literacy and wellness. She has been involved in social causes her whole life and continues this passion at Woxsen. She coordinates clothing drives with her students, sends them out to teach English classes, sources projectors and other critical equipment for the local primary and secondary schools, and promotes financial literacy both in the local schools for underprivileged youth and on campus for the cleaning staff. Having university students teach budgeting skills, debt management, savings and investment, and financial decision making reinforces the concepts while instilling social responsibility. Dr. Agarwal calls them "little acts of kindness."

These and other activities may be the reason that Woxsen received the top rating in 2021, 2022, and 2023 from the Positive Impact Rating (PIR) (2023 Report), placing it on the same level as more established Indian institutions and well above universities from developed countries. PIR, developed by Thomas Dyllick and a team from St. Gallen University, Switzerland, measures the societal impact of business schools, assessments that AACSB and EQUIS have now also begun. Woxsen is a member of these organizations, as well as of PRME.

The business school at Woxsen, however, is not the only example of ERS on campus. At the AI and Robotics Lab, students work on projects that focus on increasing efficiency, providing virtual healthcare, and improving understanding of the SDGs. At the School of Arts and Design, students are trained in up-cycling, working with local artisans and designing products using sustainable materials. Dean Dr. Adity Saxena sees designers as problem solvers and seeks to nurture the change makers of tomorrow. As an example, in a recent project, students were sent into the local community to research waste flows at a municipal garbage collection facility, and to identify recycling and up-cycling solutions.

Woxsen administration

In our work at GMI, we have seen multiple examples of sustainable curriculum transformation. Most rely on the committed persistence of an individual working within a supportive environment. In my experience, activism alone seems insufficient to dislodge the stasis present at many higher education institutions. In other words, although the will to transform outdated curriculum is a necessary requirement, without the support from above those efforts will have a difficult time gaining traction. At Woxsen, a good example of this is the ERS committee. It is a representative body led by legal counsel and professor Pavana Kiranmai Chepuri – who has both an interest in sustainability and a working knowledge of it on campus, serving as coordinator for the annual PIR and PRME submissions together with Vice President Rodriguez. The ERS committee on campus represents the voices of each school, including business, technology and AI, architecture and planning, arts and design, liberal arts and humanities, law, and sciences. Its function is to streamline approvals for teaching projects at the respective schools.

The administration is also continuing to broaden its understanding of ERS on campus. Ms. Chepuri started working with Global Movement Initiative (GMI) in 2023 to increase sustainable curriculum on campus through both regular calls and as a coordinator for virtual exercises. The weekly Zoom sessions initially begun in preparation for a celebration of sustainability initiatives on campus have now broadened into a campus-wide inquiry into sustainable curriculum. The structure is simple; each participant raises agenda items, the session is recorded, and we meet for 40 minutes weekly.

It is important to note that the GMI participants on these calls are versed in Otto Scharmer's "generative listening" and "collective creativity" (Scharmer, 2023). Often called level four listening, it is a technology of listening for possibility, using the metaphors of planting seeds and nurturing growth to drive transformational change. Simply put, once a question has been asked or a comment has been raised it becomes part of the discussion. The weekly calls serve to reinforce and broaden these nascent concepts. In other words, a question is an inquiry and an inquiry can lead to an investigation. It's not that it always does, but more often than not it raises interest and agency. One of the repeated barriers to business curriculum transformation is a lack of agency, from either administration or work overload, or a lack of collaboration. These calls provide a space for that.

Another example involves an exercise currently underway at the business school. Under the auspices of Dean Kakoli Sen, interested professors are brought together for one hour on Zoom to discuss how best to include sustainability in their courses. The exercise was developed in a recent visit by Prof. James A. F. Stoner of GMI to the university. In a kick-off session, two professors were asked to spend time reviewing the syllabus of one of their classes using the framework of Start–Stop–Continue, involving individual reflection. In the ensuing discussion, the question was raised by Dr. Shiva Sai Kiran Pothula, "What is the baseline knowledge that the students will have of sustainability when entering the class for the first time?" In India, each student comes with a different set of sustainability skills and learning from their K-12 schooling.

To address this disparity, Woxsen has created a set of "Talks" required of all students that create a common language of sustainability on campus. Further, while many definitions of sustainability exist, Woxsen uses the language of the SDGs to guide its ERS activities. The course was introduced for the fall of 2023 semester and was led by Chahat Mishra, Head of International Relations and Strategic Development and supervised by Ms. Chepuri.

Using *The Future You Talks*, an existing part of both the undergraduate and MBA curriculum at Woxsen, Mishra was able to shift the class to focus exclusively on sustainability core concepts. Importantly, it didn't require lengthy approvals or budgeting and the course was amended in under a month prior to commencement. Equally as important, it was able to tap into a large group of passionate sustainability experts globally by using video conferencing software and with students and professors increasing comfort with distance learning. By engaging a ready team of international sustainability thought leaders Mr. Mishra was able to create a series of classes that would not have been otherwise possible, and to do so in an incredibly short time frame.

In the summer of 2023, when GMI began speaking with Mr. Mishra and Ms. Chepuri about developing a foundation of sustainable concepts for all students, *The Future You Talks* were already scheduled. By shifting some of the invited speakers, adding two professors from GMI, and coordinating which speakers would address which core topics, Woxsen was able to integrate key concepts of sustainability into its curriculum in under one month. It was a required course for all students, currently over 3,500. Here is a description of the course:

> In today's rapidly changing world, the concept of sustainability has emerged as a critical framework for addressing pressing environmental, social, and economic challenges. This interdisciplinary course, "Sustainability for the 21st Century," explores the principles, practices, and implications of sustainability across various domains. Students will learn how organizations can align their strategies, practices, and policies with sustainable principles to drive positive social and environmental outcomes while fostering long-term business success.

The main intended learning outcomes (at an introductory level):

1. Demonstrate an ethical, responsible, and sustainability-oriented mindset.
2. Demonstrate a global mindset.
3. Use and critically evaluate indicators of sustainability.

	Educator	Institution	Topic	Date
1	Prof. Natalia Yankovskaya	Institute of Business Studies, Russian Presidential Academy	Introduction to Sustainability	August 2, 2023
2	Dr. Mohammad Bait Ali Sulaiman	College of Commerce and Business Administration, Dhofar U.	21st-Century Marketing	August 9, 2023
	Prof. Linda Irwin	Anderson College of Business, Regis U.		

(*Continued*)

(Continued)

	Educator	Institution	Topic	Date
3	Prof. Karim Parra Rodriguez	Luiss Business School	Carbon Finance & Investment	August 17, 2023
	Dr. James A. F. Stoner	Gabelli School of Business, Fordham U.		
4	Dr. Vikas Kumar	Bristol Business School, UWE	Sustainable Supply Chain	August 30, 2023
5	Prof. Jack Buffington	University of Denver	Social Innovation Ecosystems	September 6, 2023
6	Dr. Chung Shing Lee	St. Martin's University	Sustainable Business Models	September 13, 2023
7	Dr. Elena A. Panfilova	Transparency International	Corporate Governance	September 20, 2023
8	Dr. Carlos Scheel	EGADE Business School Tecnológico de Monterrey	Circular Economy	September 27, 2023
9	Prof. Gustavo Loiola	UN PRME i5 Project Manager	Sustainable Reporting	October 18, 2023
10	Prof. Danilo Maeda	Beon ESG Strategies	Branding Practices	October 22, 2023
11	Dr. Prince Asare	University of Cape Coast, Ghana	Sustainable Leadership	November 1, 2023
12	Prof. Mutiu Lyanda	HSE University, Russia	Design Thinking	November 2, 2023
13	Prof. Sam Obafemi	The Octopus	Community-Centric Initiatives	November 8, 2023

When I asked Mr. Mishra how he was able to put together such a diverse group of thought leaders from all over the globe to teach the course, he said "I just asked." The reality is there is nothing preventing this from happening at any institution. The recognition that there is a gap between traditional business training and the needs of the business environment should be enough to move institutions to correct the inadequacies of their curriculum. It is also important to note that by providing a separate sustainability training professors are no longer required to begin at the beginning. By providing an introductory course in sustainability Woxsen is introducing the building blocks that other courses can further develop.

That this is happening here at Woxsen University, however, is not an accident. Woxsen actively pursues honorary chairs from international professors. Its global perspective is built on collaborations with international institutions including Monmouth University, USA, and the HHL Graduate School of Management in Leipzig, Germany. This serves to underline the outward facing, international focus of a world-class institution and also serves as support for some of its latest courses and extracurricular projects.

It is also a compromise – not all core courses currently taught at Woxsen have been updated to reflect the needs of a sustainable future – but, by creating a course that provides a firm grounding in sustainability the students are more readily able to recognize the transitional nature of other classes. Some would call this "saddle bagging," or bolting on sustainability to an otherwise traditional business curriculum (Sharma & Hart, 2014). But at Woxsen the sum of the curricula – experiential learning, sustainability training, required internships – is more than just incremental change, inculcating what Isabel Rimanoczy has called a sustainability mindset (Rimanoczy, 2021). This is evident in the students and the curriculum, multiple sustainability events, initiatives, and extracurriculars they have created.

Woxsen students

Many student events involve the surrounding communities. For example, over 250 students participated in a textbook donation and visit to a Minorities Residential School in Sangareddy. This government school, designed to provide a free boarding school education for disadvantaged youth, seeks to prepare students for higher education, whether in business, in civil service, or in the military. A Woxsen alumni, Amogh Jajee, donated math and science textbooks for use in the classroom. The visit was coordinated as an ERS Project at Woxsen and included both staff and current students. In addition to delivering books, the creation of a mentorship program, *Project Legacy*, between Woxsen students and the school was discussed.

In another event and collaboration by two student clubs, the Sustainability Club and the Centre of Excellence for Diversity, Equity, and Inclusion (DEI) coordinated the donation of free sanitary pads and feminine hygiene education to over 200 female workers on campus and set up an awareness campaign with regular gynecological visits. These workers come from the surrounding villages and rely on the wages they receive working on campus, but otherwise lead traditional lives where medical attention and personal hygiene topics are not openly discussed. Ms. Sahithi, student and VP of the Centre for Excellence DEI reminded them, "Don't be shy," in the frank training session led by students which was conducted in English, Hindi, and the local Telugu language.

Further, an idea that started as a simple question, "What do we do with all the plastic waste that we see on campus?" was developed into a project that reinforced sustainable concepts, involved multiple stakeholders, and supported individual initiative. Working with the architecture department, the business school, as well as with professors and the administration, the Sustainability Club spearheaded this complicated project. Students initially collected, washed, and sorted plastic for up-cycling; then iterated multiple designs integrating the plastic bottles into the collection bin design; and finally received approval from the administration for placement on campus. Per Someshwar, then President of the Sustainability Club, "I like how it reminds students to recycle and demonstrates the effects of their individual actions."

Events like these, and others such as clearing dangerous debris from local government schools are meant to inculcate ethics and responsibility as well as to benefit the local community. "We're doing our part," says VP Rodriguez. Equally as important, many of the professors on campus that I spoke with are personally committed to social engagement. "I've always given back to the community," says Professor Shilpi Agarwal. She worked with VP Rodriguez to initiate a Rural Entrepreneurship and financial literacy program, having students and professors educate both school children and adults on the value of investment and savings.

Using the tradition of *gullak* – similar to a piggy bank – lessons focused on acquiring the minimum necessary to open a bank account, as well as how to structure investments to grow a home business. Woxsen students, who mostly come from privileged backgrounds and participated in these sessions, also serve as role models to the local youth.

In the AI Robotics and Innovation Lab, students have created an app to quantify and predict food waste. Dr. Hemachandran, director of the AI Research Centre, works on both consulting projects and training students for positions in industry, especially as Hyderabad has been recently dubbed the AI capital of India. Nawaz Asif Ali Shaik of the debate club and budding AI entrepreneur, summed it up, Woxsen is "helping me upgrade the arsenal of skills I need to take on the new challenges" of the 21st century.

In contrast to the marked decline in business school enrollment in the developed world, Woxsen has a 17% acceptance rate, with significantly more students applying than are enrolled, a 100% placement rate for the business school, and a 97% placement rate for undergraduates after graduation. That means that nearly all of the students receive employment upon completion of their studies with recruiting partners including Goldman Sachs, IBM, Providence Healthcare, and Cognizant as well as many smaller internet startups predominantly based in the Hyderabad area.

And even though there remains much to be done, and there are courses that still do not include sustainability at Woxsen, the changes are having a huge impact. When asked how to improve *The Future You Talks* for the Sustainability in the 21st-century class, the students had strong opinions. Some requested more hands-on projects, some requested smaller breakout groups to discuss the concepts with their peers, but all requested more time for questions. It seems that the class had raised as many questions as it had provided new concepts.

One large business owner affiliated with the university said that he wished he had more universities like Woxsen. "India doesn't have enough skilled labor. The candidates lack the critical thinking and experience necessary to put theory into practice." Further, for every 100 candidates that he sees, only one is capable to fill the position. And, in his opinion, sustainability is a critical skill set.

Woxsen has recently added to its curriculum a new Sustainable Leadership certificate and a course on Sustainable Finance and Accounting is in the pipeline. Professors and students are working with outside organizations, including Global Movement Initiative, Humanistic Leadership Academy, and MIT's ULab to broaden their understanding of what a flourishing future might look like. The Net Impact chapter on campus was inaugurated in 2023. It brings to mind *Building the Bridge As You Walk On It* (Quinn, 2011), in the sense of rapid curriculum prototyping and continuous improvement to existing offerings.

A parent visiting from Abu Dhabi where her husband works and where the family currently lives said "God bless this university," because it is beautiful, connected to nature, and with good values – a perfect place for her two girls. She lamented the loss of values in cosmopolitan Indian life. In another example, Someshwar, of the Sustainability Club, was impressed by Woxsen because he could leave his mobile phone on the table in the dining hall. "No one steals anything here." In my four weeks at Woxsen, I was able to verify the same. And, as a recent graduate commented to Mr. Pula – he said how proud he was to be a Woxsen graduate – it is clear that the students have got the message.

I am reminded of an earlier time when neighbors helped neighbors, community included the least fortunate, and everyone worked together to make their world a better place. Obviously, that vision of utopia does not survive critical analysis, but it does point to a possible way forward to a flourishing future. Students at Woxsen University are inculcated with both the skills and the values necessary to be leaders in our emerging global village and in a world where sustainability is a defining capability. We are often told that we have the technologies to solve the multiple problems facing us – global warming, poverty, hunger, and equitable access – but few of us are capable of seeing what that future might look like in the real world. For that, in my opinion Woxsen University can serve as a model.

Resources

"2023 Report | The Positive Impact Rating." *PIR*. https://www.positiveimpactrating. org/report2023. Accessed October 25, 2023.

Chancellor's Message – Woxsen University. https://woxsen.edu.in/about-us/chancellor-message/. Accessed December 15, 2023.

Davos manifesto 2020: The universal purpose of a company in the fourth industrial revolution. *World Economic Forum*. https://www.weforum.org/agenda/2019/12/davos-manifesto-2020-the-universal-purpose-of-a-company-in-the-fourth-industrial-revolution/. Accessed December 2, 2019.

Global Movement Initiative. https://youtu.be/NuDyFYy8Fow. Accessed December 15, 2023.

Hub, IISD's SDG Knowledge. *Goal 4 – Quality Education | SDGs | SDG Knowledge Hub | IISD.* http://sdg.iisd.org/sdgs/goal-4-quality-education/. Accessed October 24, 2023.

International Commission on the Futures of Education. *Reimagining our futures together: A new social contract for education.* https://doi.org/10.54675/ASRB4722. Accessed December 15, 2023.

Irwin, L., Rimanoczy, I., Fritz, M., & Weichert, J., (2024). *Transforming business education for a sustainable future: Stories from pioneers.* Routledge.

Laszlo, C., Sroufe, R., & Waddock, S. (2017, May). Torn between two paradigms: A struggle for the soul of business schools. *AI Practitioner, 19*(2), 108–119. https://doi.org/10.12781/978-1-907549-31-1-12

PRME principles refresh – final report. UN Global Compact. (2023). https://d30mzt1bxg5llt.cloudfront.net/public/uploads/PDFs/Principles-Refresh-Final-Report.pdf

Quinn, R. E. (2011). *Building the bridge as you walk on it: A guide for leading change.* Wiley + ORM.

Rimanoczy, I. (2021). *The sustainability mindset principles: A guide to develop a mindset for a better world.* Routledge, Taylor & Francis Group.

Rodriguez, R. *A new curriculum focuses on societal impact | AACSB.* https://www.aacsb.edu/insights/articles/2023/05/a-new-curriculum-focuses-on-societal-impact. Accessed October 25, 2023.

Scharmer, O. (2018). *The essentials of theory U: Core principles and applications.* Berrett-Koehler Publishers.

Scharmer, O. (2023). *Humanistic leadership fall webinar series.* https://youtu.be/6nAagnY_Hq0?si=S5i_xA2RgpQ99CvH

Sharma, S., & Hart, S. L. (2014). Beyond "saddle bag" sustainability for business education. *Organization & Environment, 27*(1), 10–15. https://doi.org/10.1177/1086026614520713

Stoner, J. A. F. (2021). The blessed unrest in business education. *Journal of Management for Global Sustainability, 9*(1), 1–13. https://doi.org/10.13185

Transforming our world: The 2030 agenda for sustainable development | department of economic and social affairs. https://sdgs.un.org/publications/transforming-our-world-2030-agenda-sustainable-development-17981. Accessed November 21, 2023.

Woxsen University. https://www.linkedin.com/posts/raulvillamarinrodriguez_with-a-vision-to-develop-an-outstanding-cadre-activity-6984014171587719168-X21o/. Accessed May 15, 2024.

9

INSPIRATIONAL PARADIGM

Rethinking business education

Michael J. Garanzini

Abstract

The largest global network of business education on the planet is an outcome of centuries of educational dedication in preparing students with academic and social skills to be leaders in improving the common good. This chapter describes how leaders of Jesuit business schools, influenced by Pope Francis toward the cause of environmental justice, and in recognition of societal and business changes, created the "Inspirational Paradigm." Leading Jesuit business educators developed the Inspirational Paradigm in 2018 to address responsibility of business schools to prepare a different kind of graduate through curriculum based on the centrality of ethics, the common good, and the dignity and flourishing of the individual within a market economy.

This chapter outlines why change is necessary and how a business curriculum must be based on the needs and character of the students we wish to graduate, and our responsibility to the common good. It describes considerations and questions business schools must tackle to implement the Inspirational Paradigm. Finally, it summarizes actions taken and next steps in the process to continue establishing the Inspirational Paradigm across the network of Jesuit business schools.

A new mission for the Jesuit business school

Jesuit business schools number about 90 and constitute the largest global network of business education on the planet. Their foundations sometimes date back to the early 20th century.

Whether begun to serve a local population of eager students, or part of universities that date back centuries, they exist for the formation of the worldview of the students they serve. They contribute to research needed both locally

DOI: 10.4324/9781003521839-10

and internationally for sustaining and expanding the benefits of economic growth and the betterment of community life and individuals.

Since the founding of Jesuit education in the later part of the 16th century in Europe and then in the "New World," this education had as an explicit aim, the preparation of leaders for the communities they serve. Such preparation necessitated academic skills and social skills alike. Most critical of all, the foundational program stressed the common good. That is, a civic-minded person must be concerned about the impact of decisions on the least and those without power or influence, as well as on the affluent and powerful. To abandon one's duty to the poor and the unfortunate is to exacerbate community problems and contribute to the destabilization of the society one was hoping to build, strengthen, and preserve. But did concepts like "the common good" ground Jesuit business education?

Too often in the 20th century, Jesuit business schools simply modeled themselves off of the most academically notable. Or, aspiring to be categorized among the elite, they copied the standard business curriculum without questioning whether it was fulfilling its mission to shape society for the benefit of all, and not just those with economic resources and opportunities. Preparing graduates for the world of commerce and the skills needed to manage a business enterprise meant following the rules of accreditation which purported to be value neutral and backed by research that did not question the underlying assumption of the citizen consumer.

The social upheavals of the 1970s and 1980s did not impact Jesuit business schools except to press for greater "scientific" consideration of business practices, research-informed approaches to management, and closer scrutiny of fiscal policy and its impact on business practices. The assumption that the liberal capitalist model on which the United States and Western European economic structures were built was never questioned. However, the last decade of the 20th century and the first decade of the 21st century saw criticisms from within and from without as the world grew smaller, and implications of our interconnected economies became more obvious. This period also saw several business schools take Catholic social teaching seriously, which preached the need to be concerned with all segments of a society, and its support of the rights of workers and fair labor laws. The Catholic Church's support of its many immigrant populations to the United States led to the Church's association with the Labor movement, which sometimes gave the impression it was not interested in economic development on a macro scale or that it could advocate for principles of good and fair management. However, Jesuit business schools in this country and in many others trained local business leaders just as they trained many local doctors, lawyers, social workers, and teachers.

A serious extension of Catholic thinking regarding economic justice was launched by a document that extended Catholic social teaching to the causes of environmental justice. Pope Francis, who became the leader of the Catholic Church in 2014, and the first Pope from the Southern Hemisphere, made the environment and what he calls "integral ecology" a hallmark of this religious tradition (Francis, 2019).

By *integral ecology* Pope Francis proposes that environmental challenges cannot be divorced from the social conditions that sustain and advance the degradation of the physical environment. And, drawing on his faith's religious text, he proposes that all humans on the planet hold a moral responsibility to become aware of the ways in which as individuals, as communities, as complex social and economic systems, we are responsible to one another and to future generations for the care of the planet and the economic well-being of the least as well as the mighty. No religious document has been so well received and reviled as his Encyclical "Laudato Si," a 100-page letter to the human family begging that we turn our attention to saving the planet and ourselves. It's opening sentence is a positive call to action for all: "The urgent challenge to protect our common home includes a concern to bring the whole human family together to seek a sustainable and integral development, for we know that things can change" (Francis, 2019).

Taking this call seriously, a group of business educators met in New York throughout 2018 to reflect on the responsibility of business schools to prepare a different kind of graduate. Their joint statement of purpose was eventually named the "Inspirational Paradigm for Business Education."

It can be summed up as follows:

> The Paradigm articulates an ambitious and profoundly important educational and formative agenda: the centrality of ethics, the common good, and the dignity and flourishing of the individual. While the Paradigm embraces a market economy, it deftly repositions economic forces as a potent channel to help give rise to a just social order. The implication for business schools means a bold departure from a traditional curriculum's primary emphasis on skills and concepts associated with a goal of profit maximization.
>
> *(Garanzini & Santos, 2021)*

The "Inspirational Paradigm" (IP) was created by deans who knew they were not alone in seeing the need for change. Leaders in a variety of fields – business, politics, and religion – also heard the cry of those marginalized by their socio-economic conditions and recognized that at minimum "self-interest" should play a role in refashioning the preparation of social and economic leaders. Experts in professional education have long pointed to the impact on the profession of a growing disparity between rich and poor within countries and regions, the devastating effects of climate change leading to displacement and war, and the corrosive effects of politicians and others who seek to take advantage of these situations for their own power and personal enrichment.

For the deans who reflected on our volatile, uncertain, complex, and ambiguous (VUCA) world, the lessons and encouragement of Pope Francis's encyclical "Laudato Si" became a text for inspiration. How can we rethink our business education programs in order to form them for lives of meaning and purpose? Can our business programs inspire a new kind of business leader?

This core group of business educators is by no means naïve regarding why students come to a good business school. They acknowledge that many, perhaps most, students come with a variety of motives. They are eager to increase their chances of earning a decent living and advance economically and socially. At the same time, they know that the idealism of youth, their formidable knowledge of the conditions of the environment, and the struggles of peoples around the globe has rendered may "connected, committed and concerned."

Social media accounts for some of students' knowledge or assumptions, but phenomena like global warming, violence, migration, threats to democratic institutions, and the rise of poverty have made them astute observers of the challenges they will face in the years ahead. This is especially true of the leaders among them. What educators are hoping to tap or to instill are what they call "hungers."

The measure of a school is the student we graduate

In an attempt to clearly and unequivocally state what a Jesuit education in business ought to build upon and promote, the deans developed a list of "aims" of a Jesuit business education. The list was forged from 450 years of experience in education and leadership development and a reading of what young people want for their future. Studies such as the World Economic Forum's 2023 survey of young people and the International Youth Foundation's studies of concerns of young people informed the creation of the list. Faculty are asked to address these in practical ways in their revised courses. See, for example, the World Economic Forum's 2023 "The Future of Jobs" Report (WEF, 2023) and the International Youth Foundation's report on the concerns of young people (IYF, 2023).

The IP declares that Jesuit Education seeks to develop young leaders who desire:

A more just society

The IP is predicated upon the belief that students desire a world with greater opportunity for those at the margins of society. They are expecting to find or to build a community of fellow citizens who share their passion for a more just and equitable world, and not merely acquaintances interested in maximizing profit and investor wealth.

Knowledge integration

Students want to receive an education that helps them integrate what they read and hear in the classroom with the complex problems that confront society and the individual who hopes to contribute positively to family and to society.

A global paradigm

Experiences throughout their lives have shown how interconnected and interdependent we are with sisters and brothers throughout the globe. Young men and women know that we share a common destiny whether we are talking about our political, social, or economic realities. What happens in one part of the world can easily be felt in a variety of places and in a variety of challenges.

A moral compass

Our students are eager to acquire the tools to detect, manage, or confront moral dilemmas that inevitably arise in their careers and in their communities.

Dignified and humane work and meaningful impact

Their own sense of justice has them feeling strongly that work must be respectful of the dignity of all human beings in the community, and they want to experience firsthand the struggles and the opportunities for making an impact in the lives of all with whom and for whom they work.

An adult spirituality to support them

Finally, even if they are not conscious of this deep hunger, young people recognize that the questions they face are not only about material success – for themselves and their fellow citizens – but also impact or inspire a spiritual depth that will sustain them in times of difficulty. When they look at their teachers, they wonder about more than the knowledge that she or he is sharing, but whether this is a person of integrity, whether he or she is happy, whether he or she has some deeper anchor which holds them and supports them in life's problems and challenges.

In sum, students are hoping for an education that addresses these hopes – for a life of **meaning and purpose** – and helps them feed their hunger for making a meaningful impact on the world.

Key components of the Inspirational Paradigm

What then are the implications for rethinking the business school program? Much, perhaps most, of what is currently taught is important and helpful. We are not starting from scratch. However, three areas of concern need reflection and faculty input.

1. The IP proposes that business schools must reexamine the curriculum. Does it account for and introduce more than the neoliberal model of economic growth? For example . . .

Do introductory courses and programs have the following characteristics?

- Do we offer alternative interpretations to the reigning, neoliberal paradigm in economics which is assumed in most business courses? Are their elements in these courses that point to interpretations from those who see the negative consequences of this neoliberal paradigm?
- Are there places in the curriculum where viewpoints such as Catholic Social teaching, with its emphasis on the common good, the dignity of labor, the rights of the marginalized for healthcare, education and access to meaningful employment, etc., are presented?
- Is environmental sustainability built into the curriculum in each program so that all students are aware of and knowledgeable regarding the ways the business community can contribute to this effort, and how our economic impact affects the global economy and our human future?
- Are there places in the curriculum of each program where students have direct experience of the challenges facing the marginalized in society? Do service-learning opportunities and internships bring students more closely into contact with individuals who differ significantly in terms of opportunity and access to sustainable and healthy lives for themselves and their families?
- Are students exposed to society's disparities in health care, education, technology, recreation, and leisure in either the curriculum or the co-curriculum?

2. Business education needs to address our need for ongoing formation and education of faculty.

- Are there opportunities for faculty to explore these issues of the Inspirational Paradigm, discuss their relevance for the program(s) in which they contribute? Are these recognized in tenure and promotion guidelines and policies?
- Are there opportunities for research, both individual and collaborative research projects that explore the way the economy and the business community address the issues of justice and sustainability?

3. The IP asks: Is the business school itself a model of sustainability and inclusivity?

- How well do we model sustainability by the variety of measures that are proposed for the "green" campus?
- Do we seek to market our programs to those who share these values and welcome collaborations and support businesses that support and promote these values?
- Are we expanding our "coalition of the willing" and those dedicated to this new paradigm in our business and political community?

Our project today

Following a year of discussions in various international settings and conferences, the International Association of Jesuit Business Schools has adopted the project and continues to promote its adoption. A total of 39 projects have been funded since 2021, totaling $350,000. These faculty projects have been dedicated to curriculum and program revision in light of the IP. The proposals are peer reviewed and selected. In the summer of 2023, more than 100 faculty gathered in Seville, Spain, to discuss implementation efforts and shared the results of their ideas for curricular innovation.

Materials that help grant-writers and the results of previous awards are posted on "IgnitEd," an online resource sharing platform maintained by LeMoyne University's School of Business in Syracuse, New York. Those wishing to learn more or become engaged can do so through the IgnitEd Platform at https://www.ignited.global/.

Do we have evidence this is working? Do we know if the IP is in fact inspiring faculty to rethink and reimagine what they wish to accomplish with their courses and in their programs? We can say this: The meetings and conferences continue to draw decanal leadership and faculty eager to learn more and learn from one another. University presidents and provosts appreciate the "bottoms-up" approach to this movement. At times, it seems as if things are moving slowly, but course redesign can take time. Integrating not-for-profit businesses into one's collection of students' internships or placing students in agencies which deal with social challenges, finding alumni who have dedicated themselves to social policy changes, or business leaders who have worked to adopt the "triple-bottom-line" philosophy for their enterprise takes time and effort. But students find these opportunities exciting.

From this past summer's conference, and at the urging of faculty, the International Association of Jesuit Business Schools (IAJBS) decided to support faculty with an online program in how to incorporate course principles of the IP into an introductory course. Ten faculty from a variety of schools and nationalities have volunteered to create this faculty resource. The program will be available online at https://www.ignited.global/.

The breadth of representation is impressive. Participating faculty are from Loyola University in Andalucia, Spain, Xavier School of Management at XIM in Odisha, India, the Charles Dolan School at Fairfield University in Connecticut, the McDonough School at Georgetown in Washington, DC, the Universidad de Comilla, Madrid, Spain, University of CERAP in Cote D'Ivoire, ITESO in Guadalajara, Mexico, the Gabelli School, at Fordham in New York, and the Ateneo de Manila's School of Management in Quezon City, Philippines. The project is being chaired by Dr. Gisella Vertier, of the Catholic University of Cordoba, in Argentina.

This international team of faculty is complemented by a support task force for deans which is addressing issues like how to motivate and reward faculty for adoption of the IP, how to encourage collaborations across the school and between and among schools, better ways of adopting and disseminating the results of these efforts, and how to bring new deans into these efforts. The Board of Directors of the International Association of Jesuit Universities (IAJU) is discussing incentivizing Jesuit business schools where receptivity has been slow.

Along with these efforts to support faculty and deans, a group has been tasked with developing a way of measuring progress at the school level. Its task is to determine what an "Inspirational Paradigm School" ought to look like.

- What characterizes its curricular offerings, common pedagogical approaches, student study options, mentorships, internships, and immersions?
- What options exist for working in not-for-profit and community-based organizations?
- Where in the curriculum are students given ethical tools for scrutinizing human resource policies, investment policies, managerial training programs, and accounting practices?

In sum, this effort to transform business education into something other than support of the status quo, that is, maximizing shareholder value, is relatively new. However, it has taken off and is being welcomed and well received around the world. This effort also involves the scrutiny of faculty and thought leaders from a variety of perspectives and "places" from which to assess what we are teaching in schools around the globe. It allows for critical eyes and perspectives when most of our professional contacts and colleagues are likely to be from within our own national or pedagogical bubble. Faculty with rich international research programs know the tremendous benefit of perspectives of those who do not live in our country or hemisphere or are part of the global north.

The reality of this volatile, uncertain, complex, and ambiguous (VUCA) world at times necessitates the formation of business leaders who can respond patiently and empathetically, with moral insight and a sensitivity to how all our individual and collective decisions impact the rest. A school of business that is not cognizant of this new demand is contributing to "the problem" and is not part of the "solution."

The Inspirational Paradigm creates a community of business schools around the globe to redefining a business curriculum based on the centrality of ethics, the common good, and the dignity and flourishing of the individual within a market economy. Resources and opportunities to collaborate with other faculty or administrators are open to all through the IgnitEd Platform at https://www.ignited.global/. Together, we can help our students create lives of purpose and meaningful impact.

References

Francis, P. (2019). Laudato si': On care for our common home. *Ideals and Ideologies*, 503–510. https://doi.org/10.4324/9780429286827-79

The future of jobs report 2023. World Economic Forum. (2023). https://www.weforum.org/publications/the-future-of-jobs-report-2023/

Garanzini, M., & Santos, N. (2021). *Inspirational paradigm for Jesuit Business Education, Colleagues in Jesuit Business Association*. IgnitEd. https://www.ignited.global/inspirational-paradigm-jesuit-business-education-0

International Youth Foundation. (2023). *Catalyzing change, 2023 impact report*. International Youth Foundation Impact Report. https://iyfglobal.org/impact-report/#intro-content

10

THE BARD MBA IN SUSTAINABILITY

Baked in, not bolted on

Eban Goodstein, J. Renay Loper, Unique Brathwaite, Lauren E. Graham, and Janice Shade

Abstract

Since 2012, the MBA in Sustainability at Bard college has been one of the few graduate business programs worldwide to fully integrate education for mission and sustainability across the entire curriculum. This chapter explores first the vision, history, and structure of the Bard curriculum. It then provides examples of our pedagogical approach, through deep dives into two aspects of the curriculum: personal leadership, and accounting and finance. This chapter concludes with an exploration of the program's latest frontier: the evolution of the program to focus on education for building organizational culture in support of sustainability, and in particular, on training for anti-racist business leadership across the curriculum.

In 2012, Bard College launched a new MBA that fully integrated a focus on mission-driven business and sustainability into a core graduate business curriculum. The program has grown to enroll over 130 students and was recognized as the #1 Green MBA by Princeton Review in 2021, 2022, and 2023, and ranked worldwide as the #4 "Better World MBA" in 2024 by Corporate Knights. How did this "sustainability from the ground up" MBA come to be? Given the freedom to invent a program from whole cloth, what did it look like upon launch? And how has it evolved through to today?

As a core component of sustainability management education, we are now working to embed anti-racist leadership training across the MBA curriculum. This chapter highlights five foundations of the program's success:

- Sustainability fully integrated across a core business curriculum.
- Recruitment of a talented, dedicated practitioner faculty.

DOI: 10.4324/9781003521839-11

- Highly experiential approach to education.
- Individualized career planning.
- Cultivation of a JEDI-centered culture.

While the MBA incubated in an unusually entrepreneurial academic culture at Bard College, it is possible to replicate elements of our approach to support other programs.

Genesis

Bard's MBA took shape when in the fall of 2009, one of us (Eban) was appointed Director of the Center for Environmental Policy at Bard College in Annandale-on-Hudson, New York. At that time the Center offered a single graduate degree program, a master's of Science in Environmental Policy. Eban had been an Economics Professor at Lewis and Clark College in Portland, Oregon, and was familiar with the two west-coast sustainability MBAs that had been launched in the early 2000s, the Presidio School of Management in San Francisco, and the Bainbridge Graduate Institute in Seattle. He also had business experience partnering with pioneering sustainability programs at companies like Clif Bar, Nike, and Aveda.

Eban approached the Bard College administration in January 2010 with a proposal to start a Sustainability MBA. Bard is an unusually entrepreneurial institution, and with the support of Bard President Leon Botstein, the Bard Board of Trustees gave their approval in May 2011. Working closely with L. Hunter Lovins, a Presidio co-founder and co-author of the seminal text *Natural Capitalism*, Eban developed a proposal for New York State, including an initial curricular vision that drew from Presidio and Bainbridge. Eban also raised sufficient working capital to see the program through the first three years. Katie Boyle, our Admissions Director, was hired in August 2011. The MBA was approved by New York in March 2012, and the first class of 13 students enrolled in the fall of 2012. Bard has since been running a decade-plus experiment creating a curriculum geared for business leaders managing mission-driven businesses and non-profit organizations.

The Bard MBA curriculum

Bard's program is focused on a broad definition of sustainability: "Shared Well-Being on a Healthy Planet," emphasizing equally the social and ecological dimensions (Lovin's et al., 2018). We train our graduates to build and transform businesses to make measurable and continuous progress in substantially reducing environmental footprint, while also treating workers, customers, suppliers, and communities with greater justice and equity. Our curriculum begins with an integrated, 60-credit curriculum with a strong central core. The curriculum is divided into 19 semester-long classes, in turn organized around three verticals: (1) sustainability vision, (2) leadership, and (3) business execution.

Our students need first to be able to see profitable business opportunities where others see social and environmental costs; second, they must be able to lead others toward that vision; and finally, they have to execute successfully against the sustainable business models they have advanced. Table 10.1 lays out the curriculum with each course placed in its primary vertical.

Of the 19 courses, 16 are required of all students, with space for three electives. The electives, combined with a disciplinary-focused capstone, support concentrations in Impact Finance; Circular Value Chain Management; Non-Profit Management, Sustainability Consulting, and Entrepreneurship. The reason for the strong required core is that sustainability leadership requires an understanding of the advantages of mission-driven business in all functional areas: Students must be able to see and execute on the business case in terms of lowered costs from lean and green operations, employee productivity and retention, authentic storytelling for stakeholder engagement, measuring what matters, gaining access to capital, strong partnerships, strategy development, and an innovation culture grounded in justice, equity, diversity, and inclusion.

In addition to this core curriculum, we have a very strong focus on carefully mentored experiential education. The Bard MBA begins with a two-semester

TABLE 10.1 Courses by primary curricular vertical (credits)

Sustainability Vision	Leadership	Business Execution
Principles of Sustainable Management (3)	Personal Leadership Development (3)	Accounting and the Integrated Bottom Line (4)
NYCLab I & II (6)	Leading Change in Organizations (3)	Finance for Sustainability (3)
Entrepreneurship (4)	Becoming a Sustainable Organization (3)	Economics for Decision-Making (3)
Strategy for Sustainability (3)	Sustaining a Mission-Driven Organization (3)	Elective x 2 (3)*
Capstone (6)		Operations and Supply Chains (3)
		Data and Decisions I (4)
		Stakeholders and Marketing (3)
Total Credits (22)	*Total Credits (12)*	*Total Credits (26)*

* *Elective Options in 2023–24: Impact Finance I and II, Business and Sustainable Development, Circular Value Chain Management, Sustainable Supply Webs, Data and Decisions II, Non-Profit Management.*

six-credit consultancy, NYCLab, in which student teams address real-world sustainability challenges. Recent clients have included JetBlue, Siemens Wind, Eileen Fisher, New York City Fleet, Target, and McDonalds. At most schools, this would be considered a capstone-type experience, but at Bard, the course grounds its education from day one in real-world experience. In addition to NYCLab, we emphasize student-driven innovation: All of our students must participate twice in our program-wide December pitch competition, *Disrupt to Sustain,* described in greater detail in the accounting section of this chapter. Students in their final year also complete a two-semester, six-credit, individually mentored capstone, that typically helps develop a career path post-graduation. Capstones follow four pathways: Entrepreneurial, Intrapreneurial, Consulting, and Career Switching. Through NYCLab and Capstone, 12 credits or 20% of the curriculum, is devoted explicitly to experiential education.

Our faculty are all mission-driven people deeply experienced in business sustainability, who truly value the chance to work with our MBA students. They are the inventors of our curriculum and the engine of our community. Along with Goodstein and Lovins, the core faculty to whom we owe our success include Carolyn Allwin, Unique Brathwaite, JD Capuano, Alejandro Crawford, Nick DeGiacomo, Jackie Ebner, Kevin Eckerle, Jorge Fontanez, Laura Gitman, Jesse Gerstin, Lauren E. Graham, Kathy Hipple, John Holm, Lauren Kiel, Kristina Kohl, David Korngold, J. Renay Loper, Rochelle March, Gilles Mesrobian, Stephanie Milberg, George Perlov, Judy Pryor-Ramirez, Laura Ranier, Roy Rotheim, Cristian Ramos, Lily Russell, Jennifer Russell, Andrea Spender, Michael Shuman, Janice Shade, Randy Strickland, Aurora Winslade, and Jeana Wirtenberg.

Overall, Bard's curricular skeleton has changed very little since 2012, with the faculty teaching the courses continuously putting meat on the bones. The major innovations have been the steady addition of electives, and our 2020 commitment to embed a focus on education for anti-racist business leadership across the curriculum. More on this in the final section.

Program structure, career process, and outcomes

Bard's MBA has a hybrid, low-residency structure. Classes meet in person, one weekend a month in New York City, and then online in synchronous Zoom meetings two nights a week. Students can complete the program in either two years or three years. Overall, the contact hours for the program are 66% in person and 33% online.

With this hybrid structure, our students are largely employed while completing the MBA. The program works well for new mothers and fathers, and we always have a few babies born to students each year. The classes are typically two-thirds women – very unusual for an MBA – and around 40% of our students identify as non-white. In 2020, we instituted a generous scholarship program for first generation and/or students from backgrounds historically marginalized in sustainability leadership, and about one-third of our students now receive these scholarships. Students attend from all over the United States: Around 50% of our students commute to the in-person residencies from the New York City area, with the other half traveling in.

Career results are central to our MBA mission. *We need our graduates to be changing the world at scale, in a hurry, because on a lot of critical issues, we don't have a lot of time.* The process is grounded in an Individual Career Planning (ICP) process, in which MBA career staff meet with all of our students every semester in one-on-one career planning sessions. We offer a variety of mechanisms for students to build resume experience during the program, including consulting projects, internships, case competitions, and certificate completion.

The career planning process must be individualized as our students head in multiple directions in terms of industry – from fashion to energy to food to finance – and function – from entrepreneurs to intrapreneurs, consultants, and career switchers. Four quick students' success stories are as follows: Chelsea Mozen, as head of Sustainability at Etsy, guided the business to be one of the first big public companies with a major near-term carbon commitment; Emma Jenkins entered our program as a schoolteacher and within a year of graduation was VP for ESG, Americas at Deutsche Bank; Martin Freeman came to Bard as an EMT and is now a Managing Consultant at Guidehouse. After graduation, Martin Lemos became co-director at the National Young Farmers Coalition and now works in finance for regenerative agriculture. We maintain a comprehensive, public database of our alums with their career trajectories on our program website.

With this introduction to the Bard MBA's curriculum, structure, and career orientation, we now turn our attention to a closer look at two of the course sequences in the MBA: leadership and accounting/finance. In all courses, Bard faculty teach the core MBA toolkit, while helping students see how these tools can be used to build businesses that are in business to solve social and environmental challenges.

Leading the change

Leadership – the ability to take people where they otherwise would not go – is core to sustainability education, and we aim to redefine what it means to be a business leader. Students must develop the skills to become effective *change agents* to materialize the vision of "shared well-being on a healthy planet." Students enter Bard with a commitment to business practices that uphold equity and justice for people and the natural world, not at their expense. The commitment, however, is not enough. Seeding the future we envision is about human-centered leadership and the personal discipline to develop leadership practices fit for the challenge of sustainability.

A change agent is someone whose leadership and actions are a catalyst for shifting the status quo and driving transformative impact. The Bard MBA is creating change agents who will enter corporate and social sector leadership not just to respond to but entirely shift how we materially and socially address – and prevent – mounting environmental and social challenges. *Personal Leadership Development (PLD)* is the first class in the leadership vertical (see Table 10.1) and is a first-semester course for incoming students. Students go on to take courses in *Leading Change in Organizations, Building a Sustainable Organization* (with a focus on organizational management structures); and a final semester course called *Sustaining Mission,* which addresses keeping a company mission-focused among a sea of profit-first competitors.

The *PLD* course sets the tenor and expectations for the social–emotional learning that anchors the MBA program and that contrasts with traditional MBA coursework. Becoming a change agent begins with understanding oneself. We believe that students must first "locate" themselves before they begin their sustainability business leadership journey. The leadership journey is a deeply personal process where students explore their values, mission, and vision in their leadership. Location provides the opportunity for students to identify and reflect on their view of themselves – identities, privileges, and abilities, and juxtapose them with what they believe the world needs. Throughout this process of location, students develop and strengthen their internal compass that will guide their decision making and actions as leaders facing a complex external environment.

PLD is structured around five modules that focus on specific core competencies:

1. **Vision:** Who am I and what's important to me? What are my mission, vision, and values?
2. **Emotional Intelligence:** How do my emotions affect me as a leader? Do I recognize how I affect others I lead? Do I recognize the emotions of others as I lead?
3. **Community Leadership:** How do I demonstrate my commitment to justice, equity, diversity, inclusion, and anti-racism in my leadership style? How do I lead authentically in order to empower others? How do I lead through others?
4. **Systems and Networks:** What is my personal theory of change? How am I connected to networks and systems? What is power and how are different levers of power pulled?
5. **Resilience:** How do I stay the course, or stay true when things get tough? How do I navigate paradoxes?

Each module builds on the previous one and its associated competencies and behaviors. Students engage in a series of reflective and collaborative exercises throughout each module that allow them the space to grapple with the concepts and what they mean to them individually, as well as what they mean in a collaborative context. Students apply their learnings by engaging in case studies and real-world scenarios that require leadership responses in a variety of contexts including business, community-based organizations, religion, pop culture as well as local, national, and international political settings. The objective of this approach is to support the case for new and unique leadership models that ensure a sustainable and flourishing future.

One of the core texts used in *PLD* is *Adaptive Leadership* (Heifetz et al., 2009) that provides the framing for the type of leader we believe is most successful and effective in their business practice: someone who has a strong, values-based compass guided by a justice-oriented mindset with the ability to discern adaptive from technical challenges. Key theoretical concepts such as emotional intelligence and intersectionality help students reflect on how their identities (i.e., race, gender, class) interact with systems of power and privilege, whether it is within the professional environment, the community, or at the macro level. The environmental and sustainability-focused case studies require students to confront the realities of structural racism, traditional capitalism, and gender inequity head on. Furthermore, the collaborative learning models invite students to locate their leadership throughout, uplifting their commitment to anti-racist business practices.

Personal leadership concepts like emotional intelligence, personal theory of change, and adaptive leadership can be subjective, fluid, evolving, and cumulative. The absence of an objective "right" and "wrong" means that students find themselves navigating the muddy, gray areas where understanding and navigating context, perspective, belief systems, identity, personality, and communication styles are paramount.

Challenging traditional models

Consistent with the Bard MBA ethos of challenging the status quo, as faculty we consistently challenge ourselves – and our students – to adapt to the ever-changing landscape of our world and the sustainability space. As such we continually evolve our curriculum and address critical questions including (but not limited to) "Who developed the models and cases we are exploring and who does it speak to?" "Who is represented in the materials?" "What will the student learn about *their* leadership *through* these approaches?" "How can students connect this to their sustainability leadership practices?" "How can students apply these concepts to their practice of leadership, today?" and "Have we considered the limitations of what we are discussing?" With this line of thinking, we are able to continually evolve *how* the competencies are being explored.

An example of this is our final module, Resilience. In this module, students explore how they can sustain themselves and remain steadfast sustainability leaders in the face of volatility and adversity, especially when their personal missions and visions are confronted. Students consider approaches to taking care of themselves mentally, physically, and emotionally; how to execute on community leadership in a way that empowers others in order to share the lift of leadership; as well as how to center and remember their personal missions when things get tough. And while this perspective of resilience is important, so too is understanding the historical relationship between the term resilience and marginalized communities, many of which our students are or will be working in service of (Suarez, 2021). Without acknowledging various perspectives surrounding this commonly referenced term and instead maintaining the majority perspective, we would not be honoring our commitment of creating a welcoming environment that fosters belonging, nor would we be preparing our students to effectively engage across differences in an informed way.

Most MBA programs teach leadership, and some teach personal leadership – typically organized around Emotional Intelligence. Conventional business leadership, however, involves taking organizations toward the familiar goals of growth and profitability. This can be achieved Elon-Musk style, from the top-down. By contrast for most stakeholders, being part of a for-profit business that is organized around a mission is uncharted territory. The only way to pursue mission-first business in the long run is to enable buy-in and leadership in the service of sustainability throughout the organization. This in turn requires leaders to have not just good EQ but also a strong sense of location in the world around them.

Sustainability leadership requires leaders to intimately know themselves. We firmly believe that students who depart our program equipped with tools to navigate competing value systems, the ability to recognize and navigate networks and systems of power, and who are able and lead inclusively and with empathy are indeed the leaders who will change the game.

Business execution

Seeing sustainability opportunities and leading people effectively in their direction are two of our core curricular verticals. The third is executing on the vision. This entails mastering the generic MBA toolkit, though always with an eye toward utilizing those key concepts and skills to build more sustainable enterprises. As an example, the year-long sequence *Accounting and the Integrated Bottom Line* and *Finance for Sustainability* cover the standard material in Managerial Accounting and Corporate Finance, while building in foci on measuring what matters, and ESG finance.

A broad understanding of capital markets – how they operate, and the limitations and opportunities they present – is essential knowledge for emerging business: This sequence helps students master an understanding of the "capital" in capitalism. Most of our students were not undergraduate business majors and many arrive at Bard without much accounting or finance experience. But even those who bring extensive business experience cannot "test out" of either of these core courses, precisely because we are presenting new concepts, tools, and ways of approaching financial systems and capital markets. For students with no accounting coursework background, we require a four-week summer pre-req accounting course to familiarize students with basic terminology and concepts.

The accounting course begins with a focus on the three essential financial reports – Income Statement, Balance Sheet, and Cash Flow. We move quickly to the concept of the *Integrated* Bottom Line – how material sustainability investments enhance revenue and reduce costs. At Bard, we do not use the term "triple-bottom line" – a formulation actually withdrawn by its inventor [Elkington (2018)]. Rather than viewing people and planet as "nice-to-haves" under a separate accounting structure, students need to see how sustainability investments enhance the actual bottom line. The term Integrated Bottom Line is drawn from Lovins et al. (2018). Students also engage with the alphabet soup of existing and emerging US and European reporting frameworks and regulations: GRI, CDP, SBTi, TCFD, IFFRS, SASB, ISSB CSRD, and the latest SEC guidelines. The course delves into the calculation and use of managerial accounting tools – financial ratios, for example, vertical/horizontal analysis and liquidity/solvency/profitability ratios. To understand and evaluate performance, students choose and analyze a publicly traded company based on the least three years of its 10K reports.

Here is an example of how it works:

> Elaina Z. chose Lockheed Martin. After evaluating the world's largest defense contractor's year-on-year performance from 2019 to 2022, Elaina presented a bold proposal to create a new division within Lockheed Martin to focus on climate resilience by expanding production and distribution of the company's small line of firefighting-related products. She dubbed the new division "Wildfire Operations" and went on to demonstrate how it would "stabilize our profits from domestic contracts while we develop our life-saving firefighting technologies more intentionally and publicly." Elaina's creative sustainability focus and compelling, data-supported proposal earned her a standing ovation from her Board of Directors.
>
> *(i.e., fellow students)*

A key pedagogical backbone for the entire first semester of accounting is preparation for our program-wide December "shark tank for sustainability" pitch competition, Disrupt to Sustain (D2S). On their very first day of our class, students present a 2-minute informal pitch to the rest of the class about a sustainability-related problem they would like to solve. By the end of that first day, they are organized into groups of 4–5 based on shared interest and then begin the semester-long task of honing their sustainability solution into a comprehensive pitch. This project-based learning opportunity develops skills in creating a pro-forma budget, revenue modeling, cost forecasting, and discounted cash flow calculation. First-year students focus on the financial story of their companies in the Accounting course, and the impact story in another of their first-semester courses, Principles of Sustainable Management. The D2S competition is facilitated by the use of Rebelbase (www.rebelbase.co) social entrepreneurial courseware, developed by a team led by Bard MBA Innovation Professor Alejandro Crawford. In December, the first years compete against second- and third-year students, setting the stage for the second-semester core course: *Finance for Sustainability*.

Public and private capital markets

As with accounting, the finance course is built on basic financial concepts that are enhanced with incorporation of impact and sustainability factors, especially with regard to valuation and the role of risk and uncertainty in financial decision making. A key learning objective of *Finance for Sustainability* is to understand financial systems and their relationship within global and local economies and ecosystems.

On the public markets side, students undertake company valuation and portfolio construction assignments, applying learning in valuing annuities, perpetuities, loans, and mortgages; types and valuation of bonds; public stock markets and Risk/Return through the lens of Portfolio Theory and CAPM. Students are also introduced to the ability – indeed, responsibility – of sharers to influence important social and environmental actions within public companies. Throughout, our location one subway stop away from Wall Street ensures a constant flow of top guest speakers.

The Finance curriculum includes a focus on private capital markets and alternative investment structures, emphasizing tools and strategies for investing for impact. As practitioner faculty, we bring the latest developments in impact investing and alternative financial models from our work outside the classroom, presenting real-world examples from around the world that include:

- Outcomes-based financing and other blended capital scenarios
- Impact-linked compensation (for fund managers)
- Alternative investment structures (e.g., SAFEs, revenue-based financing, redeemable equity)

The backbone, project-based learning assignment for Finance is an Ideal Portfolio assignment. Students respond to weekly prompts to further their research into finance-related topics and to encourage reflection on their own values and approach as a current/aspiring investor to, for example, fund their retirement or child's college education, to manage the pension fund for the State of New York, to create and build an endowment fund for a real or imaginary foundation, or to target social impact or the solidarity economy. Students agree the Ideal Portfolio project, while daunting at first provides the perfect capstone to their first year of accounting and finance. And we, as educators, never cease to appreciate – and learn from – the creativity that students bring to this assignment.

While many of our students will not pursue a career in finance, alumni tell us how their newfound understanding of financial reporting and capital flows within a company has improved relationships and outcomes in their current workplace. For those who do choose a finance-related career path, students pursue electives to earn the Impact Finance Concentration.

The underlying theme throughout is that sustainability is not an add on – it must be part of business decision making on a daily basis which often means reconciling financial factors with social/environmental factors in the sense of the dictionary definition of *reconcile* causing to co-exist in harmony. By grounding students in the language and concepts of traditional finance while exposing them to the power and possibility of innovations for sustainability and impact, we equip them to face the challenge of leading change within systems that may still be resistant to change.

The last two sections have explored how the Bard MBA works to embed a focus on environmental and social mission – sustainability – across the curriculum, in teaching personal leadership and introductory accounting and finance. We now conclude with an overview of the latest evolution of the MBA curriculum: a commitment to integrating education for anti-racist leadership education in all of our courses.

Anti-racist business leadership education at the Bard MBA

Like so many organizations around the world, the Bard MBA experienced a moment of reckoning when George Floyd lost his life at the hands of police in Spring 2020. Since its inception, our program inherently embraced principles of diversity, equity, and inclusion (DEI). However, to fully catalyze our definition of sustainability, there was more we needed to do toward *shared well-being* – and that was to place active emphasis on justice and, in particular, anti-racism.

Taking action on these reflections, in the fall of 2020 the Bard MBA adopted a JEDI Commitment (justice, equity, diversity, inclusion) to prepare our future leaders to (1) build fully inclusive organizations and business models, with (2) a focus on effective anti-racist leadership within their organizations. The Bard MBA is one of four degree programs embedded within Bard's Graduate Programs in Sustainability (GPS). The JEDI and anti-racism commitments of 2020 cover all the graduate programs at GPS.

For the Bard MBA, anti-racist leadership means an active focus by organizational leaders on dismantling race-specific barriers within organizations and business models, and creating consciously inclusive and equitable practices that lead to more just organizations and a more just society. Our work on anti-racism within the JEDI commitment is "both-and." Students equipped to dismantle systemic racism within their organizations, as well as within their business, policy or educational initiatives, will be well prepared to create broadly inclusive and empowering organizations across all dimensions of diversity.

An organization can invest in anti-racist activities because it may be the profitable thing to do, and/or it may be the right thing to do. These are respectfully, the *business case*, and the *justice case* for anti-racist business action (Ely & Thomas, 2020). In terms of the business case, a JEDI commitment can be a successful strategy for well-known reasons: fostering innovation, talent acquisition and retention, engagement with customers, and suppliers. However, beyond this and following Drucker's famous aphorism that "culture eats strategy for breakfast," the Bard MBA argues that *no ambitious sustainability strategy can be sustained* without an ongoing commitment to building a culture that supports the mission of "shared well-being on a healthy planet." That means a JEDI-centered culture.

Given this, and following our teaching verticals identified earlier, we seek to train our students to (1) *see* the business case for JEDI and anti-racism where others may not, (2) *lead* their organizations to understand the business case, and (3) *execute* on strategies to achieve it. These in turn require students to master personal anti-racist leadership development; understand how systemic racism manifests within business organizations and in the broader economy, and perhaps most significantly, learn how to build an anti-racist organizational culture. Note that financial success flowing from JEDI and anti-racist strategies may not be short term – the business case can be based on a long-term investment in business profitability. Beyond the business case, we also help our graduates understand how to make the justice case for investing in anti-racism – at the organizational, business model, and public policy levels.

How do we undertake this ambitious work? Again, through faculty leadership. Since 2020, working with our student DEI committee and supported by training opportunities, faculty in almost all of our courses have reworked their curricula to consciously address the themes earlier. In addition, in 2021, we introduced a summer pre-requisite for all incoming students focused on developing a common vocabulary upon entry into the program. There is no model for a business school integrating a focus on anti-racism across the curriculum, so ours has been an iterative learning journey on which we have made substantial progress (Goodstein, 2024).

A JEDI roadmap for organizational transformation

In conjunction with our curricular innovation, we have been working to strengthen our own JEDI-centered culture. These activities have been governed by a JEDI Roadmap, originally developed by MBA alumni Lauren Hill and Martin Freeman. This work is advanced by faculty, staff, and students, and is evaluated annually. The roadmap includes a strategic framework that outlines four areas where we aim to produce measurable outcomes: curriculum, representation, community experience, and thought leadership. These areas are supported by four cross-cutting activities: training, resource acquisition and allocation, partner engagement and collaboration, and accountability (Figure 10.1).

Since the commitment was made in 2020, we have issued two progress reports against this framework (Bard Graduate Programs in Sustainability, 2022, 2024). One of the major changes to the program was the creation and funding of an Opportunity Scholars program providing substantial MBA tuition scholarships to students who were the first generation in their families to attend college, and also to students from groups that have historically been excluded from sustainability leadership. In three years, the percentage of Opportunity Scholars grew from zero to over 30%, greatly diversifying the composition of our student body. Over the same time frame, we substantially increased the percentage of BIPOC (Black, Indigenous, People of Color) faculty and administrators as well. Understanding a JEDI journey is just that, a journey, we are continually evolving our roadmap and supporting activities.

Four years on since our 2020 JEDI commitment, we are now witnessing a highly public, politically driven, anti-DEI backlash that has developed in the United States, as part of a broader attack on ESG value creation strategies. This political response does not negate the underlying facts. The United States is becoming steadily more diverse, and workforces increasingly non-white, often majority non-white. For this diversity to become a source of business advantage and engagement, and not a source of continual conflict and disengagement, organizational leaders need to be well schooled in building a JEDI culture. In a hostile political environment, companies today may be "DEI-hushing," but the work continues, and creating inclusive cultures will remain critical to business success. This is even more true for businesses that live or die by commitment to mission. In the 2020s, no company or nonprofit organization that aspires to sustainability leadership can succeed without also building a JEDI-centered culture that will in turn foster their sustainability strategies.

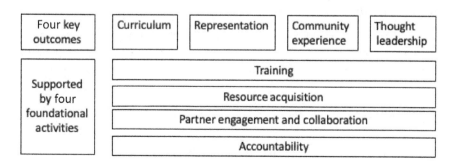

FIGURE 10.1 The Bard MBA strategic framework.

Conclusion

We are living at an extraordinary moment in the history of the human project. One hundred fifty years of unprecedented, break-neck growth in the human footprint is placing tremendous pressure on all forms of natural capital, including the climate stability of the entire planet. It is a truism to say that only through a transition to a regenerative economy we can deliver shared well-being on a healthy planet. On reflection, it is also obvious that a regenerative economy must be composed of, and dominated by, regenerative enterprises. It follows that the task of building a good future must focus on the creation and growth of sustainable for-profit businesses and nonprofits – organizations that deliver goods and services while putting social and environmental mission first, and from which financial success then follows.

Since 2012, the Bard MBA has had the freedom to invent a graduate educational program designed to train business leaders for this kind of purpose-focused economy. We offer five key lessons.

Baked in, not bolted on

To build a successful sustainable enterprise, organizational leaders need to be able to see, lead on, and execute against a myriad of sustainability revenue, cost, and innovation advantages, across all functional areas of business. This means all of their courses need to integrate a sustainability perspective – accounting, operations, marketing, strategy, data analysis, and every business vertical.

Practitioner faculty

It will be sometime before there will be a supply of PhD academics with the training, business experience, and teaching ability to deliver a quality sustainable graduate business education, particularly in this fast-moving field. Fortunately, there is a large talent pool of intellectually engaged, experienced professionals, who are at the leading edge of sustainable business. Lean into this opportunity.

Experiential education

Sustainable business is a problem-solving discipline. Integrate project-based learning, consulting opportunities and real-world exercises wherever possible. This is also critical for building student resumes for career success.

Individualized career support

Students will have a variety of career interests, from consulting to entrepreneurship to intrapreneurship and career switching. They will also want to work in industries ranging widely: fashion, food systems, finance, energy, and more.

In addition, pipelines are largely undeveloped. Career success means working with students on a one-on-one basis, from vision to storytelling to networking and through the interview process.

JEDI culture

Young people committed to sustainability today rightly demand a JEDI-focused culture within their business education, and the training to support truly inclusive businesses upon graduation. Lack of an authentic commitment to JEDI will sink a business school aspiring to sustainability in the same way it will sink a business that aspires to solve climate change but fails to sustain its people.

In making these recommendations, we recognize that Bard has been fortunate in building an MBA from the ground up, with a remarkably free hand granted by a uniquely entrepreneurial institution. This has allowed us to largely sidestep common challenges of silos, turf battles, irrelevant institutional requirements, and bureaucratic obstacles. Recognizing that some of the five features highlighted here may be hard to replicate, they have nevertheless been core to our success.

References

Bard Graduate Programs in Sustainability. (2022). *JEDI roadmap progress report*. Bard GPS Working Papers.

Bard Graduate Programs in Sustainability. (2024). *JEDI roadmap progress report*. Bard GPS Working Paper.

Elkington, J. (2018, September 13). *25 years ago I coined the phrase "triple bottom line." here's why it's time to rethink it*. Harvard Business Review. https://hbr.org/2018/06/25-years-ago-i-coined-the-phrase-triple-bottom-line-heres-why-im-giving-up-on-it

Ely, R. J., & Thomas, D. A. (2020). Getting serious about diversity. *Readings and Cases in International Human Resource Management*, 119–128. https://doi.org/10.4324/9781003247272-9

Goodstein, E. (2024) *Anti-racism in the bard MBA curriculum*. Bard MBA Working Paper.

Heifetz, R., Grashow, A., & Linsky, M. (2009). *The practice of adaptive leadership: Tools and tactics for changing your organization and the world*. Harvard Business Press.

Lovins, L. H., Wallis, S., Wijkman, A., Fullerton, J., & Raworth, K. (2018). *A finer future: Creating an economy in service to life*. New Society Publishers.

Suarez, C. (2021, March 31). *The problem with resilience – Non Profit news: Nonprofit quarterly*. Non Profit News | Nonprofit Quarterly. https://nonprofitquarterly.org/the-problem-with-resilience/

11

CURRICULAR DESIGN AND BUSINESS EDUCATION FOCUSED ON SUSTAINABILITY

The importance of an interconnected and comprehensive strategy

Carlos Alberto Restrepo-Rivillas, Alejandro Beltrán-Duque, and Gustavo Yepes-López

Abstract

This document analyzes how the dean of the School of Management at Universidad Externado de Colombia and his team faced the challenge of transforming the curricular design toward focusing on sustainability as a central element. Beyond offering courses on corporate social responsibility or sustainable development, the protagonists tell how they implemented initiatives and programs articulated to their mission and sustainable development objectives. Over several years, the team managed to make sustainability a transversal element that guided and articulated the teaching, research, and extension activities of the School in its undergraduate and graduate programs and in projects with the business environment. Through a chronological story, this chapter presents the motivations that the members of the faculty and the directors of the School had over the years to implement the initiatives, as well as their characteristics. The document presents lessons that may be valuable to other school directors interested in implementing a curricular proposal in which sustainability plays a central role.

A new challenge

The new dean of the School of Management at Universidad Externado de Colombia met with the rector at the beginning of 2008 to analyze the strategy for the coming years. At that time, various local and global factors posed challenges for management education and the School of Management. Market conditions at the national level were challenging due to new universities offering formal education programs in these subjects. At the same time, foreign universities arrived in the country with a portfolio of face-to-face and virtual programs. The demographic conditions of low birth rates reduced the market size.

DOI: 10.4324/9781003521839-12

The dean held meetings with business leaders from the country who expressed their gratitude for some programs that the school had been carrying out with them for some years, which had positive results. At the same time, entrepreneurs and managers also expressed their interest in knowing and implementing new management models to better impact their environment and respond to the challenges of sustainability, which was emerging at that time as an essential trend. The dean and his team faced the challenge of designing educational programs that would allow them to differentiate themselves in the market and respond to the requirements of their interest groups.

The dean brought together the professors, the vice dean of research, and the director of the Corporate social responsibility (CSR) research line to analyze the topic. The authors of this chapter held those positions in the School at that time. The meetings showed us that it was necessary to consider the external objective conditions in which the School operated and its members' capabilities, resources, and interests.

Colombia is a country that, like many in South America, faces severe problems of poverty, lack of legitimacy of its institutions, deterioration of forest reserves, unemployment, and low productivity of its business fabric, composed mainly of SMEs. During the meetings, it was also evident that there were different positions; some professors proposed maintaining a curriculum design focused on the orthodoxy perspective of competitiveness, financial profitability, and growth. Another group of professors favored a curriculum with an emphasis on social responsibility and the commitment of companies to social and environmental problems. Despite this, the entire team decided to take on the challenge of building a novel proposal in which both positions were possible.

Origins 2000–2007 – new challenges and ideas

This story's origins date back to 2000 when the United Nations approved the Millennium Declaration (2000). In response, the School's professors considered it essential to form a committee with Faculty and Administrative Staff members to analyze the implications of these proposals for training programs. Some of the professors on this committee participated in the School's board of directors, which made it easier for the proposed innovations to be studied and approved for implementation.

One of the committee's primary tasks was to review the curricula of our academic programs. This review aimed to incorporate content that reflected the evolving role of companies in society. Additionally, the committee actively promoted research activities, fostering a culture of innovation and adaptation within our academic community.

As a result, we implemented some specific changes. To begin, the undergraduate program Business Administration and the Master of Business Administration (MBA) implemented a course on technical assistance to standard and medium-sized enterprises (SMEs). This program, called Plan Padrinos, aimed to improve productive deficiencies and develop strategies within Colombian SMEs. In this program, students carry out intervention projects in companies with the accompaniment of a professor from the degree program. The students and teachers formed teams that went to the companies to diagnose, analyze, and propose strategies and action plans that the companies could implement to achieve early victories and generate changes in the medium term in operation and results of the company. For its development, the Plan Padrinos program had external allies such as large companies, civil society organizations, government development agencies, multilateral organizations, international non-governmental organizations, and academic institutions.

Another initial change included a Sustainable Development, Management Ethics, and Corporate Social Responsibility (CSR) course for the Undergraduate Degree in Business Administration. For this part, the School's postgraduate programs included subjects on sustainable development, corporate social responsibility, corporate governance, and environmental management.

In 2003, the Faculty members proposed creating a line of research in corporate social responsibility. They promoted several research projects and joint projects with other lines of research of the School to understand the dynamics between companies and their environment. The line of research was led by the person who would later become the director of initiatives for sustainable development. Some joint research had to do with SMEs (Beltrán et al., 2004; Beltrán et al., 2006), the business environment (Restrepo et al., 2005), companies, and the environment (Boada, 2004), and social responsibility (Yepes et al., 2007). Other investigations carried out in alliance with external organizations referred to anti-bribery practices in private companies (Transparencia por Colombia, 2008) and tax evasion by companies (McGee et al., 2007). These activities allowed the proposals to arise from a process of reflection by the School's teachers and to have academic support.

During this period, CSR professors and researchers began approaching relevant institutions on sustainability issues at the national level, such as the United Nations Global Compact, which allowed them to be linked to the local public debate on social responsibility. Likewise, they organized a massive event held in Bogotá, Exposocial 2005, which included the participation of renowned international experts. Thus, the professors were invited to be part of the committees that analyzed the technical quality standards on this topic, especially the ISO 26000 standard in Colombia.

Next, the School carried out several executive education projects and programs and in-house programs for companies on CSR issues, for which teachers and researchers were critical. The programs received support from union organizations and companies in the oil sector. This program trained the first consultants in corporate social responsibility in Colombia through a program in alliance with the Inter-American Development Bank, the Multilateral Investment Fund, and the Colombian Confederation of Chambers of Commerce. Through an alliance with the government agency to promote SMEs in the country, the teachers conducted training activities for entrepreneurs in many cities nationwide.

Another program born in these years was First Steps in Corporate Social Responsibility, a business intervention program that aims to include corporate sustainability criteria in the strategy of participating companies. In this program, students form teams and, under the guidance of a teacher, provide close accompaniment to the company. This program offered a novel consulting training process to school students through the intervention of small- and medium-sized companies. The program allowed for the inclusion of international corporate sustainability criteria.

Years later, the program was improved by including an innovative virtual platform called 3SC4L4. This platform allowed professionals to structure, design, monitor, and manage the incorporation of international sustainability criteria into business strategy. Thus, the teachers digitalized all the program processes, resulting in excellent coverage and optimal execution in the remote versions. Today, the program has external allies for its development, such as large companies, civil society organizations, government development agencies, multilateral organizations, and academic institutions interested in promoting inclusive and sustainable development in Colombia. The Colombia Global Compact has had a prominent role as an ally in this program. Currently, the program has a trademark registration that has been valid for ten years.

During these first years, the line of research in Entrepreneurship created the Business Creation Support program, in which the student received specialized advice for creating their company on technical, financial, and commercial issues. Entrepreneurs presented the projects at an entrepreneurship fair at the School's facilities, to which young entrepreneurs from other institutions throughout the country were also invited. Years later, the research team created the *Emprende* + program, a more developed version of the business creation program. In this program, entrepreneurs received support in the ideation, prototyping, business plan, start-up, and consolidation stages. It is a pre-incubation and incubation process that connects the entrepreneur with the actors of the entrepreneurship ecosystem through support and relationship activities.

These programs consolidated until they became a reference within the School. By including a businessperson in the training process, the result was the development of new methodologies, which not only allowed the teaching-learning process to be improved but also facilitated the integration of the research, teaching, and extension circuit or social projection. Given the conditions of an emerging economy, the *teachers proposed that the School offer these programs at* **no cost** *to the participants*, contributing to the School's recognition by the business community and State entities.

A growing model – 2008–2016: Curriculum changes and courses

This background allowed the new dean, who would lead the School for the next 15 years, to know that the team had the fundamental elements in place to design a new strategy and face the challenges raised during the meeting with the rector in that summer of 2008. Although the team members knew that the School enjoyed a good reputation due to its contributions to business development at the national level, we were also aware of the need to have a curriculum clearly articulated to sustainability.

The debate on the social responsibility of university institutions began some years ago due to the rise of Corporate Social Responsibility (Kliksberg, 2006) and to the leading role that the academic institution plays in society (Boyle, 2007; Guédez, 2012; Söderbaum, 2009; Vallaeys, 2008). Given the difficult prospects for the educational sector, we knew the commitment we had as an organization to social responsibility, and we proposed that this topic be part of the agenda in the meetings with the faculty members and the meetings of the School's governing bodies.

The dean and team knew we had to consider several elements. From the point of view of teaching-learning methodologies, some teachers proposed continuing to privilege master classes with a solid theoretical component, which had characterized the School in the last three decades. Another group proposed developing methodologies that prioritized interaction with actors such as companies, state entities, and NGOs in classrooms.

The teachers considered that sustainability should be a transversal element that permeates teaching, research, and extension as essential functions of the School as a social actor. Therefore, the training of young administrators had to incorporate a clear message about the role of companies and their managers in the face of the millennium goals.

On the other hand, regarding the financial management of the School, some proposed that activities aimed at different interest groups should include a sales price so that they would contribute to the School's income. Others proposed that, given the context of an emerging economy, the programs should be free for participants so that income would not come from vulnerable communities or small businesses but from large actors in the national economic ecosystem. It was necessary to add a strategic planning process that the dean and his team wanted to carry out that fall. All of this would mark the programs' and teachers' focus and operation.

In addition to the antagonistic positions set out earlier, there were three possible scenarios for the design and implementation of the solution. The first scenario intended to continue offering subjects related to sustainability in all programs, as has been done in the last decade. The second proposed adding programs to help other interest groups and vulnerable communities. The third proposed designing an operation model that integrated sustainability into research, teaching, and extension activities, involving actors from civil society and business in the area.

The balance leaned toward the third alternative where a comprehensive approach to articulating sustainability to the curriculum prevailed. That is, connecting research, teaching, and extension, as well as working with civil society and business actors in the environment. As a result, the faculty members decided to take university social responsibility as the approach to carry out academic activities, consequently affecting the objectives, goals, organic structure, and performance evaluation.

For this reason, the dean and the vice dean of research decided that the person who led the CSR research line would begin to lead a new area that would be created called Management and Social Responsibility to have a specific team in charge of leading university social responsibility. The objectives of this area would be to:

- promote solid research on the topic;
- design a comprehensive offer for formal education;
- design a compelling offering of continuing education, advice, and consulting;
- ensure an efficient and sustainable social projection;
- ensure adequate deployment of university social responsibility within the School; and
- promote permanent and effective collaboration to generate responsible actions.

Realizing that achieving our objectives required a collective effort, we sought out allies. We believed that by pooling our knowledge, resources, and capabilities, we could accelerate our progress. Thus, we proposed that the School align with the United Nations Global Compact initiative, Principles of Responsible Management Education – PRME. This was a testament to our commitment to promoting responsible actions and the responsibility of business schools.

Later, in September 2010, we linked the School to the nascent Ibero-American Network of Universities for Corporate Social Responsibility and, in July 2014, to the BoP Global Network initiative, led by the renowned business professor Stuart L. Hart. Thus, the School became a BoP Lab. This collaborative work allowed professors and researchers to present their advances in international settings and events at Universities such as Harvard, Emerson, Salem, and Columbia and in organizations such as ISO, the Association to Advance Collegiate Schools of Business – AACSB, and the Latin America Business Association – LABA.

These efforts strengthened the research line on corporate social responsibility with joint projects on topics such as principles of social investment (Centro

Regional de Apoyo para América Latina y el Caribe, 2012), anti-bribery practices (Transparencia por Colombia, 2010, 2012, 2015), and the role of higher education in CSR (Casani, 2015). In association with the United Nations Global Compact Network in Colombia, the professors proposed rewarding the best corporate sustainability management practices.

Table 11.1 summarizes some of the leading programs and initiatives that teachers and researchers proposed to have a more comprehensive strategy for curriculum design.

These programs and initiatives resulted from the relationships that professors and researchers made with other allied organizations. All of them aimed to bring responsible management to SMEs and the supply chains of large companies.

TABLE 11.1 Programs and initiatives created to achieve a comprehensive impact on the curriculum

Program/Initiative	Description
Master in Social Responsibility and Sustainability	First master's degree of that type in the country.
Women breaking barriers	Our mentoring program is designed to empower young undergraduate and graduate students, particularly women, to overcome the limitations often imposed by organizations. The program is led by teams of female mentors, high-ranking professionals from large national or multinational companies in Colombia, who guide the young apprentices in their daily activities and help them strengthen their soft skills.
Family Business Management	This program involves students and graduates who have a family business. Students and their families receive management, corporate governance, and strategy training at the School's facilities. Students or graduates, along with their siblings, parents, uncles, or cousins, share lessons on how to manage their business.
Emerging Markets Initiative	This initiative integrated intervention and training programs to support BOP companies or companies that operate in business models based on the circular economy. There, Colombian students and other nationalities form intervention teams to diagnose and propose courses of action to companies. In addition to applying knowledge in the real world, the program gives students the opportunity to live multicultural learning experiences.

(*Continued*)

TABLE 11.1 (Continued)

Program/Initiative	Description
Training for entrepreneurs in the agricultural sector	Our program operates in close alliance with the bank for the promotion of exports and SMEs, a key financial partner attached to the country's Ministry of Industry. This collaboration not only significantly expanded the program's impact but also served as a platform to validate research results and empirically contrast the developments created by our teachers.
Initiative for Individual Sector Responsibility – IRIIS	The initiative arose from an alliance with the Association of Petroleum Engineers of the country, five universities from different cities in the country, and more than ten companies in the sector. It helped generate greater commitment from people to transform this industry and obtain significant benefits for themselves and society.
Responsible Supply Network	This initiative arose from an alliance with the Colombian Network of the United Nations Global Compact. The network sought to promote the development of small- and medium-sized businesses in the country. The initiative began with six leading sustainability partner organizations, which sought to reduce risks in the management of their chains. For this, they invited suppliers, distributors, or clients to work together. There, students from the School helped improve the management of participating small- and medium-sized companies.

Consolidation and maturation – 2017–2023: connections for a new business education

In 2017, we faced new challenges that forced us to reformulate the strategy, which included adjusting the articulation of the sustainability and the curriculum. In 2015, the member countries of the United Nations approved the 2030 agenda for sustainable development. This agenda contemplated making commitments on 17 global issues to balance global social, economic, and environmental sustainability. As part of its strategic plan, the School had initiated international accreditation processes with the Association to Advance Collegiate Schools of Business (AACSB), the Association of MBAs (AMBA), and the Education Quality Accreditation Agency (EQUAA). Likewise, in the business environment, the need to strengthen commitments to sustainability and report concrete actions to the different interest groups in this area was evident.

The Dean, the vice dean of research, and the director of Management and Social Responsibility, together with the professors, undertook the challenge of building a new framework that included sustainability as an integral part of its strategic platform, guaranteed continuity of the initiatives already developed, and to overcome new challenges identified. During the fall, they collected information and held meetings with students, graduates, and managers of companies and state organizations, among others. All of this allowed them to identify the priorities and scope commitments to be incorporated.

As a result of a collegiate process, we established that the mission of the School would be "To train agents of change in management skills to qualify the contribution that organizations make to sustainable development in emerging economies" (Universidad Externado de Colombia 2017, par. 1). Since 2016, we began executing a plan for programs and initiatives, to achieve our commitment to the 2030 Agenda for Sustainable Development visible and verifiable.

Likewise, we created the Directorate of Initiatives for Sustainable Development, which focused on integrating sustainability more organically into the research, teaching, and extension circuit. Considering the guidelines of the Project Management Institute (Wanner, 2014), we made the distinction between initiative and program. Based on the new mission and considering the previous circuit, the teachers prioritized 7 of the 17 sustainable development goals (SDGs) and 12 of the 169 goals. They integrated them into the School's management model. The prioritized objectives were number 4 on quality education, number 5 on gender equality, number 8 on decent work and economic growth, number 9 on the industry, innovation, and infrastructure, number 12 on responsible production and consumption, number 16 on peace, justice and strong institutions, and number 17 on alliances, aligning initiatives with each of these objectives.

Teachers discussed and agreed to focus action on five basic principles. The first established that free services would continue for the beneficiaries of the different programs but generate income through social outreach programs. The second indicated that the School would maintain collaborative work with other institutions that shared the same purpose and contributed to better results, such as the United Nations Global Compact, the Principles of Responsible Management Education – PRME, the BoP Global Network, Aim2Flourish, the Global Reporting Initiative, the CSR Observatory, the country's companies, unions, and state entities. The third stipulated that the contents and topics included in teaching processes and courses should consider the context of the emerging economy. The use of learning-by-doing methodologies should be privileged. The fourth established that the applied research approach should be prioritized and that access to the different communities under study in the research projects should be encouraged. The fifth indicated that, in extension projects, each activity developed should generate an impact on the environment and include the different actors present.

Table 11.2 presents the grouping of the main programs developed based on the School's mission and the adopted SDGs.

TABLE 11.2 Relationship between programs and the SDGs, according to pillars of the mission

Mission Pillar	SDG	Programs		
		Teaching	Research	Extension
Agents Of Change	4- Quality education	Courses on Sustainability/Social Responsibility in Undergraduate and master's programs. Master in CSR and Sustainability	Research line of the School on CSR	Intervention project in grassroots communities: Entrepreneurship courses, Strengthening SMEs, etc.
	8- Decent work and economic growth	Course on consulting and assistance to companies included in the School's programs	Research line of the School on SMEs Development	Project to support SMEs: Padrinos Plan, First steps in CSR. Certificate in Family Businesses
Management Skills	9- Industry, Innovation, and Infrastructure	Master in logistics and supply chain management. Master in Business Innovation Management Bottom of the Pyramid Challenge Courses	Research line of the School on Competitiveness, productive chains and clusters Research line of the School on Operations and Supply Chain Management Research line of the School on innovation Research on Responsible Supply – Social Enterprises	Activities with large companies through the Responsible Supply Network. Workshops for international students on Strengthening SMEs and businesses at the base of the Pyramid
	12- Responsible production and consumption	Circular Business Courses	School's line of research on technology and production Research on Circular Business – Inclusive Business	Workshops for international students in Circular Business. Competitive SMEs Program. Conferences

(Continued)

TABLE 11.2 (Continued)

Mission Pillar	SDG	Programs		
		Teaching	Research	Extension
Sustainable Development	16- Peace, Justice, and Solid Institutions	Courses in Corporate Governance in Undergraduate and MBA	Investigations related to Bribery	Conferences and events on anti-bribery practices
	5- Gender equality	Discussions on leadership, gender, and management	Research line in Human Management and Organizations Gender research	Women Breaking Barriers Program
Emerging Economies	17- Alliances to achieve objectives	Association programs for SMEs	Research in associativity – Cooperation networks	Configuration of the responsible supply network (Large companies in the country)

As a complement to the previous and to respond to the crisis caused by the COVID-19 pandemic, we proposed creating a free virtual program called SMEs 2020. The purpose of the program was to develop skills in SME entrepreneurs that would allow them to face the challenges that COVID-19 imposed on businesses.

During this period, the School also achieved the main results it had set out to achieve. In each of the SDGs in which it developed initiatives, they executed programs, reaching a compliance of 75% in research, teaching 58%, in extension 83%, and with a compliance of 75% in average of the prioritized SDGs. The strategy guided by the Director of Initiatives for Sustainable Development always had support from external allies. Box 11.1 shows the testimony of the leader of the government agency to promote internationalization.

BOX 11.1   QUOTE 1

ProColombia's alliance with the Externado University of Colombia has made it possible to fulfil the organization's missionary commitment to "promote sustainability as an attribute of competitiveness for the promotion of non-mining energy exports, foreign direct investment, international tourism and Country Brand." Thanks to this alliance, we have managed to reach 55 companies to close gaps in sustainability and continue contributing to the sustainable development of our country. A very special thank you to the entire Faculty of Business Administration team, to everyone who has been part of this process and to the Responsible Supply Network.

Senior executive of the government agency
to promote internationalization.

BOX 11.2   QUOTE 2

For us, the Responsible Supply Network of the Externado de Colombia University has been a space of high value, accompanying us in raising awareness among our suppliers. For those companies that have had the opportunity to participate in the First Steps program, the network helped them carry out a complete diagnosis of their company, proposing early victories and a path to follow in sustainability.

Manager of an important oil company in Colombia

All of (100%) the School's students participated in at least one of the proposed programs. The School received students from other schools and fields of knowledge and international students from prestigious institutions. Likewise, it helped improve management, reduce risks, and promote innovation in more than 18,000 companies in alliance with leading sustainability organizations. Box 11.2 shows the testimony of the manager of an important oil company in Colombia.

Since 2007, at least a handful of students from different degree programs have participated with a professor and received awards from Case Western Reserve University's initiative called AIM2Flourish. This competition rewards outstanding cases of companies that contribute significantly to SDGs 11, 1, 2, 14, 9, 7, 16, and 13. Additionally, in 2021 the Master of Business Administration obtained position 15 in the MBA: top 40 ranking of the Canadian organization Corporate Knights.

BOX 11.3   QUOTE 3

We want to express our deep gratitude to the Corporate Social Responsibility program of the Externado de Colombia University for the opportunity to participate. It was an honor to work on projects for Colombian companies, where we managed to design sustainability strategies and apply recognized international frameworks in sustainability.

Undergraduate Business Administration Students

The effort led by the Directorate of Sustainable Development Initiatives, the vice dean of research, the program directors, and the professors allowed for a transformation of the programs toward a commitment to sustainability as well. This effort also contributed to achieving other important goals of the strategic plan. In particular, the School obtained accreditation from AACSB, AMBA, and EQUAA. In all of them, the evaluators highlighted the School's commitment to sustainability and its impact on the different interest groups. The teachers' mentality changed, and today, they understand that their activity in class should be associated with the purpose of generating an impact on society. The graduates linked their companies or participated in some of the programs where they, at the time, participated as students. Box 11.3 shows the testimony of an undergraduate student in Business Administration.

Large companies, state entities, and universities were interested in participating in the School's initiatives. Professors actively participate in dissemination, discussion, and dialogue activities about sustainability, reaching more than 5,000 people annually in ten countries.

As a result of these initiatives, in 2023, the School consolidated an alliance with the country's main media outlet to launch a weekly national radio program called *Caracol Sostenible*. The initiative had the support of the most important telecommunications company in Latin America.

Emerging Markets Initiative, through the TSB, BoP Challenge, CSR programs, EMI Workshops, Circular Business, and Social Business, has served 153 companies and 786 students from important international university institutions.

By December 2023, the Responsible Supply Network already had more than 30 allies, three lines of work (efficiency, risks, and innovation), seven versions of the Plan Padrinos program, 2,908 companies, and 5,869 students, and two versions of the Primeros program Steps in CSR, 606 companies, and 1,447 students.

The decisions that the School made over these years reflected a management style that emphasized teamwork, analysis of the environment, and the desire to generate initiatives that had a real impact on the interest groups and allowed us to move from reflection to action.

Conclusion

This document presents the experience of a team of teachers and directors of a School of Management in building a curricular design committed to sustainability. The School of Management at Universidad Externado de Colombia is an institution that operates in a South American country, where companies and higher education institutions face the typical limitations of an emerging economy. This chapter shows how the team overcame these limitations and implemented a curriculum proposal in which sustainability plays a central role. Beyond offering courses on corporate social responsibility or sustainable development, the School implemented initiatives and programs articulated with its mission and sustainable development objectives. In their proposal, the professors ensured that sustainability guided and helped articulate the School's teaching, research, and extension activities in its undergraduate and graduate programs, as well as in projects with the environment.

As these pages reveal, the School's journey was influenced not only by the local context but also by global trends in responsible education in administration. Led by the United Nations and numerous non-governmental organizations, these trends provided guidelines for transforming the way administrators are trained. The School's response to these trends was not just a reaction but a proactive intervention in the educational process. This intervention aimed to transform educational and business practices, steering them toward a model more committed to building a sustainable world.

The success of the sustainability-focused curriculum was not a solitary achievement but a result of collaborative efforts. The School's teachers engaged with various actors at the national and international levels, including the country's government development agencies, chambers of commerce, unions, and associations. They also participated in United Nations initiatives and formed alliances with significant non-governmental and multilateral organizations. These partnerships and collaborations were instrumental in the successful implementation of the curriculum.

An element that has become a significant success factor of this experience is that the School showed all internal and external actors that the initiatives and programs could be designed and executed in a win-win scheme. That is to say, through the contribution of companies, teachers, students, and allied organizations in the environment, it was possible to carry out programs that benefit companies and communities, and at the same time, students lived significant learning experiences in which they could apply the knowledge acquired and become actual agents of change for society. The teachers managed to combine traditional training approaches oriented toward profitability and efficiency with approaches oriented toward sustainability.

The experience benefited from the research processes carried out at the national and international levels. In that sense, another success factor was the articulation of professors to international academic networks. Beyond program design, we sought to generate a culture of innovation within, which was clearly connected to global debates in relation to sustainability. Academic events, visiting professors, joint research projects, mobility of researchers from the School, were processes that happened in parallel to the implementation of the programs.

Several lessons remain for other schools interested in implementing similar initiatives and programs.

First, there must be a medium and long-term vision. That is, sustainability initiatives connect to the School's strategic planning processes, and all internal actors understand their importance.

Second, in addition to having a strategy, it is essential to have leaders and human teams capable of putting ideas into action and making things happen. Audacity is required to create innovative actions despite the possible risks of failure. Persistence is required to continue despite obstacles. Will and discipline are powerful attitudes necessary when transforming an organization (Araç & Madran, 2014). Without a committed and well-organized team, ideas for generating a curriculum focused on sustainability can remain just good intentions.

Third, links are critical. Throughout the process, teachers received support to connect with different types of public and private actors at the local and global levels and attend conferences and work meetings inside and outside the country. Alliances are fundamental and consolidated through agreements and memorandums of understanding that translate into actions.

Fourth, as seen in this story, ensuring that the curriculum design and the School's essential functions are connected to sustainability is only achievable after some time; there are errors, and it is necessary to correct course on more than one occasion. The process involves several years of constant work, starting with impacts in the immediate environment until expanding the scope of influence at the national and international levels. Curriculum intervention requires sufficient time and patience to allow initiatives to overcome stages and mature at the pace of the organization's culture. We recognize that there may have been errors in not considering, from the beginning, the management of culture and organizational change, which would have allowed us to avoid some setbacks.

Fifth, avoiding making these processes dependent on specific people is essential. The schools must connect initiatives to a formal structure that can guarantee continuity over time, even if the people change.

References

Araç, S., & Madran, C. (2014). Business school as an initiator of the transformation to sustainability: A content analysis for business schools in PRME. *Social Business*, *4*(2), 137–152.

Beltrán, A., Anzola, O., Torres, E., Camargo, R., & Bello, C. (2006). *Mejorando la competitividad de la Pyme. Desarrollo y aplicación de modelos de gestión*. Universidad Externado de Colombia.

Beltrán, A., Torres, E., Camargo, R., & Bello, C. (2004). *Pymes. Un reto a la competitividad*. Universidad Externado de Colombia.

Boada, A. (2004). *Las empresas y el medio ambiente: un enfoque de sostenibilidad*. Universidad Externado de Colombia.

Boyle, M. (2007). Learning to the neighbor? Service-learning in context. *Journal of Academic Ethics*, *5*(1), 85–104. Obtenido de https://doi.org/10.1007/s10805-007-9045-5

Casani, F. (2015). *La educación superior como dinamizadora de la responsabilidad social empresarial: Un estudio comparado entre los futuros dirigentes empresariales en América Latina*. Universidad Autónoma de Madrid.

Centro Regional de Apoyo para América Latina y el Caribe. (2012). *Principios para la Inversión Social*. Centro Regional de Apoyo para América Latina y el Caribe. The Global Compact. https://centroregionalsp.org/wp-content/uploads/2021/02/Principios-para-la-Inversion-Social.pdf

Guédez, V. (2012). De la trisectorialidad a la cuatrisectorialidad: la Universidad como espacio para gerenciar el conocimiento de la RSE. En I. Licha, *Enseñanza de la Responsabilidad Social Empresarial. Retos de las universidades de Latinoamérica*. Sudamericana Random House Mondadori. Dirección Regional del PNUD y la Agencia Española de Cooperación Internacional para el Desarrollo (AECID), 605–620.

Kliksberg, B. (2006). Capital social y cultura, claves del desarrollo. *Cuadernos Latinoamericanos de administración*, *2*(2), 5–31.

McGee, R., López, S., & Yepes, G. (2007). *Is Tax Evasion Ethical? An Empirical Study of Colombian Opinion*. Barry University. Andreas School of Business. https://papers.ssrn.com/sol3/papers.cfm?abstract_id=973762

Restrepo, C., Isaza, J., & Acosta, C. (2005). *Competitividad y estructura de la economía Colombia*. Universidad Externado de Colombia.

Söderbaum, P. (2009). Making actors, paradigms and ideologies visible in governance for sustainability. *Sustainable Development*, *17*(2), 70–81.

Transparencia por Colombia. (2008). Primera encuesta nacional sobre prácticas contra el soborno en empresas colombianas. *Cuadernos de transparencia*(15). https://transparenciacolombia.org.co/Documentos/Publicaciones/empresa-mercado/Cuaderno15.pdf

Transparencia por Colombia. (2010). Segunda encuesta nacional sobre prácticas contra el soborno en empresas colombianas. *Cuadernos de transparencia*(19).

Transparencia por Colombia. (2012). Tercera encuesta nacional sobre prácticas contra el soborno en empresas colombianas. *Cuadernos de transparencia*(20).

Transparencia por Colombia. (2015). Cuarta encuesta nacional sobre prácticas contra el soborno en empresas colombianas. *Cuadernos de transparencia*(23). https://transparenciacolombia.org.co/cuarta-encuesta-soborno/

United Nations Millennium Declaration | Ohchr. (2000, September 8). https://www.ohchr.org/en/instruments-mechanisms/instruments/united-nations-millennium-declaration

Universidad Externado de Colombia. (2017). *¿Quiénes somos?* Universidad Externado de Colombia. https://www.uexternado.edu.co/administracion-de-empresas/historia/

Vallaeys, F. (2008). *Breve marco teórico de la Responsabilidad Social Universitaria.* Universidad Pontifi cia del Perú. http://rsuniversitaria.org/web/images/stories/BreveMarcoTeodelaResponsabilidadSocialUniv.pdf

Wanner, M. F. (2014). Implement strategy by strategic initiatives with effective program and change management. *PMI® Global Congress 2014 – EMEA.*

Yepes, G., Peña, W., & Sánchez, L. (2007). *Responsabilidad social empresarial. Fundamentos y aplicación en las organizaciones de hoy.* Universidad Externado de Colombia.

12

SUSTAINABILITY IN ACTION

An experiential learning course in international business

Anu Jossan and Ilijana Petrovska

Abstract

This chapter presents a case study of how two UK business programs, B.Sc. International Business Management and BA International Business, integrated sustainability courses as a meaningful action into their curriculum through a project called "Sustainability in Action" at their branch campus in Doha. The project aimed to educate, empower, inspire, and transform students to become globally responsible leaders who can contribute to the common good. The project involved a series of events, like local and international field trips, summits, industry expert guest lectures, beach cleanup, symposium, and poster exhibition. This chapter describes the rationale, design, implementation, and outcomes of the project, highlighting the challenges and benefits of transforming the traditional classroom curriculum into a dynamic experiential model. This chapter also discusses the impact of the project on the students' mindset, knowledge, and skills regarding sustainability and how it fostered a sense of community and engagement among the stakeholders. This chapter concludes with some reflections and recommendations for business schools who wish to embed sustainability into their curriculum and create positive change in themselves, their organizations, and the world.

A leading liquified natural gas (LNG) shipping behemoth in the Middle East served as the case company for financial valuation research in a national challenge for business school students. While the executives of the company showcased their business success, a keen business student asked how the company itself, as well as the maritime industry, see their success through the lens of sustainability. The executive responded that even though they transport energy across oceans as a business, they also bear responsibility to safeguard

DOI: 10.4324/9781003521839-13

the oceans. Through many joint ventures and with a national vision of sustainability, the executives explained the efforts of the shipping business on sustainability, a revelation for the students as they understood businesses can be way more committed to sustainability than mere lip service. The students heard a call to action – a call that resonated far beyond the steel walls of the ship with a focus on LNG – the promise of clean energy bridging continents and giving power to homes and businesses while serving as both a commodity and a conduit for change.

This event enlightened us, both the students and teachers, and continued a discussion on how sustainability can be woven into the DNA of business, especially through joint ventures. This was the beginning of a project called "Sustainability in Action" about how we, as a business school, can include actionable sustainability initiatives within the delivery of business curriculum.

"Welcome, dear students to the International Business Programme." From the first day of class, ambitious students have visions of corner offices, business attire, and global deals. They are taught to believe that they are embarking on a voyage toward prosperity – a voyage fueled by profit and ambition. Most international business program curricula are focused on teaching how to maximize profit and value for shareholders, and preparing students for business that exploits resources and consumes unsustainably. Traditional business models prioritize money over environmental and social impact with little sustainability beyond Corporate Social Responsibility (CSR) reporting. The business curricula are like well-charted maps leading students toward profit and treasures. We teach them to read balance sheets, negotiate contracts, construct business strategy, and optimize supply chains. But somewhere in the margins, sustainability has been scribbled in faint ink – a footnote usually lost in the pursuit of growth.

The work by Muff et al. (2013), however, advocates a paradigm shift for business schools, urging them to prioritize being "best for the world" over "best in the world" by transforming their vision, curriculum, pedagogy, research, and engagement with stakeholders. They propose a holistic and systematic approach to business education that aims to develop globally responsible leaders, to facilitate business organizations to serve the common good, and to actively serve the transformation of business and the economy. In an era fraught with pressing global sustainability challenges such as climate change and resource depletion, why should a business school focus on profit maximization at the expense of preparing students for a sustainability mindset? Business schools play a pivotal role in shaping mindsets and practices for future leaders and should have a much more active role in fostering a generation of business professionals who understand the interconnectedness of economic, social, and environmental systems. By integrating sustainability into their curricula, business schools can equip graduates with the skills to navigate complexity and drive positive change, thereby fostering ripple effects that extend globally.

Sustainability frameworks in business education

In our business program, we transcend traditional lectures, creating narratives through engaging case studies and collaborative group work. Here, the conventional classroom setup takes a back seat, making room for more contemporary and dynamic experiential learning. The program also includes a sustainability framework, with a common objective across all business education, and the integration of environmental, social, and governance (ESG) principles. The sustainability framework integrated into our business curriculum is as follows:

- The triple-bottom-line (TBL) framework (Elkington, 1997) at the business level emphasizes the three dimensions of profit, people, and planet and considers how businesses can make an impact beyond financial performance. TBL is often taught in business schools through lectures and rarely through guest lectures and group projects. Students explore real-world examples and how companies balance these three dimensions. For example, as part of the strategic management module, students engage in a TBL analysis of Patagonia, an outdoor clothing and gear retailer, or complete a coursework component where they analyze a case company's TBL initiatives. Student engagement with the framework includes assessing TBL through both case content and website content and making recommendations.
- The 17 United Nations Sustainable Development Goals (UNSDGs) (UNSDG, 2014) as a global-level framework is an agenda seeking to embrace global sustainable development in every institution. At the undergraduate level (years 1 and 2), the SDGs are taught in terms of national adoption, business practice relevance, and company alignment. Students create business plans and projects addressing specific SDGs and assess how their recommended solutions contribute to global sustainability.
- The Corporate Social Responsibility (CSR) framework (Carroll, 1991) highlights a company's ethical responsibility toward society, including philanthropy, ethical sourcing, and giving back to the community, while accepting the basic economic responsibilities of business (making a profit to survive). The CSR framework is mostly lecture-based with teachers discussing both principles and case studies. This framework fits best as part of a business ethics and strategy management course and is included in strategy and change management concepts. In our own subjective experiences, developing CSR strategies for a real or fictional company is part of a strategy management course but was traditionally given short shrift, mostly assessing the impact of CSR initiatives on various stakeholders, shareholders, and long-term growth.
- The circular economy framework (McDonough & Braungart, 2010) aims to minimize waste by designing processes and products that promote

reusing, recycling, and regeneration, including cradle-to-cradle design and closed-loop systems. This framework is introduced as part of the supply chain and logistics courses where students analyze supply chains, product life cycles, and waste reduction strategies, and propose circular economy business models.

- The stakeholder theory framework (Freeman, 1984) proposes a holistic approach to business when considering welfare and well-being by including the interests of all stakeholders (employees and communities), going beyond a shareholder perspective. This sustainability framework includes stakeholder mapping as well as an understanding of the control and interest aspects of a particular business environment, and is taught either as a part of Strategy and Change Management or alternately in Conflict Management. Classes are designed to explore the framework and its implications in terms of conflicts between stakeholder interests. Students conduct stakeholder analyses for real companies including force field analysis, identifying the forces that promote or hinder a particular change within an organization and creating a change management scenario with a new strategic direction or change. They identify key stakeholders and propose strategies to address their needs, which is often more about "inclusivity" of interests from a sustainability perspective.

- The Integrated Reporting framework (IIRC, 2013) combines both financial and non-financial information – especially ESG factors – to provide a holistic view of a company's performance. The framework is increasingly important in green financial statement reporting, and students are taught how best to integrate non-financial ESG factors into published business documentation, serving as appreciations for actions that improve the public good. Students analyze company reports and assess materiality as well as other ESG elements to consider how non-financial factors impact financial performance.

However, adding these frameworks to core courses such as financial management, strategy, and change management as is regularly done in traditional business schools often relegates sustainability to an occasional act of goodwill. At most, students dissect a hypothetical scenario through a case study with some discussion on the topic. Even with experiential and collaborative learning, classroom approaches often fall short without any impact or mindset shift in the student, an inefficient way to create a generation of business leaders who care. Teaching these frameworks within the confines of a classroom is no better than a boring speech, with a case study discussed and no action taken or generated. The students absorbed theories, but theories alone will not weather the storms beyond the classroom. These concepts need to resonate with the golden promise of balancing the drive of economic prosperity with social well-being and environmental stewardship. But here lies the irony – under such conditions a classroom becomes a vacuum where ideas and discussions fade into abstraction.

The frameworks stripped of soil, wind, and human touch become a theoretical relic where the Earth is just a blue dot on a PowerPoint slide. For students to truly understand the importance of striking a balance between growth and development and sustainability, they must witness the damage caused to the Earth by growth and development practices, feel the weight of profit margins at the cost of unsustainable actions, and hear the stories of sustainable practitioners who work as change agents. TBL's true classroom is a factory floor, a beach with plastic garbage, a bustling market square, or a recycling expo. There, theories and frameworks collide with reality and balance sheets come to life.

Sustainability in action project

This project began in the vibrant corridors of our university when a group of enthusiastic students united around a common goal – to champion sustainability in their community. Led by a team of resolute business instructors, they embarked on a journey of collaboration, action, and the determination to be effective. Participating in this project were students enrolled in either the BSc International Business Management Programmes' Introduction to Global Business Sustainability course or the BA international Business programmes' Sustainable Development and International Business Law. These students knew that business could be a force for good, but they also knew that it would cause harm if not done responsibly, with courses in theory and practical exposure through the sustainability in action project. The Sustainability in Action project was a testament to the vision of this group of students and a faculty who wanted to do more than just teaching concepts. Together, they sought to share their knowledge of sustainability not only within the university but also with industry partners, fellow students, and faculty members alike. Their mission was clear: to educate, empower, and inspire. With meticulous planning and unwavering dedication, the project unfolded in stages. From brainstorming sessions to project proposals, from approvals to preparations, every step was carefully orchestrated to maximize impact.

The heart of the project involved four distinct events and actions, the aim of which was to make the students realize that profit maximization is not the only choice and fostered a mindset of caring about their future through necessary sustainable actions. First, there were enlightening company fieldtrips both locally and internationally as well as captivating industry guest lectures.

One such excursion led them to a local sustainable construction consultancy called Cundall, where they explored sustainable engineering and design solutions across the built environment (About Cundall, 2024). This consulting company, one of a select few who have achieved carbon neutrality as a business, presented their projects. They are now aiming toward net zero for all projects by 2030. "Zero Carbon Design 2030 (ZCD2030) is a global initiative that aims to engage everyone at Cundall – every office, every discipline, every level – to help our clients to achieve their net zero carbon goals" (Zero Carbon Design 2030, 2024). The students were thrilled about this visit and their feedback highlighted what they learned about sustainable office environments.

Students also had a chance to visit Georgia to see a multinational (MNC) food and beverage company (Pepsi GE, 2024) before the end of the semester, where they had the chance to taste sample Pepsi max with no sugar, and see firsthand Pepsi's ESG efforts with sustainable packaging, and contribution to circular economy. We also visited a chocolate factory in Georgia (Barambo, 2024), and the students were able to ask questions and offer suggestions about minimizing water usage and sustainable cocoa farming. Beyond the waning lectures, students were able to obtain practical knowledge of sustainable methods in corporations. We as educators and facilitators were awestruck, as we started to see some mindset changes and an awareness of sustainable business in our students. It reinforced how higher education can have the potential for transformational experiences that nurture mindset changes and behavioral shifts toward sustainability (Wynsberghe, 2022).

Second, our students participated in the sustainability in action project Beach Cleanup (ARIU_Derby, 2023), a firsthand demonstration of student and faculty commitment to social responsibility. As stated by Boulton et al. (2019), the impact of civic participation can boost morale and create a better working mentality. As they worked tirelessly to restore cleanliness to the beaches, the exercise fostered a sense of community and environmental stewardship. A beach cleanup can be meaningful and impactful as the personal interaction with the environment creates more empathy and psychological benefits (Wyles et al., 2017). While time spent near the sea is found to be restorative and impactful on improved health and well-being, a purposeful effort to clean up the beach also helped students to understand the impact of all business productive activities on nature. Students cleaning the beach experienced real-world challenges that did not fit neatly into textbooks or in their minds.

The pinnacle of their efforts in this project was the Sustainability in Action Symposium. This student-led symposium was an excellent opportunity for selected final-year business students (Sustainable Development and International Business Law module) to present their course research on global sustainability initiatives and to receive feedback from industry practitioners who also shared their own experiences and insights. Students presented their findings about how MNC operations have been detrimental to the promotion and protection of human rights in developing countries, and discussed the soft law implementation, voluntary mechanisms, and binding frameworks to regulate MNC activities in the international sphere. The industry feedback was supportive – not criticizing, but critically analyzing distinct aspects of the proposals from different areas of module and assignment research – on sustainability practices in the world.

The industry practitioners, including luminaries such as Mr. Jose Retana, Sustainability director of FIFA World Cup 2022; Ms. Sabika Shaban, Founder of Qatar Disability Resource (QADR); Dr. Mohammed Al Humaiqani, Senior project manager of Gulf Organization for Research & Development (GORD); Mr. Martin Bauerle, Operational manager at Cundall measuring air quality; and Ms. Jennifer Marie Tungol, CEO of Ateliers Artea Worldwide specializing in plant-based fashion products, each presented their best industry practices and connected academic research topics to real business cases. Students heard from these top executives and managers who are already impacting the world through their sustainability initiatives. The fruitful discussion fostered a higher level of critical thinking in the students and opened connections with industry leaders, as well as possible further collaboration in sustainability areas.

It was especially important to hear about the sustainability achievements of FIFA World Cup Qatar 2022, as the most important Sport Event in Qatar that year. This event was the first tournament to be certified at the international standards ISO 20121 for event sustainability management systems, setting a new mega-events sustainability standard. Examples included the program for stadium energy management, including water and waste management, through design, construction, and operations, bringing Global Sustainability Assessment System building certification to all eight stadiums. Benefits include 30% more energy-efficient stadiums, 40% less water usage, 79% of stadium construction waste either reused or recycled, and 15% of construction materials obtained from sustainably sourced materials (Inside FIFA, 2022).

The founder of QADR presented different practices on how university students could involve the students and people with special needs, presenting the best practices and inspiring young people to make better inclusion in future (Qatar Disability Resource, 2023). She showcased some of the best practices and tools that QADR offers to help people with disabilities in accessing education, healthcare, recreation, and employment opportunities.

The GORD project manager presented best practices in the construction industry and how much of it starts in the development stages, including in architectural and urbanistic planning and showcasing the Msheireb as one of the best cases in Qatar (GORD – About Us, 2023). The Cundall Operations manager measured the air quality in the university classroom, presenting to the students the importance of workspace balance with nature and air quality for better work efficiency. His explanation about how indoor air quality affects the health, comfort, well-being, and productivity of the occupants was an eye-opener for all of our students. The plant-based fashion CEO was another eye-opener, as few are aware of sustainable fashion opportunities, and this was a unique opportunity to see, hear, and touch, including a banana leaf shirt, and jewelry from recycled plastics (Ateliers Artea Worldwide, 2023).

Each industry expert shared how profit alone is a hollow victory, like hoarding gold without sharing it with the village or how a business that ravages the planet is like an emerald shattered into shards. They shared the social dimensions for sustainable business – how it thrives when its people thrive – and that sustainability is the most important cause. They also shared their battle scars revealing how they navigated through rough patches. These experiences led the students toward better learning outcomes, to a deeper understanding of and the ability to critically evaluate the meaning of sustainable development as well as the laws applicable to international business transactions, and to creatively solve international business problems through the practical application of sustainable development theory and practice. Sustainability ceased to be a footnote; it became a mindset that molded the student's business perspectives.

Fourth, after the inspiring symposium presentations and workshops, the junior students had the opportunity to showcase their coursework on Introduction on Global Business and Sustainability in a poster exhibition. The aim of the exhibition was to display the student's ability to apply the United Nations Sustainable Development Goals (UNSDGs) to practical scenarios of different countries' contexts and sectors and display their research and analysis on practical challenges and opportunities. The speakers from the symposium also attended the exhibition, asked questions, and gave feedback to the students, creating a dialogue and exchange of perspectives. The poster exhibition gave the students a chance to apply theoretical knowledge to practical scenarios, communicate it to a diverse audience, and receive constructive feedback from experts and peers.

According to Reinders (2020) and UNESCO (2023), projects and initiatives like these matriculate with Education for Sustainable Development, which in turn empowers students to become engaged and accountable citizens who can make a difference in the world by addressing the sustainability challenge. As the symposium and exhibition ended, the echoes of inspiration lingered in the air, a reminder of the transformative power of collective action. From an afterthought to a core value, students' perspectives on sustainability have grown throughout this project.

Transformation and benefits of the sustainability in action project

Imagine a race where different industries compete to make changes for the future. Some are fast and agile; others are clumsy and slow. Where does the education industry fit in this race? Isn't it often clumsy and slow, and resistant to change? For example, technology that can support better learning and teaching outcomes was long ignored until there were no other choices, as in the pandemic and the in-person shutdown of schools and colleges or when AI could no longer be ignored. The education industry has since started embracing technology. But following what happens is not a clever way to run the race. The massive adoption of sustainability as an action in the curriculum is not a choice, but an inevitable step for creating a mindset of change. With just six years left to achieve the UN SDG goals, where are we with the sustainability goals? If not in our schools and colleges, where else can we create a generation of future business leaders with a perspective that is different from current leaders to achieve the sustainability goals?

With the Sustainability in Action project, our university embarked on a transformative journey to reshape our curriculum and to nurture a sustainability mindset in our students. While industry professionals played a critical role in this endeavor, it is important to clarify how their involvement directly contributed to the project. Throughout the initiative, students were actively engaged with real-life sustainable business cases and people who pioneered the changes. As stewards of this project, we, the teachers, and mentors of the program, were purely driven by the desire to help students make the transition from classroom theory to real-world application through the tangible illustrations provided by our industry partners. The metamorphosis began with a meticulous evaluation of the existing curriculum, including identifying the effectiveness and gaps in addressing sustainability concepts, as well as the need to create students with the mindset for sustainable action. This massive shift from a conventional syllabus-based curriculum delivery to a dynamic experiential model was a considered evolution in our approach to teaching and learning. As an outcome, the students came to realize that neither success nor money nor maximization of profit mattered as much as a sustainable world where survival was assured.

The Sustainability in Action Project was implemented as a carefully but passionately operated project and for that, many buy-ins were needed from the management, faculty, and students. With their involvement, the project was supported with ideas and determination. The introduction of firsthand experience such as international and local industry field trips, guest lectures, and engaging projects replaced the traditional lectures. The classroom became a dynamic space where theories collided with reality and the project became a linchpin connecting theoretical frameworks with tangible actions, fostering a deep understanding of sustainability principles. Quantifying the transformation worked out by this multifaceted project was challenging as it involved many subjective aspects of mindset shifts, learning and unlearning.

However, the learning outcome was still evident with the final reflective pieces the students put forward in their written work and presentations. Most of the students referenced this perspective shift. Of the many feedbacks we have received: The "Sustainability in Action symposium has introduced me to real life methods the companies nowadays are implementing to promote sustainability in operations," "I was not aware that sustainability could be worked in daily lives – who would think that clothes and accessories could be made from bamboo and sugarcane? Until the point of touching it, I never thought it was a real concept." Before and after analyses of this project revealed a significant improvement in the student's comprehension of sustainability frameworks and their practical applications.

The vision of a revamped curriculum delivery requires many coordinated efforts and a shared vision. The journey of transforming a traditional class-based curriculum to a more active sustainability-embedded one is not an easy task and is not an end in itself. The challenges we faced were daunting, the arrangements required were different from the routine set of traditional courses and needed coordination with industry experts, event planners, and university human resources. Resistance came from many corners and the traditional and routine path was a more comfortable road. The enthusiasm of the program leader and the module leaders of the program, however, made up for the resistance with persuasive communication which highlighted the positive impact of the novel approach. A dedicated support system in the form of project management office meetings comprising the faculty, students, and sub-committees and overseen by the program leader was instrumental in aligning the project goals and trickling down the inspiration and engagement needs. Navigating logistics requirements for field trips and coordinating with industry practitioners needed meticulous planning and execution. One of the students who was acting as a project lead said:

> I was coordinating with all industry practitioners for different speeches, and I could add them to my network. Talks with them motivated me to think of sustainability as a key area to look into in any business I will be in the future.

And what an incomparable experience the students had! Their engagement and passion as well as a concern for their fellow beings, nature, and the future made these daunting arrangements rewarding. The outcome was the promise of a more engaged and conscious cohort fueled by care and determination. There is more to be done, but the starting point with sustainability as a core value of the learning experience has been realized. In future, courses more actionable sustainability learning, additional assessments, and other redesigns are necessary to better align the principles and practices of education for sustainable development. The incorporation of industry feedback into the curriculum is also necessary, to enrich the content of the course and provide the students with real-world perspectives on the challenges and opportunities in sustainable business practices.

Echoing Einstein's observation that "We can't solve problems by using the same kind of thinking we used when we created them," the solution lies in modifying our perspectives for raising a generation that can comprehend sustainability as a way of life. If only we can change the way we see, we can change the world we see, and it must start with our perspectives. As the famous US Advisor on climate change and Yale professor, Gus Speth once said

> I used to think the top environmental problems were biodiversity loss, eco-system collapse and climate change. I thought that with 30 years of good science we could address those problems, but I was wrong. The top environmental problems are selfishness, greed, and apathy . . . and to deal with those we need a spiritual and cultural transformation, and we scientists do not know how to do that.

Inner Development Goal (IDG) is a nonprofit organization that researches, collects, and communicates science-based skills and qualities that help us to live purposeful, sustainable, and productive lives (Inner Development Goals, 2024). The IDGs aim to change the inner perspectives of human beings on sustainability, which is closely related to education. IDG-related activities can be integrated into the curriculum of business schools to foster inner development and global responsibility among students. These activities can complement any business course by enhancing the human capacity to change and adopt sustainable business ideas with high cognitive involvement.

By integrating inner development and sustainability hand in hand into the business curriculum, we as business schools can prepare the next generation of leaders who have the mindset to create positive change in themselves, their organizations, and the world. Business schools must embrace a broader mission of one that teaches beyond financial gains to encompass well-being and environmental stewardship, where sustainability is not an optional add-on but an essential lens through which we see business education. Imagine a world where business leaders are not driven by greed, but by purpose, a world where they care not only for profit but also for people and the planet. In such a world, we learn to transform ourselves, our organizations, and our society through inner development and sustainable actions. This is the world we can create by changing the way we teach business.

References

About Cundall. (2024, February 11). Retrieved from Cundall: (https://www.cundall.com/about).

ARIU_Derby. (2023, March). https://www.instagram.com/p/Cpu7lRIMrSH/?igsh=ZjlvM3lhZWg2bjYy%29&img_index=1

Ateliers Artea Worldwide. (2023). Retrieved from Ateliers Artea Worldwide-FB: https://www.facebook.com/ateliersartea/

Barambo. (2024, February 11). Retrieved from Barambo: https://barambo.ge/en

Boulton, C. A., Hughes, E., Carmel, K., Smith, J. R., & Hywel, W. T. (2019). Student engagement and wellbeing over time at a higher education institution. *PLoS One, 13.*

Carroll, A. B. (1991). The pyramid of corporate social responsibility: Toward the moral management of organizational stakeholders. *Business Horizons*, 39–48.

Elkington, J. (1997). *Cannibals with forks: The triple bottom line of 21st century business*. New Society Publishers.

Freeman, E. E. (1984). *Strategic management: A stakeholder approach*. Pitman.

GORD – about us. (2023). Retrieved from GORD: https://www.gord.qa/about-gord/about-us/

IIRC, I. I. (2013). *Integrated reporting framework*. IIRC.

Inner Development Goals. (2024). Retrieved from IDG: https://www.innerdevelopmentgoals.org/

Inside FIFA. (2022, February). Retrieved from FIFA: https://www.fifa.com/fifa-world-cup-qatar-2022-sustainability

McDonough, W., & Braungart, M. (2010). *Cradle to cradle: Remaking the way we make things*. New Society Publishers.

Muff, K., Dyllick, T., Drewell, M., Shrivastva, P., & Haertle, J. (2013). *Management education for the world: A vision for business schools serving people and planet*. Edward Elgar Publishing.

Pepsi GE. (2024, February 11). Retrieved from Pepsi GE: https://pepsi.ge/

Qatar Disability resource. (2023). Retrieved from Eartna. QA: https://www.earthna.qa/node/217

Reinders, H. J. (2020). Sustainable learning and education: A curriculum for the future. *International Review of Education*, *66*, 29–52.

UNESCO. (2023, November 17). *What is education for sustainable development?* Retrieved from UNESCO: https://www.unesco.org/en/education-sustainable-development/need-know

UNSDG. (2014). Retrieved from UN: https://sdgs.un.org/goals

Wyles, K. J., Pahl, S., Holland, M., & Thompson, R. C. (2017). Can beach cleans do more than clean up litter? Comparing Bean cleans to other coastal activities. *Environment and Behaviour*, 500–535.

Wynsberghe, R. V. (2022, May 18). *Education for sustainability, transformational learning time, and the individual -collective dialectic*. Vancouver, British Columbia, Canada.

Zero Carbon Design 2030. (2024, February 12). Retrieved from Cundall: https://www.cundall.com/about/zero-carbon-design-2030

13

MARKETING PRINCIPLES FOR A SUSTAINABLE WORLD

Transforming the foundation

Abigail B. Schneider

Abstract

As the business function intended to drive growth by developing, promoting, exchanging, and distributing products, marketing has consequences for consumers, society, and the environment. Yet mainstream textbooks often provide a sole focus on the principles, processes, and practices of marketing without discussing the larger societal and environmental contexts in which marketing takes place. This chapter describes how an undergraduate-level Marketing Principles (Introduction to Marketing) course was transformed to fully integrate social and environmental sustainability concepts. Importantly, the course revision discussed was intended to not only incorporate social and environmental sustainability topics but also help students develop a critical lens and understand how business principles and processes are not objective fact but rather subject to historical, social, and cultural biases. The aim was, thus, to expose these subconscious biases and rewrite the narrative of what marketing can – and should – be. Ultimately, the goal was to build a bridge from mainstream marketing to a regenerative future.

Introduction

I distinctly remember prepping my Marketing Principles class for the first time. It was the summer of 2014, the months between when I defended my dissertation and started my new tenure-track job as an assistant professor. I sat inside my apartment, pouring over the pages of the textbook I had chosen, while outside my window, the Denver city skyline towered in front of an iconic Rocky Mountain backdrop. That image – human-made construction, commerce, and the energy that fuels it, juxtaposed with the sheer awesomeness of the non-human natural world – was apropos of the content I wished to cover in my course.

DOI: 10.4324/9781003521839-14

Yet, finding a textbook that grappled with the challenges of climate change and environmental degradation in the context of marketing or even questioned any aspect of capitalism was impossible to find. With the exception of a few rare outdated and/or off-topic titles, every marketing principles textbook promoted the same neoliberal narrative of unfettered growth fueled by advertising, promotion, and selling. It was the same message that causes embarrassment and even shame whenever I sheepishly admit to being a marketing professor to new acquaintances. Whenever people ask me what I do, I always have to qualify "marketing Professor" by saying, "but not the kind who teaches students to sell things that people don't need to people who don't want them."

I wanted to tell a different story of marketing. A story about hope. A story that made me proud to be a marketing professor. And it was clear that I was going to have to write that story myself.

Textbooks provide a blueprint for classes. They lay out a framework for syllabi. And they create a schema in students' minds of what a field is (and what it is not). The narrative of the discipline is often implied based on what is not said (and on the matter-of-fact tone of what is). Words printed on a physical (or even digital) page are often taken to be the Truth. Especially in business classes, unlike in liberal arts disciplines, the information espoused in textbooks is often considered to be objective fact, and it is rarely challenged – the textbooks define concepts, present tools, and outline processes, but the larger context of marketing is rarely interrogated.

Marketing *is* the 4 Ps. The product life cycle *is* the product life cycle. The sales process *is* the sales process. Students do not consider the historical, political, cultural, and rhetorical nature of the content of marketing textbooks. They do not always consider how the content that is included in the textbook is a choice – conscious or not – made by authors and editors (often male and white from the global north) who carry their own biases.

So, as I sought to rewrite the story of marketing, I also sought to teach students to think critically and to explicitly consider the contextual nature of the information they were consuming. I didn't want them to just digest the new story; I wanted them to consider the gaps in the old and to be able to compare and contrast the two narratives so that they would not take either for granted. It was critical for them to see where the field of marketing had been and to trace where it was going so that they could understand why it needed to change. The old story still permeates corporate America, and students need to be able to identify what most marketers take for granted as standard practice in order to forge a new path toward a sustainable world.

So how did I do this? I started where many marketing professors start – the textbook. I chose a title that struck a balance between being informative and engaging and that was relatively inexpensive, but any standard marketing textbook will do for this part of the exercise. Then, for each topic covered by the textbook, I curated "counter-content," content that could help me construct a different narrative for the discipline. This content included academic journal articles, popular press articles, book chapters, TED Talks, documentaries, podcast episodes, and more (see Table 13.1 for an outline of the topics and counter-content).

I also required that students write a brief response to a specific prompt that required them to compare and contrast the "old" and the "new" narratives of marketing for each topic (e.g., when studying strategic planning, students were asked, "What are the goals of business? How do a company's objectives influence its practices and processes? What role might ethics and social responsibility play in an organization's strategy?"; other discussion prompts can be provided upon request). The responses, which I termed "entry tickets," were due prior to the start of each class, and we discussed them in person or on Zoom depending on the modality of the course (students first discussed their responses in small groups, and then I held a full-class discussion; note that such an assignment could also work for an asynchronous course's discussion forum assignment).

At the end of the class discussion, I summarized the main points raised by the students and highlighted the tension between the "old" and "new" narratives (e.g., "the old narrative maintains that the goal of business is to maximize short-term profits for shareholders and to achieve growth. The new narrative, however, argues that business should maximize both short- and long-term values for all stakeholders, including the environment. A company's objectives serve as a "north star," driving its practices and processes, so running an environmentally and socially sustainable business requires that the firm's objectives are aligned with sustainability goals. Failing to manage for sustainability can be viewed as a strategic risk. As one student noted, "Growth often times means change." That is, instead of – or in addition to – growing quantitatively, businesses should incorporate ethical standards into their strategies in order to grow qualitatively."). My own key takeaways comparing the "old" and "new" narratives are included in Table 13.1.

Those included in the development process

No idea is ever conceived of in a vacuum, and that is true of this course revision. Ideas for such a course started percolating long before I ever taught it, and I was influenced by numerous leading thinkers from both academia and industry such as Stuart L. Hart, Tony Cooke, Jody Fry and members of the One Planet Education Networks (OPEN), Isabel Rimanoczy and members of LEAP! UN PRME Working Group on the Sustainability Mindset, Linda Irwin and Jim Stoner and members of the Global Movement Initiative, Nathan Havey, and the countless guest speakers who spoke in my class (e.g., Dana Bacardi, Jennifer Purdum, Juan Mayorga, Joe Conrad), including some former students who are now leaders in the corporate sustainability space (e.g., Sade Akindele, Paul Hunter).

My academic colleagues were also influential, as I used many of their existing articles as content (e.g., Sunaina Chugani, Michael Luchs, Shalini Bahl) or published new articles with them to underscore the topics in the course (e.g., Linda Irwin; Schneider et al., 2022). Nathan Havey and I also founded a podcast series, Growing Good Business, which I plan to include in future iterations of the course. Growing Good Business is "a podcast showcasing forward-thinking business leaders who are re-creating the business paradigm to honor humanity and our planet's life support systems." The mini-series includes nine episodes featuring groundbreaking figures such as Raj Sisodia, Co-Founder and Chairman Emeritus of Conscious Capitalism; Lisa Conway, VP of Global Market Sustainability at Interface; and Leith Sharp, Former Director of Executive Education for Sustainability Leadership at Harvard. The podcast can be found on Spotify, Apple Podcasts, at https://www.regis.edu/academics/colleges-and-schools/anderson/seed-institute/growing-good-business or wherever you get your podcasts.

Importantly, many of the podcast episodes were recorded live, either in person or via Zoom, in order to generate a conversation and facilitate networking between the hosts, guests, and attendees. Sustainability professionals often work in silos or find themselves as the "token" sustainability champion at their organization, so finding and maintaining a community among sustainability professionals is critical for sharing knowledge and moral support. The people who informed this course are among those in my community who give me the energy to persevere with the work of transforming business higher education; and their knowledge and ideas were critical for designing the course.

Summary of resources or tools used

My course revision incorporated academic journal articles, popular press articles, book chapters, TED Talks, documentaries, podcast episodes, etc. Table 13.1 at the end of this chapter illustrates each topic covered along with specific resources that I used to tell the new story of marketing and the key takeaway(s) from that story. Note that I have also rearranged the order of some of the textbook chapters in order to more effectively tell the new narrative.

In addition to the resources outlined in Table 13.1, I invited guest speakers to come to my class to complement the material. Finally, students completed a marketing plan project for a local nonprofit organization, There with Care, in order to underscore how the tools of marketing can be applied to prosocial, and not just material, consumption contexts. More information about this project can be found in Schneider (2022).

Impact

While I hope that this chapter will prove useful in providing other marketing instructors with a blueprint for integrating social and environmental sustainability concepts into their courses, the impact of my work, thus far, has largely been on students.

When asked what aspects of the course contributed most to their learning, as part of the end-of-semester student evaluations of teaching, students repeatedly noted the readings, entry tickets, small group discussions, and large group discussions. Students appreciate the interactive lessons and find the class to be fun, engaging, and interesting.

A follow-up informal survey of students revealed that those surveyed generally found that, compared with other business classes they had taken, this course incorporated sustainability topics to a greater extent; they found that it incorporated social justice topics about the same as or a little more than other classes. Given that the course is taught at a Jesuit university, it is perhaps not surprising that other business classes do incorporate social justice topics to some extent. Students believed that the supplemental readings were valuable and said that the readings very much influenced how they think about the field of marketing. As one student noted, "Before this class I didn't think much about the way our financial actions and business affect our planet's health, after the class I now see all the many ways we are constantly damaging our planet at the expense of profit." Another student, Callie Burns, noted that she is "incredibly grateful . . . that sustainability and social justice [topics were] implemented in nearly every class."

I think that it is important to note, however, that one should approach teaching such a class with minimal expectations. I was not asked by my superiors to teach a course that incorporated sustainability topics, and I do not believe that it has impacted my yearly evaluations one way or the other. Promoting sustainability in my own classes and others' classes will not secure me a promotion or a raise. And my student evaluations of teaching were strong before I heavily incorporated sustainability topics into this class. In sum, I think that faculty should not teach such a class expecting to receive accolades from students, peers, or superiors or expecting any institutional support.

Instead, I think that the driving force has to be one's passion and conviction that the future of our planet and the ability for our institutions of higher education and for humanity and other living beings to exist depends on the dedication of those tirelessly fighting for a different way from wherever they are and within whatever sphere of influence they occupy. Indeed, it is tireless, often thankless work, and I believe that it is important for faculty who are dedicated to transforming business education to be in community and provide support to one another for the essential work that we are doing. Such is an important contribution of the Global Movement Initiative and other groups such as the United Nations PRME Working Group on the Sustainability Mindset and the One Planet Education Networks (OPEN).

Later, I will discuss some of the challenges specific to this course as well as some key learnings and recommendations.

Personal learning outcomes and recommendations

After teaching this class, there are a number of learnings and recommendations that I would like to share related to the broad topics as follows:

Facilitation: While classes may still include some lecture, unlike many traditional business classes where the faculty member lectures, unchallenged, on content that is presented as objective fact, this revised version of Marketing Principles requires that faculty members be able to facilitate potentially challenging conversations about controversial topics. It is critical that students feel safe expressing their views (even if those views challenge this new narrative of marketing), and faculty should try to ensure that all students' voices are heard. During the large group discussion, each small group should have an opportunity to report out (a group recorder and reporter can be selected in advance by each team).

Empathy for a Diversity of Lived Experiences: Instructors should be aware that some students may be personally impacted by some topics. For example, a student from Vietnam may have family members who are directly impacted by global supply chains. Mexican American students may be able to relate to marketing that targets "the Hispanic market" in ways that promote negative stereotypes. I have found that discussions are enriched by these personal experiences, but some examples may be triggering for some students.

Volume of Work and Accountability: Given the additional reading that is required by this course, I recommend requiring the entry tickets in order to hold students accountable. The entry tickets also give more introverted students time to prepare their responses prior to the group discussions. At the same time, given that the entry tickets require additional work, students will want feedback on each entry ticket to ensure that they are on the right track. I often share examples of top entry tickets and email students to congratulate them on particularly insightful and well-written responses. Such engagement requires additional work on the part of the instructor.

Volume of Work and Setting Expectations: This version of the course is more work than students may expect in an introductory class, so it is important to properly set expectations and explain the purpose of the content and why it is useful. Students have noted in the end-of-semester evaluations of teaching that the course is challenging but rewarding.

Relevance. In addition to the supplemental content listed in Table 13.1, it is important to keep the class current and relevant by updating the content and the format of the content (e.g., readings, videos, podcasts, etc.), to address current issues of interest to students. Developing experiential learning exercises around the content is another way to keep the course relevant and to maintain student engagement.

TABLE 13.1 Alternative marketing content

Topic	Reading	Counter-Content	Key Takeaway(s)
An Overview of Marketing & the Marketing Environment	Lamb et al. (2021, Ch. 1)	Kotler (2011) Irwin & Schneider (2020)	Marketing is not just about selling "stuff" and driving growth; the tools and processes of marketing can instead be used to curb resource degradation and drive other prosocial and pro-environmental efforts.
Ethics and Social Responsibility	Lamb et al. (2021, Ch. 3)	Senge et al. (2010, p. 177) Klein (2000, p. 75) Wright and Nyberg (2015, pp. 16–22, 73–75, 85–87) Bakan (2004, pp. 16–21, 25–53)	Ethics and social responsibility should not be a "token" chapter and class topic but rather the foundation that permeates every aspect of the course. Students should be critical of CSR efforts and challenge companies to make substantive changes in service to society and the environment. Friedman's assertion that "the social responsibility of business is to increase its profits," should be questioned in light of its consequences and not treated as just another perspective.
Strategic Planning	Lamb et al. (2021, Ch. 2)	Senge et al. (2010, pp. 119–133)	Strategy should incorporate long-term thinking and risks related to climate change to create sustainable value.
Global Marketing	Lamb et al. (2021, Ch. 5)	Stiglitz (2002, Ch. 1) Watch Chiang (2012) John Oliver Fast Fashion (Avery et al., 2015b, April)	Globalization is a complicated issue with myriad positive and negative outcomes.
Marketing Research	Lamb et al. (2021, Ch. 9)	Grassegger and Krogerus (2017)	Marketing research is a powerful tool for understanding consumers' wants and needs. In the age of AI and big data, it is imperative to protect consumers' privacy and use their data responsibly.
Consumer Decision Making	Lamb et al. (2021, Ch. 6)	Bahl et al. (2016)	Instead of learning to manipulate consumers as future marketers, students can learn to be mindful and wise consumers in order to avoid being manipulated by marketers.

(*Continued*)

TABLE 13.1 (Continued)

Topic	Reading	Counter-Content	Key Takeaway(s)
Business Marketing	Lamb et al. (2021, Ch. 7)	Illing (2019)	Marketers generalize and stereotype in order to put consumers into boxes and push products to them; identities should not be commoditized and commercialized. Marginalized and vulnerable communities should not be exploited for the sake of profit.
Segmentation and Targeting Markets	Lamb et al. (2021, Ch. 8) Lamb et al. (2021, Ch. 4, pp. 53–60 only)		
Developing and Managing the Product	Lamb et al. (2021, Ch. 11)	Klein (2000, pp. 3–26) Kesslen (2020)	The rise of the brand meant that products themselves no longer mattered and could be produced around the world for a fraction of the cost at the expense of people and the planet.
Product Concepts: Packaging, Labeling, and Branding	Lamb et al. (2021, Ch. 10)	Jaffee (2014, pp. 147–153) Godoy (2016)	There is a complex reality behind the eco-labels intended to simplify purchase decisions. For example, certifications such as Fair Trade and Organic often maintain colonial hierarchies such that producers in the global south are subject to rules and regulations maintained by the global north; additionally, some certifications are ineffective and/or have unintended consequences for marginalized communities (e.g., GMO labeling could lead to additional spending on R&D, the cost of which would be disproportionately passed on to vulnerable consumers). Packaging presents an exciting opportunity for sustainable innovation.

(Continued)

TABLE 13.1 (Continued)

Topic	Reading	Counter-Content	Key Takeaway(s)
Services and Other Intangibles	Lamb et al. (2021, Ch. 12)	Watch Pallotta (2013)	Nonprofit marketing is just like for-profit marketing with a few exceptions. When nonprofit organizations are held to different standards, they are put at a disadvantage when it comes to being able to solve social and environmental challenges of great magnitude. Overhead, such as marketing, is critical for growing the resources available to nonprofits.
Pricing Concepts & Setting the Right Price	Lamb et al. (2021, Ch. 19)	Watch Morgan (2015): The True Cost Cline (2012, Ch. 2)	The human and environmental cost of production is not reflected in the price tag.
Marketing Communications	Lamb et al. (2021, Ch. 15)	Senge et al. (2010, pp. 330–332)	Instead of spending copious amounts of money on traditional advertising intended to manipulate consumers into buying the product, marketers can use promotional tactics such as education that meaningfully engage with consumers and treat them with dignity.
Advertising, PR, and Sales	Lamb et al. (2021, Ch. 16)	Bakan (2004, pp. 121–138) Klein (2000, pp. 87–98) Lewis (2017)	Our public spaces are being colonized by a culture of consumption.
Social Media and Marketing	Lamb et al. (2021, Ch. 18)	Schneider et al. (2022) Watch Harris (2017)	The effects of social media are paradoxical with consequences for consumer and societal well-being. Certain features of social media platforms exploit how our brains function to make users addicted, and the technology can pose a threat to democracy.
Personal Selling and Sales Management	Lamb et al. (2021, Ch. 17)	Watch Avery et al. (2015a, February): John Oliver Pharmaceutical Sales	Aggressive selling in certain industries can introduce dangerous incentives and put profits over patients.
Supply Chain Management; Marketing Channels and Retailing	Lamb et al. (2021, Ch. 13)Lamb et al. (2021, Ch. 14)	Klein (2000, pp. xv–xviii) Friedman (2020) Watch NPR (2013): Planet Money Makes a T-Shirt	There is a story behind every product's journey from raw material to retail outlet to consumer, and it is important for consumers to understand the human and planetary resources required to make their products.

In addition to my own learnings and recommendations, I asked the students who were surveyed to provide recommendations from the student's perspective. These students reinforced the value of the entry tickets and the class discussion format over a lecture format. One student, Sayuri Toribio, emphasized that faculty members need to "give examples that students will actually care about." Similarly, Callie Burns suggested experiential learning opportunities as a way to make the class relevant to students.

In terms of recommendations for other students (which instructors can share in an effort to set expectations in their classroom), the students surveyed suggested that students know "what [they] are getting into" but be open-minded. Given the workload, these former students also recommended that others keep up with the work.

Conclusion

The principles and processes of marketing have consequences for consumers, society, and the environment. Yet textbooks often simply define concepts, present tools, and outline processes while failing to provide the historical and cultural contexts from which those concepts, tools, and processes emerged and failing to consider the possibility that different – more sustainable – concepts, tools, and processes could exist. The status quo is taken for granted and not challenged. As David Foster Wallace suggested, we are fish in water . . . and the oceans are warming. We need to become aware of the impact of marketing on people and our planet and change – fast.

References

Avery, K., Carvell, T., Gondelman, J. & Hoskinson, J. (2015a, February 8). Marketing to Doctors (S2. E1) [TV series episode]. In T. Carvell, J. Oliver., L. Stanton, J. Taylor, & J. Thoday (Executive Producers), *Last Week Tonight With John Oliver*. HBO.

Avery, K., Carvell, T., Gondelman, J. & Hoskinson, J. (2015b, April 26). Fashion (S2. E11) [TV series episode]. In T. Carvell, & J. Oliver. (Executive Producers), *Last Week Tonight With John Oliver*. HBO.

Bahl, S., Milne, G. R., Ross, S. M., Mick, D. G., Grier, S. A., Chugani, S. K. & Boesen-Mariani, S. (2016). Mindfulness: Its transformative potential for consumer, societal, and environmental well-being. *Journal of Public Policy & Marketing*, 35(2), 198–210.

Bakan, J. (2004). *The corporation: The pathological pursuit of profit and power*. Free Press.

Chiang, L. T. (2012, June). *The voices of China's workers*. TED. https://www.ted.com/talks/leslie_t_chang_the_voices_of_china_s_workers?language=en

Cline, E. L. (2012). *Overdressed: The shockingly high cost of cheap fashion*. Portfolio/Penguin.

Friedman, V. (2020, July 13). Los Angeles apparel factory shut down after more than 300 Coronavirus cases. *The New York Times*. https://www.nytimes.com/2020/07/13/style/los-angeles-apparel-dov-charney-coronavirus.html#:~:text=But%20on%20July%2010%2C%20the,June%2C%20and%20one%20in%20July

Godoy, M. (2016, March 16). Bill blocking GMO labels stalls in Senate, but battle is far from over. *NPR*, https://www.npr.org/sections/thesalt/2016/03/16/470677241/bill-that-would-block-states-from-mandating-gmo-labels-stalls-in-senate

Grassegger, H., & Krogerus, M. (2017, January 28). The data that turned the world upside down: How Cambridge analytica used your Facebook data to help the Donald Trump campaign in the 2016 election. *Vice*. https://www.vice.com/en/article/mg9vvn/how-our-likes-helped-trump-win

Harris, T. (2017, April). *How a handful of tech companies control billions of minds every day*. TED. https://www.ted.com/talks/tristan_harris_how_a_handful_of_tech_companies_control_billions_of_minds_every_day

Illing, S. (2019, February 16). How capitalism reduced diversity to a brand: A law professor explains how corporations commodify people of color. *Vox*, https://www.vox.com/identities/2019/2/11/18195868/capitalism-race-diversity-exploitation-nancy-leong

Irwin, L., & Schneider, A. B. (2020, December). A paradigm shift in marketing: Creating value for a more sustainable future. *The Solutions Journal*, *11*(4).

Jaffee, D. (2014). *Brewing justice: Fair trade coffee, sustainability, and survival*. University of California Press.

Kesslen, B. (2020, June 17). Aunt Jemima brand to change name, remove image that Quaker says is 'based on a racial stereotype'. *NBC News*. https://www.nbcnews.com/news/us-news/aunt-jemima-brand-will-change-name-remove-image-quaker-says-n1231260

Klein, N. (2000). *No logo*. Flamingo.

Kotler, P. (2011). Reinventing marketing to manage the environmental imperative. *Journal of Marketing*, *75*(4), 132–135.

Lamb, C., Hair, J., & McDaniel, C. (2021). *MKTG13: Principles of marketing*. Cengage.

Lewis, P. (2017, October 6). 'Our minds can be hijacked': The tech insiders who fear a smartphone dystopia. *The Guardian*. https://www.theguardian.com/technology/2017/oct/05/smartphone-addiction-silicon-valley-dystopia

Morgan, A. (Director). (2015). *The True Cost* [Film]. Untold Creative, LLC.

NPR. (2013, December 2). Planet money makes a t-shirt: The world behind a simple shirt, in five chapters. https://apps.npr.org/tshirt/#/title

Pallotta, D. (2013, March). *The way we think about charity is dead wrong*. TED. https://www.ted.com/talks/dan_pallotta_the_way_we_think_about_charity_is_dead_wrong

Schneider, A. B. (2022). Implementing the marketing plan: How depth-of-engagement in community-based learning impacts students and their nonprofit partners. *Journal of Nonprofit Education & Leadership*, *12*(4).

Schneider, A. B., Chugani, S., Kaur, T., Stornelli, J., G. Luchs, M., Bakpayev, M., . . . & Pricer, L. (2022). The role of wisdom in navigating social media paradoxes: Implications for consumers, firms, and public policy. *Journal of Consumer Affairs*, *56*(3), 1127–1147.

Senge, P., Smith, B., Kruschwitz, N., Laura, J., & Schley, S. (2010). *The necessary revolution*. Broadway.

Stiglitz, J. E. (2002). *Globalization and its discontents*. Norton.

Wright, C., & Nyberg, D. (2015). *Climate change, capitalism, and corporations*. Cambridge University Press.

14

DEVELOPING A 21ST-CENTURY SUSTAINABILITY LEADER

John (Jed) Lindholm

Abstract

Teaching with Sustainable Development Goals (SDGs) provides teachers with a framework for connecting with students on multiple levels. Business education goes beyond a company's operating effectiveness and a profit and loss statement. Twenty-first-century business education requires teachers to teach with sustainability as a goal of student awareness and the United Nation's SDGs as a specific indicator of student learning. This chapter presents one teacher's use of SDGs to connect with students at a personal level, through their passions, at an organizational level, through use of the school's (Worcester Polytechnic Institute) sustainability plan and climate action framework, and finally through showing how SDGs can be aligned at the company level in Environmental, Social, Governance (ESG) programming. Given the global concern for sustainability at many levels, I believe, educators who use SDGs in their curriculum will strengthen student awareness of how sustainability is categorized, measured, reported, discussed, and provided a leadership skill for their future.

Sustainability is one of the most important 21st-century business challenges and teaching objectives. Sustainability occurs through people working together toward the common goal of well-being. Just as an entrepreneur sees a need in a community and then begins to think deeper on how to provide a product or service to fill that need, a teacher can use the objective of being sustainable as a way students learn. As educators, we know students are struggling with making sense of the climate crisis, developing approaches to the threats for the health of life on land and under the sea, developing new awareness of ways to protect environmental biodiversity, the continued existence of poverty and hunger throughout the world, and the disequilibrium of wealth.

DOI: 10.4324/9781003521839-15

How can we, as individual teachers, address our student's concerns for their future in a way that gives them confidence to learn the subject matter we are teaching, see their potential for making positive change happen, and excitement for their future while addressing concerns for climate change, economic equity, social justice, and other human challenges? As transformational business educators, we can use Sustainable Development Goals (SDGs) to personalize and empower students by linking SDGs throughout school curriculums, school programming, and school outreach activities. In aligning and expanding SDGs as teaching tools, we are taking the first steps in transforming business education. We, as educators, want to actively include current events and concerns in our material and by using SDGs, we are using global concerns as the way to prepare students for their future. A student's positive future, just like a teacher's, does not happen alone but happens through working with others.

Following the use of SDGs as global goals in 2015, I began using SDGs in my teaching in 2016. Since then, I've been using SDGs as a central framework for teaching leadership in student assignments, student discussions, class projects, intra- and inter-departmental course connections, and as a way to orient research and teaching activities. SDGs provide business educators 17 topics to teach from, as well as 17 areas to connect with each student's passions. SDGs provide teachers with a way to connect with students on multiple levels: personal, social, and organizational.

The first-level connection is personal. I explore and develop questions such as "What SDG interest students? How do students see themselves connecting with an SDG? How do students see SDGs being needed in their communities? How is math, science, language, business, or any of their other classes connected with the SDGs?"

FIGURE 14.1 SDGs.

The second-level connection, social, I try to make through SDGs is through student networks. How do students see and understand SDGs? Do students see SDGs as interconnected, and if so, how? Are SDGs part of their home, work, school, and community activities? Where are SDGs being used to address the climate crisis?

The third-level connection I try to make through my teaching is through the student's organizational connection with the school or outside organization. How are SDGs being used to guide my school's (or other organization's) operational practices? How are SDGs being measured at my school? Does my school have a sustainability plan? Most recently, I've introduced a connection between SDGs and Environmental, Social, Governance (ESG) programs, which provides a direct connection between business operations and sustainability concerns for the planet and people.

It is through using SDGs daily, which reinforces the direct connection with students on the personal, social, and organizational levels that business education is being transformed. Through SDG connections, I've seen students become aware of their personal power to live sustainability, their community power to open new conversations with others about living sustainably, and their organizational/entrepreneurial power to ignite their capacity to change eco-environmental processes. This organizational/entrepreneurial power includes value creation and innovating that has led to new product design ideas for charging devices, and creating new educational materials to help others better understand why and how to become sustainable.

This chapter presents my experiences in using SDGs as a core teaching process and business management content that presents sustainability as a central topic to connect goals for teachers-students. Whether you're a teacher who is a little interested in sustainability or is passionate about sustainability, you can use this chapter as a guide in using SDGs as a one-on-one teaching framework, as a tool to direct students outside the classroom (though projects and civic work), and finally how SDGs are connected to business operations ESG programming.

My use of SDGs in the classroom began as an introduction of the SDGs, which students used to define their leadership model, as well as research and report on current business concerns with other students. The group formation then grew into deeper study and analysis outside the classroom that identified possible solutions for new product redesign, customer educational information, or both. Using sustainability as a teaching topic and SDGs as business issues, a teacher expands both the content that is taught and the way students think about solutions. Over the past year, student awareness of SDGs has expanded to include how sustainability and ESG programming overlap but are different in their challenges and objectives. The deeper connection between SDGs and ESG allows teachers a teaching path to teach business management with a longer-term goal of creating sustainable value.

First-level connection – student to teacher (passion and purpose)

Increased concern for sustainability issues is changing how leaders lead businesses. Concern for sustainability is driven by customer, investor, and governmental goals. A student's passion, when included as part of discussions in leadership through SDGs, provides a path to uncovering and developing a person's purpose and passion, which creates a self-supporting energy for learning.

Irna Cozma's Harvard Business Review article (2023) describes the importance of connecting a person's passion as a driver for full engagement in work that a person values. She goes on to describe a person's purpose as a larger, broader concept that brings together a person's values and purpose in decision making. This connection between teaching from a place of passion and purpose is the foundation for developing high-level student-teacher engagement. All the SDGs are directed with a purpose of personal and environmental wellness that, when studied in the class and applied in the world, creates a natural cycle of experimentation and reflection that can develop lifelong curiosity for learning.

Ask yourself, what person doesn't want to work toward SDGs of eliminating poverty, ending hunger, and ensuring good health and well-being? Or, if a student identifies with the planet, an SDG of climate action, life below water, and life on land. Using SDGs as universal challenges, which include both social and technological areas of interest, a path for deep and strong connections between teachers and students can be created.

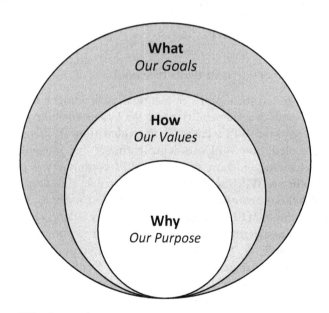

FIGURE 14.2   Why, how, what.

The breadth and interconnection of SDG issues provide a teacher with multiple channels to engage a student. The strongest signal a teacher uses to connect with a student is from the heart to the mind, and then the hands. The framework of Why-How-What helps a teacher sequence discussions and materials that begin with connecting a student's passion to a purpose that then moves them outward toward action (values) and toward a goal. Stephen Wyatt (2021) uses this model to show the importance of leaders knowing <u>Why</u> we do things as our Purpose then moving into <u>How</u> we work as our values that implement our purpose, which results in <u>What</u> we do as people and organizations in the Goals we work toward.

My goal in teaching 21st-century leadership is for students to become aware of SDGs and to leave the class knowing at least three SDGs. My course learning objectives include a developed understanding of major leadership theories, a deeper understanding of the organizational contexts in which leadership occurs, and how they are aware of their personal leadership profile. Through active involvement in this course, students will be able to:

1. Tell their leadership story and their personal leadership style(s).
2. List the four (4) domain frameworks of the *Sustainable Mindset*.
3. Describe their leadership model within an environmental context.
4. Explain their connection to three or more Sustainable Development Goals (SDGs).

In the class, SDGs are connected to Worcester Polytechnic Institute's (WPI's) sustainability plan to make deeper connections with students on how sustainability is put into action at WPI.

Second-level connection – students to school

SDGs are integrated into WPI's operational environment and educational programs through a sustainability plan. WPI's sustainability plan is being used to change how WPI's energy is provided, how WPI's buildings are heated and cooled, how WPI's students learn and live with sustainability as a common element, and how the whole WPI community is part of a sustainability solution. WPI's school of Arts & Science, Business, Engineering, and Global School are using SDGs to connect disciplines. Sustainability-focused programs at WPI include the following: (Undergraduate program): Architectural Engineering, Civil Engineering, Environmental Engineering, Environmental & Sustainable Studies, International Development, Environment, and Sustainability (IDEaS), and Sustainability Engineering; (Graduate programs): Civil Engineering, Community Climate Adaptation, Environmental Engineering, and Science and Technology for Innovation in Global Development. The breadth and depth of sustainability topics taught

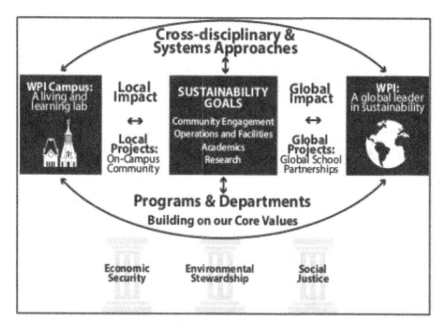

FIGURE 14.3 WPI sustainability plan elements.

throughout WPI are matched by the operational changes in WPI's energy sourcing. Through comprehensive change, students begin seeing how sustainability is connected to the ideas taught in classrooms and the operational activities of the organization.

WPI's climate action

WPI's operational strategy is to achieve carbon neutrality as soon as possible. To do this, WPI has partnered with Harrison Street and BC Energy to reduce greenhouse gas emissions and operate WPI's energy facilities. As a teacher, we see how students' attention is piqued when we can demonstrate examples of ideas in action. WPI's sustainability plan provided the framework for leadership to identify the why, how, and what to change to address climate change. From using localized examples of companies and organizations that are addressing sustainability issues, especially Affordable and Clean Energy (#7) & Climate Action (#13), student connections to their school or organization deepen.

WPI's passion and purpose in addressing climate change is seen in its recent history of updating its campus. Beginning in 2012, WPI has been working, building by building, to address climate change. Figure 14.4 is a timeline of how WPI has been working toward using sustainable energy.

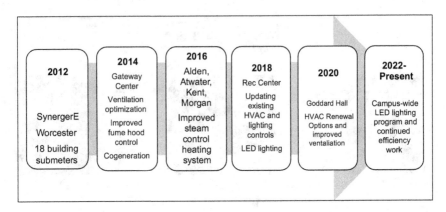

FIGURE 14.4 WPI climate action timeline.

WPI's climate action plan, released in January 2024, announced the goal to "reduce CO_2 emissions by >70% by 2040" and benefits from Inflation Reduction Act incentive as follows:

- Energy Conservation Measures (ECMs) allow for up to 10% reduction in campus electricity usage and reduced sizing of future energy systems.
- Geo-exchange phased in with building upgrades providing for an estimated 50% reduction in utilities and maintenance costs.
- Cogeneration provides resiliency and hedge against future commodity prices with the ability to transition to renewable fuels.
- Rooftop solar at ten buildings providing up to 1.5MM kWh/yr of on-site green energy generation.
- Microgrid & Immersion Center at Gateway campus to demonstrate technologies, create savings and revenue opportunities, and provide an academic learning space for students.
  - Net-zero carbon emissions achievable with off-site renewables will be assessed in parallel with the electrification plan.
  - Academic and career opportunities with Public–Private Partnership (P3) and partners.

The immediate timeframe for climate action changes:

- Within two months:
  - create internal structures.
- Within one year of start date
  - Complete greenhouse gas inventory, identify near-term opportunities, and submit evaluation of progress.

- Within two years of start date

  - Compete Climate Action Plan, and submit annual evaluation of progress.

- Each Subsequent Year

  - Review and revise, if necessary, and submit annual evaluation of progress.

WPI's Climate Action Plan is an example of secondary-level connections teachers can create with students when showing how SDGs are being used to change operations in the schools we teach in, and organizations students work and learn in. By including long-term, 10+ years, and short-term, 3+ months, these goals allow students to see change at multiple levels. A key point in making multiple-level connections is to empower students of the change WPI is trying to make in the classroom (personal level), in the campus (social level), and in the physical buildings (organization level) in working toward sustainability through working toward SDGs.

In the spring of 2024, WPI began reporting, through campus-wide discussions, student awareness of SDGs and WPI's actions toward addressing them. This was the first SDG student survey. There were 28 students who completed the survey. Key summary points from students include:

> *It would be great if WPI took a more **holistic approach to sustainability and the SDGs** that could then be **reflected in this report with a focus on integration**. Seems like the way we educate students about these specific SDG wasn't as clear or prominent as it could be. Was more grant and research focused. **Not much of a spotlight on our undergraduate programs or courses** related to these SDGs.*
>
> *I love that we **track the SDGs to the IQPs**. That should be in the report.*
>
> *Student entrepreneurs are focused on many of the SDGs.*
>
> *I feel that there is an opportunity to greatly **increase our showing in the category of Partnerships for the Goals** category. Our entire Global Projects Program could be listed, front and center, as our institutional orientation toward Partnerships for the Goals. At each of our 40–50 project centers around the world, center directors recruit and maintain networks of partners who are working directly with communities to address challenges that are pertinent to the SDGs.*

Third-level connection – student to world (ESG and value creation)

As background on the SDGs, the 17 sustainable development goals (SDGs), also known as the Global Goals, were adopted by all United Nations Member States in 2015 as a universal call to action to end poverty, protect the planet, and ensure that all people enjoy peace and prosperity by 2030. The SDGs are intended to be broad, interdependent, and specifically aim to address global challenges involving poverty, inequality, climate change, environmental degradation, peace, and justice. SDGs interconnect and, ideally, are considered within the context of the other goals. For example, ending poverty goes together with strategies that improve health and education, reduce inequality, and support economic growth. Addressing poverty can also include addressing climate change and working to improve our oceans and forests.

Students learn leadership as global awareness. Sweden is presented as a good example of how implementation of SDGs is part of the Government's overall strategy for ensuring that Sweden remains a strong, prosperous country – a society that is using sustainability as the focus for future generations. The Swedish government reviews components of its society's most important immediate goals and uses the SDGs as a policy driver to prioritize those goals in a systematic and integrated manner (Sustainable development.UN.org.).

For example, by 2030, Sweden is committed to achieving human rights, gender equality, addressing inequalities within and between countries, universal social protection, strengthening empowerment and participation, and transitioning toward resource-efficient, resilient, and climate-neutral economics. By using target dates and goals for governmental and business operations that are based on SDGs, students see how a county (Sweden) is integrating SDGs into operations. We use this as a model of how a company can use SDGs within their ESG efforts. Knowing that ESG is a company-defined program, students learn that 21st-century leaders work toward communicating how SDGs and ESG are separate but interconnected.

ESG

Environmental, Social, and Governance (ESG) is a program built from SDGs that is intended to guide corporate activities toward improving environmental, social, and governing activities. ESG criteria are used by investors and organizations to evaluate the sustainability and ethical impact of investments and business practices and provide business teachers a direct connection between global-level SDGs and the programs that direct a company's sustainable strategy to operations. ESG reflects the three main factors in measuring the sustainability and ethical impact of a business' operations on an investment in a company. When assessing a company for investment, the ESG rating (low, medium, or high) considerations play an increasingly important role in evaluating the sustainability of a company's operations (Pourahmadi, 2024).

Many investors frequently find that the ESG information helps in the identification of the company's risk and future performance. Environmental issues provide a wide scope covering climate change, greenhouse gas emissions,

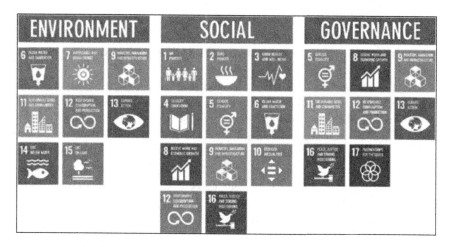

FIGURE 14.5 SDGs into ESG programming.

waste and pollution, natural resources, and environmental conservation. Social issues involve human rights, labor practices, product responsibilities, health, and safety. Governance issues involve areas of board diversity, executive remuneration, corporate governance structure, and transparency. A core theme throughout my leadership course is for 21st-century leaders to be curious in making connections among challenges. SDGs and ESG are presented as an example of how business operations (ESG) are being updated through expanded concerns for achieving SDGs.

The integration of SDGs into ESG requires organizing the 17 SDGs into three areas: Environment, Society, and Governance business activities. There is some overlap between SDGs in multiple areas of ESG, but this overlap allows teachers and students to develop deeper awareness of the interconnectedness among different areas of sustainability and balancing trade-offs. These trade-offs are opportunities for seeing order within complexity. By using the 5P's (Planet, People, Prosperity, Peace, and Partnership) of sustainability, proposed by the UN, a teacher can introduce students to a process for personalizing sustainability. After students realize SDGs are manageable, a teacher can lead them to work with the 241 indicators within the three ESG areas. When SDGs are grouped into ESG, teachers and students can think of link investor's, who often refer to this as SDG-aligned investing, which is an emerging topic in the ESG investing world (Neto, 2023).

As I have integrated SDGs into my teaching, I've found SDG-ESG alignment as an effective way to demonstrate to students how business is practicing sustainability. The following six tables present SDG-ESG-aligned goals and examples of 2030 measurable indicators. These tables help show students how companies can organize their ESG program by using SDG goals and indicators. Using ESG as the structure of SDGs, both teachers and students see the order and cross-over among the SDGs. SDGs are complex, interrelated goals. Within ESG, there are four SDGs grouped into the Environment area, five SDGs grouped within the social area, and one SDG grouped within the governance area (11 SDGs).

The remaining six SDGs are found across two or three ESG areas, which creates a high level of complexity for many people, but the point to remember is that sustainability is a complex topic, which is why it is both exciting and challenging to teach. Teaching from SDGs to ESGs provides teachers robust contextual and analytical material to connect with their students. The current issues of climate change, economic security, access to health care, and social justice engage students to learn about current events and create discussions around future solutions.

ESGs are not measured by the UN but are used by companies to demonstrate their operational risk to insurers, investors, customers, and employees. ESG is a program aimed at reporting company operations that minimize its detrimental impact on environmental, social, and governance concerns. SDGs have 241 indicators targets for 2030. While numerous, these indicators provide teachers with specific time-bound targets that students can research, track, and report on.

Using conceptual awareness of the SDGs, operational awareness of ESG programs, and specific measurable indicators of each SDG there are well-documented teaching targets, which can be measured at global or local levels. The following six tables present SDG goals that are grouped within ESG categories with the total number of 2,030 SDG indicators. Each table includes examples of the indicators. These SDG-ESG indicators are presented to student to clarify how sustainability goals are measurable at global, national, regional, and local levels. The teaching objective is to ask students to identify one, two, or three measures within ESG area and research the area and goal (Indicators, 2020).

TABLE 14.1 SDG-ESG environmental goals

ESG with the 5P Categories	Total SDG Indicators (2030)
1. Environment (Planet)	**41**
Goal 6. Ensure availability and sustainable management of water and sanitation for all	11
Goal 7. Ensure access to affordable, reliable, sustainable, and modern energy for all	6
Goal 14. Conserve and sustainably use the oceans, seas, and marine resources for sustainable development	10
Goal 15. Protect, restore, and promote sustainable use of terrestrial ecosystems, sustainably manage forests, combat desertification, and halt and reverse land degradation and halt biodiversity loss	14

Examples of the SDG Environmental indicators:

SDG 6: Clean water and sanitation

- Proportion of population using safely managed drinking water services
- Proportion of wastewater safely treated
- Water stress levels and water scarcity
- Water-use efficiency and water-use productivity

SDG 7: Affordable and clean energy

- Proportion of the population with access to electricity
- Renewable energy share in the total energy mix
- Energy intensity measures (energy use per unit of GDP)
- Investments in energy efficiency and renewable energy technologies

SDG 14: Life below water

- Coverage of protected marine areas
- Fish stocks overexploited or within sustainable levels
- Marine pollution levels (e.g., plastic debris, oil spills)
- Ocean acidification levels and impacts on marine ecosystems

SDG 15: Life on land

- Forest area as a proportion of total land area
- Extent of protected areas for biodiversity conservation
- Trends in biodiversity loss and extinction rates
- A proportion of degraded land was restored and rehabilitated

These are just some examples of the environmental indicators within ESG. Monitoring company progress on these indicators helps track the global efforts toward achieving environmental sustainability and addressing pressing environmental challenges.

Examples of the SDG Social indicators:

Goal 1: No poverty

- Percentage of employees paid a living wage
- Programs/initiatives addressing poverty alleviation in communities where the company operates
- Proportion of population living below the national poverty line, by sex and age
- Proportion of the population is covered by social protection floors/systems

TABLE 14.2 SDG-ESG social goals

ESG with the 5P Categories	Total SDG Indicators (2030)
2. Social (People)	**88**
Goal 1. End poverty in all its forms everywhere	12
Goal 2. End hunger, achieve food security and improved nutrition, and promote sustainable agriculture	14
Goal 3. Ensure healthy lives and promote well-being for all at all ages	26
Goal 4. Ensure inclusive and equitable quality education and promote lifelong learning opportunities for all	11
Goal 5. Achieve gender equality and empower all women and girls	14
Goal 10. Reduce inequality within and among countries	11

SDG 2: Zero hunger

- Prevalence of undernourishment
- Prevalence of moderate or severe food insecurity
- Prevalence of stunting among children under 5 years of age
- Prevalence of wasting among children under 5 years of age

Goal 3: Good health and well-being

- Employee health and safety record
- Access to healthcare benefits for employees
- Initiatives promoting health and well-being in communities

Goal 4: Quality education

- Investments in employee training and development
- Support for educational initiatives in communities

Goal 5: Gender equality

- Gender diversity on the board and in leadership positions
- Pay equity between genders
- Policies promoting work–life balance and parental leave

Goal 10: Reduced inequality

- Measures of income inequality within the organization
- Diversity and inclusion initiatives
- Community investment programs targeting marginalized groups

TABLE 14.3 SDG-ESG governance goal

ESG with the 5P Categories	Total SDG Indicators (2030)
3. Governance (Prosperity)	**25**
Goal 17. Strengthen the means of implementation and revitalize the Global Partnership for Sustainable Development	25

TABLE 14.4 SDGs across three ESG areas

ESG with the 5P Categories	Total SDG Indicators (2030)
4. Environment, Social, Governance (SDG goals found in all three ESG areas)	**25**
Goal 9 (Prosperity). Build resilient infrastructure, promote inclusive and sustainable industrialization and foster innovation	12
Goal 12 (Planet). Ensure sustainable consumption and production patterns	13

These are just some examples of the social indicators within the ESG. Monitoring company progress on these indicators helps track the global efforts toward achieving social sustainability and addressing pressing social challenges. Examples of the SDG Governance indicators:

SDG 17: Partnerships for the goals

- Total government revenue as a proportion of GDP, by source
- Proportion of domestic budget funded by domestic taxes
- Total official development assistance (ODA) as a proportion of gross national income (GNI)
- The number of countries reporting progress in multi-stakeholder development effectiveness monitoring frameworks that support the achievement of the Sustainable Development Goals

Examples of the two SDGs indicators found across all three ESGs:

SDG 9: Industry, innovation, and infrastructure

- Investment in infrastructure
- Research and development (R&D) expenditure
- Access to Information and Communication Technologies

SDG 12: Responsible consumption and production

- Domestic material consumption per capita
- Waste generation per capita and recycling rates
- Carbon footprint and greenhouse gas emissions per capita
- Sustainable procurement practices in government and private sector

Examples of the two SDG indicators found in Environment and Governance ESGs:

SDG 11: Sustainable cities and communities

- Proportion of urban population living in slums or informal settlements
- Air quality measurements (e.g., PM2.5 concentration)
- Access to green spaces and urban parks
- Proportion of population using sustainable transport modes

SDG 13: Climate action

- Greenhouse gas emissions by sector (e.g., energy, transportation, industry)
- Proportion of the population is covered by early warning systems for extreme weather events

TABLE 14.5 SDGs across E&G areas

ESG with the 5P Categories	*Total SDG Indicators (2030)*
5. Environment and Governance	22
Goal 11 (Prosperity). Make cities and human settlements inclusive, safe, resilient, and sustainable	15
Goal 13 (Planet). Take urgent action to combat climate change and its impacts[b]	7

TABLE 14.6 SDGs across S&G areas

ESG with the 5P Categories	*Total SDG Indicators (2030)*
6. Social and Governance	40
Goal 8 (Prosperity). Promote sustained, inclusive and sustainable economic growth, full and productive employment and decent work for all	17
Goal 16 (Peace). Promote peaceful and inclusive societies for sustainable development, provide access to justice for all and build effective, accountable, and inclusive institutions at all levels	23

- Climate finance flows to developing countries.
- Adoption of climate change mitigation and adaptation measures

Examples of the two SDG indicators found in Social and Governance ESGs:

SDG 8: Decent work and economic growth

- Employment-to-population ratio
- Average hourly earnings of female and male employees

SDG 16: Peace, justice, and strong institutions

- Homicide rate
- Proportion of children under 5 years of age who are registered at birth with a civil authority

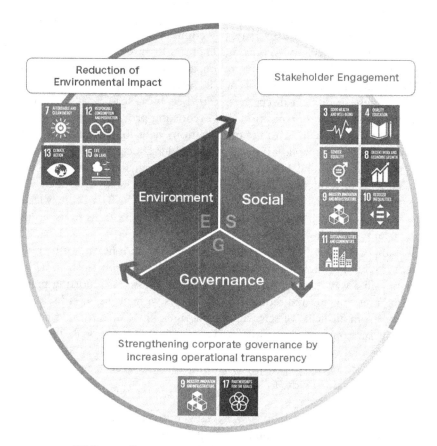

FIGURE 14.6   ESG compliance reporting.

- Corruption Perception Index (CPI)
- Rule of Law Index

Teaching with SDGs and then moving into business' use of ESG is a multi-layered process that can be made easier when teachers organize the 17 SDGs into the 5Ps (The 5Ps of the sustainable development goals – ESCWA, n.d.) and then into three ESG categories. The excitement in this process is in the "sense making" process of learning with students on how sustainability is being developed through business involvement, measurements, and reporting to multiple stakeholders.

Every company has a different level of ESG impact, and differences across industries create student awareness of differing operational challenges each company operates within. The result of this process is a transformational change for the student, the teacher, and the organization. ESG is one element investors use to assess the sustainability initiatives of companies.

My integration of ESG into teaching is just beginning to address how Governance issues are being implemented at the company level. Governance concerns track issues of board diversity, pay equity and executive compensation, corporate governance, and reporting. Figure 14.6 presents a useful view of how ESG reporting communicates a company's environmental impact, stakeholder engagement, and transparency in governance operations. ESG provides business students a direct avenue to become a leader, a Sustainability Champion, within an organization. ESG reporting provides a great opportunity for students to work with the organization's data collection, organization and analysis of sustainability impacts, stakeholder concerns for sustainability, as well as the costs and benefits of operating sustainably. While my course is a first-level introduction to leadership, I cover leadership styles, behaviors, characteristics, cultural differences, etc., I use SDGs as the 21st-century leadership challenges, which ESG has been created for organizations to use in their sustainability activities.

The importance of ESG reporting to business operations cannot be understated. ESG is the direct connection between talking about sustainability to operating in a way of being sustainable. ESG as a business reporting practice is only going to grow and requires collaborators with strong interdisciplinary expertise from all fields of science and management that can build accurate reporting on company operations to be used at local, regional, and global levels (Shauhrat et al., 2024; Tettamanzi et al., 2022). Finally, ESG is a value creator. By focusing on improving environmental and social health conditions, ESG is adding value by the following:

- Lowering company liability: By tracking business operations in environmental and social areas, a company is actively minimizing risks of regulatory fines, lawsuits, and supply chain disruptions.

- Lowering operational costs: In the long run, operating in ways that lower energy usage, water consumption, waste generation, and operating inefficiencies should lead to lower operating costs.
- Increase brand reputation: More consumers are looking for companies that behave in sustainable ways and are concerned with issues that go beyond the bottom line.
- Access to financial markets: Investors in all markets are looking for ESG ratings as a way to invest.
- Access to talent: Research is showing that millennials and Gen Z employees are more concerned with working for companies that are operating sustainably.
- Stakeholder engagement: Communicating on ESG areas with employees, customers, communities, and regulatory bodies increases trust and commitment.
- Innovation and long-term value: Operating with concern for ESG reflects a forward-looking operating strategy that results in added value both internally and externally.

Further discussions

SDGs provide teachers with an effective framework for connecting with students, integrating course materials with local and global concerns, and providing a pathway for students to develop careers that create sustainability for themselves and their world. Sustainability is a way of thinking, teaching, and living that begins with a person's attention to caring for the natural and social community around them. We often think of the natural environment first when talking about sustainability, and rightfully so, but as teachers using sustainability to frame our teaching, we expand student awareness of sustainability beginning with their personal interests and passions outward into the natural and social world. Using ideas and programs of sustainability, SDGs, and ESG in the business world, provides teachers a path to create a teaching environment that personalizes sustainability as a way toward mental and physical well-being. This is a way of teaching sustainability from the inside out. Teaching to becoming sustainable one student at a time.

Twenty-first-century students are learning through significant global events. The COVID-19 pandemic, which is still with us in new variants of SARS-CoV-2, wars in Ukraine and Gaza, changes in workplace expectations with the technologies that are being used or the way work is conducted as on site, remote, or hybrid locations. *Teaching what is sustainable and how to be sustainable is deep, complex, and rewarding path.* Connecting SDGs to ESG, both conceptually and technically, is needed in more schools of management. In the United States, management education has yet to establish an effective pedagogy for teaching sustainability of the planet and people.

To be effective, teaching through SDGs involves developing a student's "systems mindset" that uses operational oneness found in ESG. In teaching leadership, I present SDGs as areas for students to explore to identify their passion and purpose. Knowing that climate change, biodiversity health, economic equity, healthcare concerns, and social justice are impacting our student's mental well-being we need to update our teaching methods by using SDGs. Future discussions on using sustainability and SDGs should involve more curriculums using student-centered SDG teaching, comprehensive use of Collaborative Online International Learning (COIL), and project-based ESG-aligned learning. Management education that uses sustainability and SDGs as disciplinary and interdisciplinary frameworks is the only way we can effectively prepare students for the world today and the future.

References

The 5Ps of the sustainable development goals – ESCWA. (n.d.). https://www.unescwa.org/sites/default/files/inline-files/the_5ps_of_the_sustainable_development_goals.pdf

Cozma, I. (2023, October 26). *Values, passion, or purpose – which should guide your career?* Harvard Business Review. https://hbr.org/2023/10/values-passion-or-purpose-which-should-guide-your-career

Neto, M. A. (2023, May 16). *SDG-aligned investment: A new development paradigm.* SDG Action. https://sdg-action.org/sdg-aligned-investment-a-new-development-paradigm

Pourahmadi, V. (2024). *The evolution of environmental, social, and governance (ESG) and Sustainability in 2024.* 15 Rock Home. https://www.15rock.com/blog/the-evolution-of-environmental-social-and-governance-esg-and-sustainability-in-2024

Shauhrat, C., Senadheera, S., Pavani, D., Piumi, A., Rajeev, C., Jay, R., & Yong, S. (2024, January). Navigating the challenges of Environmental, Social, and Governance (ESG) reporting: The path to broader sustainable development. https://www.mdpi.com/2071-1050/16/2/606

Tettamanzi, P., Venturini, G., & Murgolo, M. (2022). Sustainability and financial accounting: A critical review of the ESG dynamics. *Environmental Science and Pollution Research, 29*(11), 16758–16761. https://doi.org/10.1007/s11356-022-18596-2

Wyatt, S. (2021). *Management and leadership in the 4th industrial revolution capabilities to achieve superior performance.* Kogan Page.

15

MAPPING AFFECTIONS

Cartography as a pedagogical tool for teaching ecocentrism in business schools

Fernanda Cassab Carreira, Maria Clara Araujo Secall, Mario Monzoni, and Ricardo Barretto

Abstract

In this chapter, we – three instructors and a student – share our experiences from an elective sustainability course held in 2023 at a Brazilian business school. The course, running since 2010, aims to challenge conventional sustainability approaches by exploring subjectivity, ecocentrism, and direct engagement with nature. In this specific semester, our primary objective was to highlight the often-overlooked importance of mangroves as life-nurturing ecosystems within sustainability discussions. To achieve this, we opted for affective cartography as a teaching tool to inspire students by encouraging affective connections with the environment and challenging prevailing notions of sustainability. Throughout the course, we implemented three key practices: (i) bringing nature into the classroom; (ii) providing firsthand environmental experiences through field trips; and (iii) using art to express emotions toward nature. A noteworthy outcome was the rich tapestry of analogies and metaphors that students derived from their experiences in the mangrove swamp and engaging in group discussions throughout the semester. The success of incorporating affective cartography as a pedagogical tool highlights its potential for widespread application in business school due to its interdisciplinary and transdisciplinary nature; compatibility with diverse teaching methods; emphasis on active listening and creative expression; and flexibility in both format and materials.

Introduction

Can you envision teaching about organizations and sustainability through observing an ecosystem and the communities dependent on it? What about

DOI: 10.4324/9781003521839-16

using an affective cartography as a pedagogical tool so that students can materialize what they have learned?

In this chapter, we share our experiences from a sustainability course held in 2023 at a Brazilian business school. On that occasion, we chosen the mangrove to be our field experience – as the United Nations had just declared 2023 as the Decade of the Ocean, a ten-year initiative to identify, generate, and utilize critical ocean knowledge for sustainable ocean management. We present here the fabulous insights our management students glean from observing living beings like crabs, mud, mangroves, and tides, as well as from the people who rely on the mangroves for their livelihoods.

Our narrative unfolds through the perspectives of us, the educators – Fernanda, Mario, and Ricardo – along with one of our students, Clara. We use the mangrove in our course, but you can replace it for another relevant ecosystem of your region. The point is to take students out into nature and where there are communities that depend on a particular ecosystem.

When crafting the course, we set several objectives:

1. Engaging students in exploring subjectivity and affect, recognizing that one of the contributors to the ecological crisis lies in our peripheral connection to the world, leading to a lack of protective actions (Maggs & Robinson, 2016).
2. Facilitating transformative learning grounded in direct interactions with non-human entities.
3. Spotlighting the significance of ecosystems such as mangroves as cradles of life, sources of sustenance and culture for many traditional communities, while paradoxically being one of the most overlooked ecosystems in sustainability discussions.
4. Investigating how human forms of organizing and living could draw inspiration from ecosystems such as the mangroves.

To address these objectives, we opted to incorporate affective cartography as a pedagogical tool within the course framework. The urban planner we invited to facilitate activities enlightened us about the concept: Affective cartography is a process where the cartographer (the map author) seeks to comprehend the world around her/him. It involves placing oneself on the map and reflecting on one's position within it, prompting considerations about identity, gender, race, ethnic representation, knowledge of one's surroundings and networks. Additionally, it encourages questioning the very production of the public space one has access to and the circuits from which one may be excluded.

Before delving into the experience, let's provide a brief overview of the course, known as Integrated Education for Sustainability (FIS in Portuguese and hereafter), which has been part of our administration degree program since 2010.

A little bit about FIS

The FIS was created by a team of researchers from the Center for Sustainability Studies (FGVces), one year after the São Paulo Business School (FGV-EAESP) joined the PRME, Principles for Responsible Management Education, a United Nations initiative for business schools. It is an elective course offered to undergraduate students majoring in business administration, public administration, law, economics, and international relations. Since 2010, over 500 students engaged in FIS, approximately 18–20 students each semester. More information about FIS can be found in Resources at the end of this chapter.

In 2022, the course was awarded the gold prize in the sustainability education in Latin America category of the Wharton School's QR-Reimagine Award for its innovative teaching methodology. Our methodology comprises two main components conducted concurrently:

• The Reference Project: A real challenge given by the FIS teaching team on the first day of class, requiring collaborative effort from students to deliver by the semester's end. Students will have to go into the field, interact with various stakeholders, and produce a project with social impact that serves as a public good. The projects always vary and are tied to the Sustainable Development Goals (SDG).
• The Self Project: A process of self-discovery facilitated by the FIS team, aiming to reestablish the students' subjectivity and emphasize that learning about sustainability entails allowing oneself to be personally impacted – or affected. For that, we bring a transdisciplinary teaching perspective, meaning that we incorporate diverse learning methods that leverage art, the body, imagination, and the knowledge of traditional peoples (Carreira et al., 2023).

Why mangroves: how to choose your ecosystem

As researchers at a sustainability study center, we are always looking for trending topics to work on with our students. Next, we share our rationale, how and why we chose the mangrove, so that it helps you to do the same exercise for other ecosystems in your region.

We started with the big picture. As we know, the oceans have gained increased relevance in recent years due to their role in global climate regulation, the escalating levels of pollution, predatory fishing, and the imperative to preserve lifestyles dependent on them, among other factors. Given the extensive scope of these issues, we chose to focus on mangrove forests for several reasons, beginning with the ecological ones. We present them below as categories that you can use for your own selection process, which can be focused on an ecosystem or a natural place of interest close to your school or sometimes even a park nearby.

- **Ecological relevance in local and regional contexts:** Mangroves are positioned at the interface of land and sea, representing crucial transitional ecosystems and function as vital nurseries for marine life, supporting an impressive diversity of species. Despite covering only 0.16% of Brazil's territory, their socio-environmental importance transcends their physical footprint (Escobar, 2022), playing a pivotal role in fish breeding, sustaining between 23 and 80% of marine fish stocks, providing sustenance to the local population, and enriching the oceans with essential nutrients, contributing to the protection of coral reefs.
- **Connection with climate change issues:** Mangroves serve as significant reservoirs of "blue carbon," storing substantial amounts of GHG and filtering pollutants, moderating extreme weather events, and providing protection against coastal erosion.
- **Potential threats:** Despite their vital functions, mangroves face ongoing threats from human activities such as settlements, overfishing, deforestation, and pollution. Often, societal neglect stems from stereotypes and political decisions, diverting attention away from their inherent value and importance to focus on other environmental issues.

Besides the previous biological reasons, there are some more subjective points that should be considered when choosing the ecosystem you will work with:

- **Metaphors and symbolism:** Taking a more profound perspective, mangroves embody the essence of life. They host a complex web of interactions among diverse life forms, offering sustenance and inspiration for both human and non-human communities reliant on them. Therefore, they are an endless source of life, poetry, and wisdom – a sanctuary of life where constant emergence reveals itself in its most exquisite and fundamental form.
- **Connection with urban life:** The diverse characteristics of the mangrove presented us with numerous opportunities to engage with students both in the classroom and during field trips. We discussed with them the adverse impacts of various business sectors, including tourism, logistics (including ports and roads), and industrial fishing. We also highlighted our impact as consumers when we choose hotels built on former mangrove areas, for instance. Additionally, we introduced topics related to climate change, socio-economics, and biodiversity, offering a multitude of exploration possibilities.

In terms of course design, visiting mangroves was relatively easy for us to organize as we had many local partners, but it could be a challenge if you don't have that. Our suggestion is to look for partnerships, NGOs, or researchers

The Challenge
Reference Project first semester 2023

The challenge of **FIS 26** is:	This Reference Project (RP)
	Involves (to take into account)
	• Reflecting critically on our interdependence with the mangrove forest;
	• Understanding the concepts of ecosystems, ecosystem services, and their valuation;
	• Mapping the main sources of human pressure on this ecosystem;
Create an affective cartography that illustrates how mangroves contribute to sustaining life on the planet.	• Approaching the mangrove in its complexity: its connections with climate change, biodiversity, gender, inequalities, cultural, political, and socio-economic issues.
	Demands (to realize and deliver)
	• Create a cartography that:
	○ Is transdisciplinary, addressing the issue in its multidimensionality and multi-referentiality;
	○ Is accessible to society;
	○ Be illustrated, with inspiration from the manguebeat counterculture or other related arts;
	• Create a complementary document that:
	○ Records the process of mapping mangroves so that other people can also make their own;
	○ Presents reflections on how human ways of organizing can be inspired by mangrove ways of organizing;
	• Raise funds, if necessary, to deliver the final product;
	• Launch the cartography at the Evaluation Board (31/05/2023): invite participants, create the dynamics of the presentation, and prepare to answer questions;
	• Submit the final version of the map, taking into account the contributions of the Evaluation Board, on the day of the final exam. The submission will become a public asset, accessible on the FGVces website and on the UNESCO Decade of the Ocean platform.

Flor do Mangue. Sculpture by Frans Krajcberg

FIGURE 15.1   FIS – challenge about mangroves.

that have already projects going on in the ecosystem you want to study. If you teach online, you may use these criteria to transfer these experiences to an online course (Carreira et al., 2023).

For us, the mangrove ecosystem was also ideal for provoking a debate on ecocentrism and sustainability. The challenge we created for the class is described in Figure 15.1.

Ecocentrism versus sustainability

This semester, we opted to delve into the concept of ecocentrism, challenging the prevailing notion of sustainability. Business schools continue to endorse weak sustainability (Kurucz et al., 2014), without questioning the dominance of rationality, technology, scientism, economic progress, and companies as the primary solutions to ecological crises. This approach neglects the exploration of alternative forms of organizing (Parker, 2018), including those based on other ontology, and might be on the way to other forms of teaching in business schools, such as the affective cartography.

When we asked ourselves how to move away from the mainstream perspective the answer was right in the essence of the semester's Reference Project: go *ecocentric*! But how could we do that as human beings that we are? Sometimes you have to take bold steps and trust that learning by doing is as valid a process for teachers as it is for the students. Our first step was to challenge the very concept of sustainability.

Despite sustainability originating from an ecological perspective, it was co-opted by global capitalism, seeking a compromise between irreconcilable positions of technocentrism and ecocentrism (Figueiredo & Marquesan, 2022). And while sustainability prioritizes human needs, ecocentrism is rooted in a relational ontology emphasizing co-dependence and interconnection among all beings (Gasparin et al., 2020). Therefore, we envisioned that an ecocentric perspective could stimulate new imaginaries and that could be well represented through the affective cartography. *"What if we could observe the world through the eyes of other beings?"* That became a motto for the students within the challenge statement (Figure 15.1), where we emphasize that mangroves sustain "lives" beyond just human lives.

For this, we developed a transdisciplinary educational journey: We brought students into contact – in the classroom and during field trips – with experts from various formal knowledge areas (e.g., oceanographers, biologists, economists, urban planners), as well as from traditional and popular knowledge realms (e.g., leaders Quilombos and Caiçaras, artists). The term "quilombo" originated during slavery in Brazil, referring to settlements formed by escaped African slaves seeking autonomy and freedom. Today, it also denotes recognized communities descended from quilombos, entitled to preserve cultural traditions, and granted specific rights by the Brazilian government. "Caiçaras" refers to traditional fishing communities along the Brazilian coast, with a strong connection to the marine environment. Like quilombos, the term also designates recognized communities entitled to preserve their traditions and ways of life, with specific rights granted by the Brazilian government.

We reflected that all this knowledge and voices could be part of an affective cartography. We also created some embodiment experiences for the students to feel closer to nature when they were in the school premises, and to help them imagine humans as part of interdependent ecosystems, as well as what might be the world perspective of a non-human being.

The affective cartography: bridging humans, non-human beings, and organizations

Fernanda: *The idea of affective cartography as a format for delivering the challenge given to students came from a school project done by my 10-year-old son. Prior to this, I was unfamiliar with "affective" cartography. Upon further investigation I realized that it could be a very interesting tool to use with management students, as it involves emotionally listening to people – and that we include non-human beings.*

Using cartography to build bridges between humans, non-humans, and alternative forms of organizing based on an ecocentric perspective was a novelty, as affective cartographies are usually created from an anthropocentric viewpoint. We wanted this bridging process to unfold through active listening and observation of nature, acknowledging our interconnectedness with the natural world. By exploring nature's diverse possibilities of organizing, we sought to expand our students' perception of reality. To this end, we focused on three pedagogical practices that consistently proved effective throughout the semester.

Bringing nature into the classroom

To spark students' imagination, we designed various activities to bring nature into the classroom. From the 28 classes and two field trips during the semester, we have chosen only a few to share here, but we will be happy to exchange more if the reader is interested.

The first class was inspired by O'Doherty's paper (2020), which used the film *Leviathan* to explore another aspect of the human-nature relationship and to create affectiveness and not-knowing spaces through aesthetic learning. In previous semesters, two FIS students based their undergraduate theses on mangroves and gender issues, resulting in the documentary *Mangrove's Mother Brasil* (2018). We chose to set up the classroom like a cinema to watch it together (with popcorn). Afterward, we facilitated a discussion with "the filmmakers." We were bringing the mangrove and the women living there into the classroom.

Fernanda: *The video provoked critical reflections on dominant social imaginaries that establish the dilemma between (economic) development and conservation, gender issues, work organization, ways of life . . . But what caught my attention the most was that the video helped the class to create an imaginary* *about the mangrove and the people who live there without having gone to the field yet, as the class took place before the field trips, and a significant portion of the class had never entered the mangrove.*

In another class, we invited a seasoned naturalist educator to lead a session centered on deep nature observation. Each student brought a natural element (e.g., a stone, leaf, plant) to form a circle. With closed eyes, we passed these elements, engaging touch, smell, and hearing. Afterward, we silently drew our elements with intricate detail, followed by crafting poems. Some shared their creations aloud, unveiling a collection of beautiful poems and detailed drawings that highlighted our profound connection with nature and creativity.

Another impactful activity was taking students to our school garden. In a class led by the specialist in cartography, we learned how to collect relevant data for our upcoming field trip to the mangroves, which would later be used in cartography. Inspired by the categories of data collection (sight, hearing, taste, touch, smell, and proprioception), Ricardo proposed a class to prepare our bodies for the field trip. The session began indoors, transitioning to the garden to explore non-human elements. Returning to the room, we recorded our findings on the blackboard. In the debriefing circle, students expressed initial discomfort in the garden during introspective activities, perceiving it as judgmental and fostering superficial relationships. However, they discovered overlooked aspects of the garden, including flowers, trees, and animals.

Sharing newfound sensations and feelings, students reflected on the experience, emphasizing the importance of slowing down, a sense of belonging, a desire for more natural spaces within the school, showing us that redefining school spaces has an important impact on students' imaginations (Michels et al., 2020).

Ricardo: *Taking part in a situation that connects the body, the environment and psychological aspects of the group allowed students to understand how perception varies with the conditions and relational aspects of each experience in life. That helped the group make sense of how relevant onsite research is and what a game-changer body awareness can be to provide in-depth acknowledgement of socio-environmental dynamics.*

Having experienced these classes, the students took on the responsibility of leading two activities. The first arose from necessity when one student fell ill and missed the initial mangrove field trip. To ensure he could still experience the journey, we tasked the group with recreating the mangrove, boat, and expert conversations in the classroom. Armed with a variety of materials, including magazines, paints, fabrics, cardboard, and strings, the class was given 50 minutes to bring the experience to life. We asked them to imagine what they could see, feel, hear, and learn based on what they experienced. The outcome was remarkable, showcasing the class's organizational skills and the wealth of intricate details. For video highlights of this class, see the Resources material at the end of this chapter.

The second activity involved students organizing a public event named the "kick-off." This event served as the launch of their project, where they introduced themselves by creating a group name and logo. They also presented the semester's challenge and facilitated a discussion with specialists and individuals passionate about mangroves, gathering valuable insights for their project.

Clara: *Based on the experiences we had, the main objective of the event was to create an enchanting atmosphere that would bring out the essence of the mangrove in participants, awakening affections and reflections throughout the event. We designed a real mangrove forest inside the room, transforming it into an immersive and captivating environment. Craft paper roots filled the space, while leaves and figures of the main mangrove animals adorned the walls, providing a sense of immersion in nature. The room was divided into distinct mangrove elements – water, mud, life and weave – each characterized by its own atmosphere and visual elements.*

This innovative and affective approach not only positively impacted the guests but also showcased the educational potential of the space during the kick-off. By providing a tangible experience, the event conveyed the ecosystem's influence on the group and enlightened the audience about the beauty, significance, and potential of the mangrove. Transforming a room into a living representation of the mangrove broadened people's understanding and connection to this unique ecosystem, an educational and transformative journey through nature. The space's role is evident in its capacity to spark curiosity, encourage reflection, and instill a sense of care for environmental preservation.

Clara: *Rather than just transmitting information, we invited participants to experience the ecosystem in a unique way, stimulating all the senses and inviting contemplation. The classroom was transformed into an active learning space, where participants were challenged to explore, question, and interact with the environment around them.*

To map you need to be in the territory

Experiential learning is one of the pedagogical approaches of the FIS methodology.

Fernanda: *We believe not only in the power of taking students on field trips, getting them out of the classroom and into direct contact with other realities and* *environments, but also in the need for all sustainability professionals to have contact with the territory. It's not possible to work with sustainability from inside offices.*

For this reason, throughout the semester, we organize two field trips. We design an itinerary focused solely on communities with alternative forms of organizing unfamiliar to management students, excluding visits to businesses or government entities. We included numerous visits to mangroves along the coast of the state of São Paulo.

During the trips, a crucial aspect was the creation of digital-free zones: Students refrain from using cell phones, computers throughout the entire trip. Cell phones were stored in a box – the "cell phone spa" – on the first day and returned on the last day. This practice is highly appreciated by students. It is such an interesting discussion, especially when digital addiction has been considered an epidemic. But we won't go into it here; it deserves its own chapter.

We wish to emphasize some impactful practices we implemented during our field trips, leaving a lasting impression on both the students and us. In the first trip, Ronaldo Christofoletti, the UNESCO representative for the Decade of the Oceans in Brazil, guided us through a visit to the mangrove, offering scientific insights into why this ecosystem is considered the cradle of life. He discussed the resilience of the ecosystem, its survival in adverse conditions, sparking profound reflections among the students, later documented in the cartography. His on-site teaching brought a unique dimension compared to a traditional classroom setting.

We also took the students on a project called "School Boat," run by the environmental department of the municipality of Bertioga and aimed at public primary schools. In it, environmental educators take the children on a boat trip to the mangroves, explaining in a playful way how this ecosystem works. We asked them to replicate the same activity with our students, including games, riddles, and songs. We wanted it to serve as inspiration for our students in their assignments throughout the semester, as well as reinforcing the content.

In the second trip, we visited mangroves located in environmental preservation areas, where students witnessed the dilemma between preservation and sustainable use. Brazilian law dictates that no one can enter preservation areas, adversely affecting traditional communities dependent on fishing and the mangrove. Students engaged with these communities, hearing testimonials about the challenges of discontinuing ancestral activities and being compared to more predatory practices like industrial fishing. Discussions unfolded about how these communities were not consulted on defining these environmental protection areas. This experience impacted the students and later facilitated discussions on the importance of being on-site to listen to people before making decisions that affect them.

Lastly, during one of our visits to the mangroves, we proposed a unique activity: a 15-minute period of profound silence where all students simply observed the mangrove. This seemingly straightforward exercise turned out to be revealing for most of the class. Some shared how they could perceive everything scientist Ronaldo had explained in theory about the mangrove's functioning, while others experienced the sensory richness of the environment, from unique smells to sounds, colors, and creatures emerging from the mud.

The main takeaway from these field trips was the power to create **enchantment** with nature and with the possibility of organizing ourselves differently. At the outset of the semester, when we inquired about the students' initial impressions of mangroves, the prevailing responses revolved around notions of dirt, unpleasant odors, and poverty. However, these perceptions underwent a profound transformation over the months. Undoubtedly, the effect this has on the students and on us as teachers changes our engagement with sustainability in a way that no classroom experience can do.

Clara: *One of the great memories that comes to mind was on March 29, 2023, when we sailed the river of the Mandira extractive reserve. The visit took in the river bordered by mangroves and ended at the oyster farm of the Mandira Quilombo. The view was one of the most beautiful I've seen in my life – seeing the reflection of the mangroves in the canal was magical, as if everything were mangroves. This opportunity struck me at first as a recognition of the privilege of having this experience. As if I were immersed in a magical and enchanting environment, witnessing the beauty of nature. An instant feeling of care and protection came over me.*

During the boat trip, the feeling of entering an enchanted forest was very strong. It became even more magical when, along the way, we encountered various animals that we hadn't had the chance to meet before, such as the alligator and the spoonbill. The environment became a veritable open-air classroom, since everything we had talked about and learned about the mangroves came to fruition during the walk. Understanding the Mandira Quilombo's relationship of respect, equality and care for the mangrove region was inspiring. The idea of preserving as a way of maintaining affections and sustaining lives in the region was tangible – as if the mangroves were an extension of the reserve residents' homes. Therefore, understanding, above all, that we are nature too.

The relationships that are formed there and the way in which society organizes itself touched me deeply. The simplicity, respect and sense of collectivity have changed the way I see and understand the world. I left feeling very inspired and with many reflections on development, ways of organizing socially, ways of living, aspects to value in life, the relationship between man and nature and, above all, the importance of mangroves for sustaining life on the planet.

Although the visits were an important part of the experiences with the students, the real enchantment and immersion in the ecosystem were awakened in different, simple, and profound ways. The mentioned movie and the construction of a mangrove in the classroom emerged as crucial strategies for connecting students to the challenges of the biome, even before physically entering it. Thus, carrying out sensory exercises that bring students closer to the reality being studied becomes an effective way of connecting them with a reality that otherwise seems distant.

Clara: *My connection with the mangrove didn't come about strictly through visiting the ecosystem itself, but mainly through a series of sensory exercises proposed by our teachers. The movie we watched was crucial in beginning to understand the power and importance of this ecosystem, while the body exercises allowed us to dive deeper into the content we were studying. From simple contact with clay to a meditation guided by the characteristic sounds of the mangrove, and even the transformation of the classroom into an environment that reproduced the mangrove with simple materials, they brought the mangrove into the classroom. These activities proved to be extremely creative and effective in sensitizing us to the complexity and relevance of this ecosystem.*

Art for expressing affections

Finally, arts-based methods are becoming more usual in teaching sustainability within business schools and at FIS they are central: We experience painting, sculpture, dance, music, digital art, bringing in artists, attending exhibitions, as each person becomes sensitized in a different way. Therefore, we prefer a greater diversity of methods rather than choosing one.

This semester, we gradually brought the students closer to the arts. We started by suggesting individual activities, usually done at home. Then, in one of the classes, we divided the students into small groups to create a prototype of a cartography and present it to the others. Only then did we suggest that they work in a single group to produce the cartography.

Fernanda: *These smaller group activities allowed students to further cultivate affection among themselves. While painting or drawing, they engaged in conversations, shared their stories, and actively listened to one another.*

Metaphors and analogies: affective listening to the mangroves and their communities

As one of the individual assignments in the course, we prompt students to reflect on the analogies, metaphors, and lessons they discern from their experiences in the mangrove swamp and group discussions along the semester. Table 15.1 illustrates the diverse insights gained from observing ecosystems and engaging with traditional communities that organize

TABLE 15.1 Metaphors and analogies: organizational learnings from the mangroves

What if organizations, inspired on mangroves, valued/promoted/embraced...

Proposals for organizational learnings	Students' metaphors and analogies
Viviparity The maternal care exhibited in the context of viviparity serves as a metaphor for the organizational environment, underscoring the significance of cooperation and mutual support for growth and survival. What if organizations: (i) cultivate a culture of cooperation and mutual care; (ii) invest in talent development to fortify the team and equip it to tackle forthcoming challenges; (iii) draw inspiration from nature to foster a culture of innovation and continuous learning?	*Viviparity is when the mangrove seed sprouts while still attached to the mother plant and its initial life stage is nourished by it, generating the propagule. We met the propagule, but this affective and caring relationship, in which the offspring continues to be cared for by the mother, suspended in the air, until it is ready for the harsh conditions of the mangrove swamp, has not been explored as much. Viviparity is obvious in mammals during gestation, but it is rare in plants, with the mangrove tree being the classic example. (S1)*
Resilience and Adaptation Mangrove resilience teaches us about facing adversity, welcoming diversity, and exercising patience in order to thrive in challenging contexts. What if organizations: (i) develop resilience to overcome unforeseen challenges and maintain stability; (ii) promote diversity to incorporate a variety of perspectives and stimulate innovation and collaboration; (iii) harness the harmony inherent in diversity, acknowledging and appreciating distinct experiences and viewpoints; (iv) maintain connections – with people, other organizations, nature, and oneself?	*[. . .] the mangrove sustains lives in the sense that there is a sacrifice at stake. It seems to use its resilience to withstand damage rather than other lives. (S1)* *Resisting even when everything stresses you out. Learning to live with differences. (S4)* *. . . the adversities that the animal faces in the ecosystem can be similar to the adversities that human beings face in the current configuration of society, with a strong need to adapt to changes in the environment, which is not a peaceful environment, with tidal variations, among others. (S7)* *The mangrove is an inhospitable environment full of instability, . . . despite all these factors, it still has the capacity to create and recreate life and, in this way, create a form of stability. (S10)*

(Continued)

TABLE 15.1 (Continued)

What if organizations, inspired on mangroves, valued/promoted/embraced...

Proposals for organizational learnings		*Students' metaphors and analogies*
Simplicity	The mangrove teaches us to thrive with simple mechanisms, such as filtering nutrients from the water. Similarly, organizations can discover quality of life in the simple things, valuing everyday moments and small joys. What if organizations: (i) celebrate small achievements and moments of joy; (ii) simplify processes and procedures whenever possible to reduce stress and prioritize efficiency; (iii) foster a culture of gratitude and recognition to cultivate a positive and fulfilling environment?	*... the simplicity of life can also be a lesson we can learn from the mangrove. While the ecosystem may seem complex in its structure and functioning, it is also able to thrive with simple mechanisms, such as the ability to filter nutrients and sediments from the water. Thus, the mangrove, like the relationship between communities and nature, reminds us that happiness often lies in the simple things and that valuing weekdays and small joys can bring a meaningful quality of life.* (S5)
Weaving relationships: dialogue and protagonism	Active listening and dialogue are crucial in our lives, in relation to both nature and human interactions. Recognizing that we are part of a wider fabric of relationships leads us to value compassion, respect, and empathy in our interactions. What if organizations: (i) establish open and inclusive communication channels, encouraging the exchange of ideas and perspectives; (ii) cultivate an atmosphere of active listening and dialogue, promoting peaceful conflict resolution and consensus building; (iii) encourage understanding of the needs and concerns of diverse stakeholders?	*We need to listen to the people who are involved in the dynamics of the mangrove – and of life.... You can't build a resilient and sustainable territory if there is no dialogue with the beings and voices present there.* (S10) *... this ecosystem creates a greater sense of respect, compassion, sensitive listening and dialogue in the way we live and behave towards the world. This applies to the government when building public policies, to society when thinking about development for all, and to personal and interpersonal relationships.* (S10)

(Continued)

TABLE 15.1 (Continued)

What if organizations, inspired on mangroves, valued/promoted/embraced...

Proposals for organizational learnings	*Students' metaphors and analogies*
A life worth living	Living near the mangrove imparts lessons on cherishing the simplicity and harmony inherent in natural cycles, highlighting the need of balancing urban life with a connection to nature. Observing nature offers precious lessons about resilience, adaptability, quality of life, and interdependence. What if organizations: (i) respect natural cycles and finding balance between urban life and nature; (ii) understand the interconnectedness and importance of each person and resource in the organization; (iii) promoting a culture that values moments of tranquility and gratitude for the little things; (iv) encouraging informal learning and the exchange of knowledge among employees?	... when leading a conventional city life, we grapple with the dilemma of whether it is worthwhile maintaining this fast pace and productivity in an environment that lacks tranquility and undergoes constant change, often wishing to "drop everything" and move to a more natural setting, adopting a lifestyle akin to traditional communities, in the pursuit of happiness. However, ... departing from this unstable environment means having to give up the benefits of it: for urban dwellers and the traditional way of life, money; while for the crab in the mangrove, the wealth of biodiversity and nutrients. ... the concepts of personal and professional quality of life differ significantly between city dwellers and local extractive communities, yet the ultimate goal remains personal and professional fulfillment, even if the "means" to achieve it differ. (S7) Today, after my alarm clock went off more than four times, I got up 30 minutes late, got dressed in a hurry, got in my car, drove to the college through [I don't know how many red lights because I couldn't miss the call, attended two classes, ... I practically gobbled up the food, got in the car again and drove to the office where I do my internship, where I spent five hours, and drove home in the evening. Three weeks ago, [we] were visiting three different mangroves and talking to people who make their living from them and where they spend most of the hours of their days and, therefore, their lives. A fisherman can never be late for work

(Continued)

TABLE 15.1 (Continued)

What if organizations, inspired on mangroves, valued/promoted/embraced…	
Proposals for organizational learnings	Students' metaphors and analogies
	like me or you, because his boss is the moon, which determines what the tide will be like, which in turn will make the water level in the mangrove rise or fall more, altering the "sweet-salt" ratio… and influencing the amount of fish, oysters or crabs he can take from the mangrove to his house that day. His time to get up, go out and fish is determined by nature and not by an arbitrary and artificial convention. The fisherman doesn't leave his house flying through red lights, without checking the sky, because the rain will alter, but not necessarily prevent, his work that day. Everything in the mangrove is extremely connected…. Each being, living or nonliving, plays a unique and irreplaceable role in an extremely complex and harmonious system. The disappearance of one species puts all the others at risk – including the human lives of present and future generations living in coastal regions. Fishermen and their families don't eat in restaurants in the center or buy from supermarkets where the food arrives in trucks sent by suppliers, after endless processes. [They] know exactly where their food comes from, because they have had to rely on what they have learned from their families, surrendering to the unpredictability of nature, and sticking their arms in holes to collect crabs, or even cultivating oysters for weeks, respecting the animal's time until it is ready…. the fishermen don't finish their working day in the mangrove and go home, because for a collective of people who live off the mangrove, materially and culturally, an ecosystem that they have learned to handle not in schools, universities or companies, but through the words of their fathers, uncles and grandparents, it is never possible to leave the mangrove, due to the centrality it occupies in their lives. (S8)

themselves in alternative ways, emphasizing the valuable contributions such experiences can make to management education and students' personal development. We use codes to ensure the anonymization of students: S for Student.

The power of affective cartography as a pedagogical tool

Affective cartography has proven to be a powerful and revealing pedagogical tool for use in business school classrooms. It has the potential to bring together various pedagogical approaches that have been used by teachers in sustainability education: (i) it is necessarily inter- and transdisciplinary; (ii) it can be done individually and collectively; (iii) it requires deep listening to stakeholders; (iv) it allows the use of art; and (v) it can be physical or digital, made of different materials and formats.

Our teaching approach, heavily influenced by art and complemented by a group with many students talented in drawing and painting, resulted in a completely hand-painted cartography, made on 80 × 100cm paper, colored pencils, permanent markers, and watercolor paint. After completion, the group digitized it with the intention of making it accessible to society. See the Resources section at the end of this chapter for the completed cartography.

Clara: *The central message was the journey of transformation we experienced during the FIS. The spiral tells this story and symbolizes the affection cultivated with the mangrove, starting with a period of "non-affection," when we were oblivious to its power. Then we illustrate the experience of interacting with the ecosystem and raising awareness through dialogue with experts and local communities. The narrative evolves into the group's period of "metanoia," as we recognize ourselves as an intrinsic part of nature. The cartography culminates in the group's state of enchantment and affection, where we come to perceive the mangrove as an enchanted forest, full of learnings, teachings, connections, and a part of our own essence. We have also provided a step-by-step guide on how to conduct affective cartography.*

Following the final presentation, the group sent printed copies of the cartography to all visited communities and experts who conducted lectures, to provide feedback on the project, ensuring it returned to the respective territories. The cartography was selected to be featured on the UNESCO Platform for the Decade of the Oceans, the first project by business students to be included in the platform, which typically features projects in the natural sciences fields (UNESCO Platform for the Decade of the Oceans).

This semester we learned a lot. Undoubtedly, affective cartography can be a powerful pedagogical tool to use with management students. And the mangrove provided us with amazing content to work on the concepts of ecocentrism and alternative forms of organizing. We encourage our colleagues to try out this approach and are available to exchange thoughts on the experience.

References

Carreira, F. C., Barretto, R., Santiago, I. C., & Brunstein, J. (2023, January 13). *Ensino Remoto em tempos de Pandemia: Oportunidades Para Uma Aprendizagem Transformadora*. Revista de Administração de Empresas. https://www.scielo.br/j/rae/a/KjnKHWt9wwr7kLPgGXVWcyt/?lang=en

Escobar, H. (2022, December 19). *Recheados de "Carbono Azul", Manguezais Ganham destaque no combate às Mudanças Climáticas*. Jornal da USP. https://jornal.usp.br/ciencias/recheados-de-carbono-azul-manguezais-ganham-destaque-no-combate-as-mudancas-climaticas/

Figueiredo, M. D. De, & Marquesan, F. F. S. (2022). Back to the future: Ecocentrism, organization studies, and the Anthropocene. *Scandinavian Journal of Management, 38*, 1–9. https://doi.org/10.1016/j.scaman.2022.101197

Gasparin, M., Brown, D., Green, W., Hugill, A., Lilley, S., Quinn, M., . . . & Zalasiewicz, J. (2020). The business school in the anthropocene: Parasite logic and pataphysical reasoning for a working earth. *Academy of Management Learning and Education, 19*(3), 385–405. https://doi.org/10.5465/AMLE.2019.0199

Kurucz, E. C., Colbert, B. A., & Marcus, J. (2014). Sustainability as a provocation to rethink management education: Building a progressive educative practice. *Management Learning, 45*(4), 437–457. https://doi.org/10.1177/1350507613486421

Maggs, D., & Robinson, J. (2016). Recalibrating the anthropocene. *Environmental Philosophy, 13*(2), 175–194. https://doi.org/10.5840/envirophil201611740

Michels, C., Hindley, C., Knowles, D., & Ruth, D. (2020). Learning atmospheres: Re-imagining management education through the dérive. *Management Learning, 51*(5), 559–578. https://doi.org/10.1177/1350507620906673

O'Doherty, D. (2020). The Leviathan of rationality: Using film to develop creativity and imagination in management learning and education. *Academy of Management Learning and Education, 19*(3), 366–384. https://doi.org/10.5465/AMLE.2019.0197

Parker, M. (2018). *Shut down the business school: What's wrong with management education*. Pluto Press.

UNESCO Platform for the Decade of the Oceans. https://www.linkedin.com/feed/update/urn:li:activity:7107725384409833473/ https://oceandecade.org/publications/how-to-make-an-affective-cartography/

Additional Resources

Cartography instructions. https://eaesp.fgv.br/sites/eaesp.fgv.br/files/u641/fgvces-fis260how_to_make_an_affective_cartography.pdf

Completed cartography. https://eaesp.fgv.br/sites/eaesp.fgv.br/files/u641/fgvces-fis26-presentation.pdf

FIS Information. https://www.youtube.com/watch?v=_cPkzyjgrPI

Instagram video of student simulation. https://www.instagram.com/p/CpS0IhXuuEq/?img_index=1

Transferring to online delivery. http://dx.doi.org/10.1590/S0034-759020230106x

Video highlights of the course. https://www.instagram.com/p/CpS0IhXuuEq/?img_index=1

16
JUST DOING IT

James A. F. Stoner

Abstract

Late in August 2019 I discovered I would be teaching an undergraduate Principles of Management course in the fall semester – a couple of weeks away. I decided to align that core course with the need for a sustainable world. I had almost no spare time to adapt a graduate-level Principles syllabus I had used a couple of years earlier, so I cobbled together the course week by week. This chapter describes that course revision journey, what the course looked like as it eventually emerged, and what I learned in the process. The basic theme of this chapter is very simple: even under less-than-optimal conditions, doing so was fun, surprisingly easy, and rich in ideas for doing more along the same lines. The hoped-for audience of this chapter is folks who will be aligning their own courses with the need for a sustainable world. The purpose is to encourage them simply to do it.

Introduction

This chapter reports a course revision journey, the context of that journey, some things I learned from making the journey, and what I might do if I were to take the next step in such a journey. This chapter is intended to provide a sense of how easy it actually is to align a core/required business course with the need to create a poverty-alleviating, sustainable/flourishing/regenerating world. The context of the journey is the opportunity and need to transform all of business education – teaching, researching, and positive activism – to be major contributors to meeting the great sustainability challenges of the 21st century.

DOI: 10.4324/9781003521839-17

The big takeaway

Revising and leading a core Principles of Management/OB course in 2019 alerted me to the need to grapple with what sophomore undergraduate class members already knew about global unsustainability. I believe that all business school courses should be grounded in the realities of the 21st century, especially the need to create a sustainable/flourishing/regenerating world and that we should start with that need – not add it into our courses in dribs and drabs as "nice to's." Starting with the need for business education to focus on creating a sustainable world is, in my opinion, fundamental to the business education enterprise.

The fall of 2019 question for me was: "What can faculty members who are changing their courses assume the students in class know about the seriousness and extent of the world's global unsustainability crisis? And, if they know very little, does each faculty member in each course need to provide some sort of introduction to that situation?"

I started my course with an introduction to the global unsustainability situation because I guessed (correctly) that my sophomore students would not have received a solid introduction to what I consider to be the global unsustainability realities of the 21st century in their first year's classes. As I delivered and reflected on the introduction I was providing, I was mindful of how tedious it would be if students had to sit through similar introductions in every one of their core-required courses – finance, marketing, accounting, economics, operations, ethics, etc. . . . and maybe even their advanced courses – the same topic over and over again. And how frustrating it would be to the profs who had to squeeze such an unfamiliar topic into a course where they already had far more content they wanted to "cover" than they had class time for.

So, "a blinding flash of the obvious": If we are to transform business education to be a major contributor to creating a sustainable world, something I think we definitely need to do, we should start with a first course of some reasonable length that addresses the great global unsustainability challenges of the 21st century, and how the business education we are delivering is going to contribute to meeting those challenges.

For me the "bottom line" of this chapter is the conclusion that we should start all business education with a solid introduction to the global unsustainability challenges of the 21st century. Then, we should teach our students and ourselves how we can contribute to meeting those challenges. That introduction should reveal and explicitly reject the neoliberal narrative – the assertion that THE purpose of for-profit firms should be to maximize shareholder wealth. These bedrock foundation pieces of the malignant form of our business and political economy can justly be labeled "cancerous capitalism" (Stoner, 2023). I also believe that rejecting these destructive framings should not be side-tracked by facile talk of "triple-bottom lines"; that too often equate to maximizing shareholder wealth when daily business decisions are actually made.

How my 2019 course revision journey came into being and unfolded

Surprise – no problem . . . . well . . .

Ooops – surprise – As I noted earlier, two weeks before the start of the fall of 2019 term at my university I discovered I would be teaching an undergraduate core intro to management course and not the upper-level MBA seminar in global sustainability I had expected to teach.

No problem – I had taught Intro to OB/Management in the MBA program for about four decades and at the undergraduate level 30 or so years ago. In leading those courses I used pretty much the same syllabus for grad and undergrad students and all of the courses went well. My usual 19-page MBA syllabus was full of fun stuff, at least fun for me. And my teaching performances seemed okay – I would occasionally win best teacher awards when my colleague, Frank Werner, was periodically barred from repeating his monopoly on the award. *So, no problem –* do what I had done many times, just in a new but less familiar environment – the undergrad program.

Well, maybe a minor problem: My schedule was chock-a-block full, and I had little free time to fine-tune the grad-level syllabus for the undergraduate course. Well, *not much of a problem.* I could cobble together a modified syllabus and fine-tune it as the course evolved. Thank goodness I have an almost off-the-scale score on the tolerance for ambiguity metric (Purdue University).

So, no problem

Well, maybe a bit of a problem: That fall undergrad course was the last course I was scheduled to teach as my three-year phased-retirement buyout was coming to an end. No problem there, *EXCEPT* I decided that I was unwilling to teach the OB/Management course in the traditional manner I had been teaching it – virtually no attention to issues of global sustainability – straight people and organizational and systems management topics. My sustainability teaching was reserved for upper-level, optional "saddle-bag courses" for those who were concerned enough about a dying planet to invest some classroom time to learn what was happening to their world and perhaps do something useful about it.

So, maybe a bit of a problem – no time to prep before the start of the term and only a desire to "go down to bare metal" to ground the course in the need to create a sustainable world . . . and a modified syllabus to guide us on that journey. That modified syllabus was not 19 pages long. It was six and a half pages long with

* three pages devoted to the first two assignments,
* one page devoted to a summary list of planned topics and readings, for the planned 14 class sessions, and
* a half page of playful mantras for the course.

In other words, a pale shadow of its traditional 19-page predecessors.

SPOILER: As this chapter reports how that 14-class-session journey unfolded, let's throw in a *No Suspense Spoiler: things turned out pretty well.* The class members did not stage a revolt. I had fun and I think they and I learned a lot. I would do it again – but better next time, of course. And because this chapter is about changing a course to be grounded in the need for a sustainable world, it is especially important to note that an awful lot of what I taught for decades in the "old" business-as-usual course seemed still to be stuff I would want to teach in the "new" sustainability grounded course.

A MAJOR THEME – Basically what I am saying in this chapter is *that developing and teaching a core business course fully aligned with the need to create a poverty-alleviating sustainable/flourishing/regenerating world is no big deal and can be done pretty easily.* I assert that all core-required and upper-level business courses should provide both the *appropriate* "traditional" skills and concepts we have taught for decades and should now include – actually be "grounded in" – appropriate skills, concepts, and mindsets (e.g., Rimanoczy, 2014, 2016, 2020) that enable our graduates to build careers that are simultaneously personally rewarding and that heal the planet. I also say that I think every one of us should alter our teaching, researching, and positive activism to do so now!

Why changing business education is such an exceptional opportunity

Early in the telling of this story it may be desirable to note how important my Global Movement Initiative (GMI) colleagues and I feel it is to change business education – teaching, researching, and positive activism. Addressing this topic now makes sense to me because it is the reason I "threw away" much of my syllabus at the last minute and created a somewhat new course week by week in that 2019 fall term. Obviously, I hope many readers will be in agreement on this topic and will do something similar to what I did . . . or share what they have already done or have started to do . . . in aligning their courses with the need for a sustainable world.

When the teaching, researching, and positive activism of all the world's business schools are focused on transforming ourselves, our business and other institutions, and our societies to create a socially just, poverty-alleviating, sustainable world, they will make an enormous contribution to creating such a world. The resources of the world's business schools are enormous, but unfortunately for many years they have not contributed to creating a more sustainable world. Instead, they have inculcated and legitimized the mindsets and the use of management and business tools to create the painfully unjust and clearly unsustainable world we now have . . . . . or maybe better said: "has us."

Transforming business education into a vehicle for creating a sustainable world will have two very positive impacts. First, merely ending the currently destructive business school teachings and researching that can be harshly labeled "doing the work of the devil" is a major positive step forward. Second, shifting those resources and mindsets toward creating a sustainable flourishing, regenerating world may be the most effective vehicle available to us for creating such a world.

The big advantage for every faculty member is that each of us can start doing so today. None of us needs permission to teach and research the realities of the 21st century and to inspire our students to deal with those realities. The big payoff is that engaging in "deep change" in what we teach (Quinn, 1996) yields many rich intellectual insights and challenges, much satisfaction of our curiosity, potentially rich colleague collaboration opportunities, and – of course – fresh publishing opportunities!!

Starting the course – how I tried to frame the course for class members

First and second classes: We started the course with the first five parts of the Hovey and Beard case – a puzzle case I have been using to kick off courses and executive programs for about four decades – and a team formation and building process I have been using for a similar length of time. We also set up the homework assignments for the next two weeks.

Framing "the big picture" for the course – an unsustainable world: I told class members, and repeated a few times during the term, that the course will assume the global unsustainability situation is severe, that we need to change how business operates, and that business schools are obligated to train graduates for three work situations:

1. *Business as usual*: Working in companies committed to making as much profit as possible with only minor concerns about their impacts on the environment, global poverty, future generations, social justice, the lives of workers in the company, etc.
2. *Transitioning companies*: Companies that are actively trying to become much more aligned with the need for a sustainable and socially just world. Such companies may be merely pursuing the "business case for sustainability" – how to make more money by doing less harm – but they are trying to figure out how to go beyond that goal.
3. *Sustainable companies*: Companies that actually are running themselves in ways that are profitable – because they need profit to flourish – but that run themselves in ways that do not damage and ideally heal our broken planet as they produce the goods and services we all need to flourish. Such companies would see profits as a *means to an end* and not as *THE end*.

I told the class that all business schools need to teach the skills and concepts that business-as-usual companies expect them to have, and that many of those skills, but not all of them, are appropriate for the other two types of companies.

Our graduates need to have those traditional business skills and concepts that business-as-usual companies expect them to have because most of the jobs currently are in business-as-usual companies. It is great if our graduates can find type two and type three companies but they're most likely going to have to go to work for business-as-usual companies.

I suggested that all business school graduates need those traditional business skills and concepts, but what they also need is a very different mindset. That alternative mindset rejects the idea that the purpose of the firm is to maximize shareholder wealth. Our students and graduates need to have mindsets that support creating purpose-driven careers and creating purpose-driven business firms and other institutions that heal the planet as they provide the goods and services we need to flourish.

Oh, yes: the syllabus. In the first class, I also handed out the syllabus and warned the class that the syllabus was not the 19-page lots-of-details syllabus of a traditional Principles of Management course. I said we would be venturing into somewhat unknown territory and building the bridge as we walk on it (Quinn, 1996) and that the syllabus should be looked at as an early plan for what we might do.

The course had five major components

1. A series of email messages, most related to global sustainability issues and most from the class members' "boss" in a full-time job they hypothetically hold during the course – the syllabus labeled those email-based assignments "skill exercises," in researching, listening, and writing that are fundamental to a successful career in any type of organization.
2. Four disguised perennial-issue cases that are vehicles for the prof to give content-focused mini-lectures – dramatic, memorable, and important management/career points.
3. Team-based activities and supporting information to develop team management and participation skills during the term.
4. A somewhat playful, and perhaps somewhat frivolous (in a good sense) way of being in the course supported by some specific assignments.
5. A set of assigned readings, mostly with classic management/OB types of articles and books.

Framing the class members' role in the course: One of the first things we did was to try to frame the course for the class members. A key part of the course design included asking the class members to assume that they are in a particular job with a particular boss and to respond to seven separate requests from the boss or others. Class members were asked in those requests

- to respond to the boss's request,
- to post their responses on Blackboard,
- to reflect on how they responded to the boss's request,

- to report how many hours they worked on the assignment,
- to list the resources they used in researching their responses to the boss, and
- to read and comment appreciatively on a fellow class member's essay.

The centrality of the boss memos

The second class finished the discussion of the Hovey and Beard case that had started in the first class and then the course started the process of using student essays written and posted on Blackboard by all class members. In those essays, class members' role was a valued young assistant ("subordinate") to an unusual boss. The boss kept sending messages to his/her assistant requesting very brief (4 hours) explorations of a question or topic and a report back to the boss very soon . . . the four-hour target was intended to be respectful of the student's/employee's time. Most of the sustainability content of the course arose from those essays.

The first of these two email messages from the boss asked the student/employee to "make the strongest possible case for the belief . . . that climate change (global warming weather weirding, global unsustainability, etc.) is the 'greatest hoax ever perpetrated on the American people.'" The second email message, a week later, requested the assistant/student to write a similar essay on the theme that "climate change is real."

Typical class sessions: After the first few weeks, the class settled down to a reasonably regular pattern:

1. Recording team scores (on a large spreadsheet) for a playful out-of-class activity ("Samurai Learning Team" scores).
2. Team bidding for an opportunity to read the book *The Max Strategy* (Dauten, 1990).
3. A short meditation about 5 to 7 minutes long led by a class member who volunteered each week.
4. An activity that took most of the class time – such as a case, experiential exercise, mini lecture by the prof, team term-project presentations, some discussion of the week's essay, and/or some team working time – and a 10-minute break in the middle of the two-hour class. Toward the end of the term, three classes were devoted to team term-project presentations. A middle of the term class session and a late in the term class session were planned to be devoted to a mini-midterm and a final exam. However, those sessions transmogrified themselves into something different.

Discovering situational ignorance and building on it

OOOPS: Surprise in the second class – After we had formed and built teams in the first class, I discovered the class members were already in teams for at least one other course that term. *Sigh.*

With considerable reluctance I chose to use those extant teams from the other course in and to disband the teams, we had formed in the first class. *Ouch* – That choice was not an obvious one, because I consider the way the class members and I compose teams in the first class (to maximize diversity) as well as the short six- or 12-minute team-building activities we follow immediately, to be a key part of building effective teams. It is also an opportunity to start learning a key skill and mindset that can be used in building future teams.

Well, as Hal Levitt used to say, "not to worry." We continued to do team-building skill development activities in the new teams, and it worked out pretty well. Later, that decision turned out to be a wise one, or perhaps just a lucky one.

OOOPS: surprise in the fourth week: learning what the class members were doing in that other course

About the fourth week of the course, I learned that the students in that other course were working on hypothetical "consulting" projects for various companies and would be making major presentations on their projects at the end of the term.

Opportunity. This discovery led to an in-flow, new assignment from "the boss" – each team was asked to identify a major sustainability challenge facing the team's client company.

I mention the second- and fourth-class session discoveries and subsequent events mainly to emphasize that changing a course in this manner – kind of moment-by-moment as the course unfolded – might involve a series of surprises, and to emphasize that the students and I could adjust without undue angst.

Perhaps equally important is the value of seizing opportunities to integrate each course with things happening in other courses, even when those opportunities are not planned in advance but, instead, appear unexpectedly as the academic term unfolds. For those of us inclined to believe that "rapid response usually trumps careful planning," those surprise opportunities are often a blessing.

Reflections on what I learned, would do the same, and would do differently

Now some reflections on how I feel about what happened in the course, what I would do and not do next time, and why knowing some specific characteristics of me might be relevant for readers to think about in terms of their own characteristics and situations.

What I learned

1. **That first course for everyone:** As I emphasized at the beginning of this chapter, perhaps the most important learning for me came from the early

discovery of the need for a first course, before other courses, on the realities of global unsustainability and the need for business curriculum change. Ideally that course would offer a broad framing of the challenges of the 21st century, each business school's explicit statement of the purpose of for-profit business enterprises, and the tragedy of defining the purpose of the firm to be maximizing shareholder wealth. It would note that profit in businesses, and financial surplus in other organizations, is necessary to maintain organizational health and continued societal contribution but that "profit is a *means to an end*, not *the end* of business activity."

2. **Commitment:** As Soren Kierkegaard noted, "Life can only be understood backwards; but it must be lived forwards." And looking backward, I realized that the one major thing I had on my own journey was a commitment to align my course with the need to create a sustainable world. I did not need time to prepare, nor money, nor orders or requests to change my course, nor even permission to do so. All I needed was commitment and the knowledge that once we commit all sorts of unexpected and wonderful things happen. One of my favorite quotations: "Until one is committed, there is hesitancy" (Goodreads). There was no time to prepare the course before the term started. There was no payment or "course release" for doing so. No one asked or told me to do so. And I did not ask permission to "align my course with the realities of the 21st century." All I needed was to commit to doing so.

3. **Fun:** Maybe almost as important as those first two points is the fact that for me redesigning and teaching the course was a lot fun and hopefully will be the same for others. Preparing for class was sometimes a bit stressful. The revision process was pretty "last minute-ish" some weeks because in week n I might be deciding what to assign for the next week ($n + 1$). I really was "building the bridge each week as I walked on it." Before class, I was sometimes photocopying class hand-outs I had just finished drafting minutes earlier. Twice, when the copying machine threw a tantrum, preparing for class was very stressful. And I survived and have wonderful memories of the students and our shared adventure.

4. **Lots of "old" stuff still fits:** I choose to use a lot of the materials, classroom activities, and mini-lectures I had previously used in the "business-as-usual" versions of the course for decades. I think this point is important, maybe even very important. As we go "down to bare metal" in transforming our courses, there is still much of what we have always done that we will need to keep doing . . . and our students will continue to learn from . . . and with us. Many of the skills and concepts we teach are needed in any of the three types of companies we described earlier.

5. **Listening to the environment:** It was really valuable to be alert to the business program environment and flexible in moving forward in that environment. Part of the course I am most pleased with is the three new

boss-request email assignments 5, 6, and 7 that emerged organically and spontaneously out of something happening elsewhere (in another course).

6. Cutting the prof lots of slack . . . and becoming proactive

The way this course was presented had to be a tricky process for many students, because it evolved during the term – away from what appeared to be a somewhat firmly set syllabus into some situations where next week's assignment was decided upon this week and may have seemed to come from almost nowhere. I am sure that process was much more difficult for class members with a low tolerance for ambiguity rather than a high tolerance for ambiguity, but somehow everyone seemed to be able to handle the fluidity of the course as it evolved.

Not only did they handle the fluidity, or perhaps because of it, but also class members became progressively more proactive as the term evolved. They began to bargain successfully with me about such things as devoting a few extra minutes of our very precious class time to working in teams even though doing so was not in our schedule for a particular evening. Somehow along the way, the mini midterm exam seems to have disappeared – replaced by other things we did in class instead.

And most dramatically of all, they somehow bargained me out of a final exam! They explained to me, over a couple of class sessions, how doing a teacher-tests-the-students-in-an-exam was inconsistent with the collaborative culture that had emerged. They bargained me into a final graded activity that was to be a class in which each team would make a class presentation that was a valuable learning experience for all and captured important parts of the course or its key essence.

As I reflect back on that "negotiation," I'm still a little mystified about how they talked me into that approach. But it is a pleasure to report that the presentations were all excellent. Interestingly enough, two of them were on Dale Dauten's book *The Max Strategy* (Dauten, 1990), the book that all class members had to read, but which I promised "would not be on the midterm or final exam."

What I would do the same

If I were in a similar situation in the future – teaching a Principles of Management course to sophomore students with little or no prior substantive exposure to the realities of our global unsustainability crisis – I think I would keep pretty much to the final syllabus and course that evolved. Most of the changes would occur in doing better what I did in my first attempt. However, if the students came into the course with a deeper knowledge of the sustainability challenges of the 21st century, I could eliminate the two essays on "climate change is a hoax" and "climate change is real" and free-up some class and homework time for other use.

What I would do differently

1. **A small tweak might make a big contribution to the course**. I think the class member emails responding to the boss's requests worked really well. However, I rarely had time to read and respond to them before class and we rarely had class time to discuss particularly interesting messages from various class members.

   I would like to experiment with a decoupling of the essay assignment – in the first part of each week's assignment the class members would still post on Blackboard their response to the boss's request in which they also report what they did to create their response, their reflections on what they did, and how much time they invested in the assignment. They would no longer write an appreciation of a class member's *previous week's* email to the boss. They would submit their essay each week about four days before the next class (a bit tight, I admit, but maybe doable since they would know about each essay assignment from the beginning of the term). Two days before the next class, they would read some class member essays for the upcoming class and write an appreciation of one of those current week's essays. I would read all of the essays and all of the appreciations, and we would invest at least a little class time discussing – and celebrating – some of them.

   Something like that. Maybe it would work.

2. **Great challenges of the 21st century**. I would be explicit about calling for the course and all business education to be committed to meeting "the great challenges of the 21st century," using a description of those challenges like:

   1. Dealing with global warming – better yet: "Avoiding global roasting,"
   2. Avoiding Nuclear Armageddon,
   3. Becoming the kinds of people who can flourish on this planet in ways that heal it,
   4. Discovering how to produce the goods and services we need to flourish in ways that heal the planet, and
   5. Creating a poverty-alleviating, cultural, economic, environmental, political global system that works for 100% of humanity.

   (adapted from Stoner & Peregoy, 2021)

   And I would be explicit about how business school teaching, researching, and positive activism are ideally suited to contribute to meeting at least four of those five challenges.

3. **Listening.** In this course and for many decades, I have said in all courses that "listening is the most important of all management skills" – "Listening for the gold" as my student and colleague Brent Martini often says and very much like what Otto Scharmer describes as "Level 4 listening – generative

listening" (Scharmer undated). I would play Scharmer's 8–1/2-minute video in the references in class early in the term.

4. **Sustainability mindset.** In the context of the third and also the fourth of those 21st-century challenges, I would somehow squeeze in the work of Isabel Rimanoczy and her colleagues (e.g., Rimanoczy, 2014, 2016, 2020) on the sustainability mindset.

5. **Humanistic and shared leadership**. In the context of the fourth and also the third of those 21st-century challenges, I would somehow also squeeze in the work of the Humanistic Leadership Academy (Humanistic Leadership Academy, undated), companies like the Barry Wehmiller Company (Chapman & Sisodia, 2015) and the "shared leadership" work of Ernie Turner and Swee Heng Tan (Turner & Tan, 2023).

6. **The third email request from the boss.** I would either figure out how to make the third email message request from the boss – the one about traditional hierarchical, command-and-control management – work better or simply drop it. The class member essays on the topic were the least satisfactory ones of the seven class members wrote. I think the problem is that I did not give the class members enough assistance in grappling with that topic. My bad. But maybe the topic is not high enough priority to struggle with.

7. **Multiple choice exam questions written by class members.** For many years, I have asked class members to write multiple-choice questions on the course's assigned readings and on the assigned cases. I would use those questions to create very short mini exams that the class members would answer as individuals and in their teams at the beginning of class. I did that in part because I think writing one's own exam questions is an excellent way to dig into assigned readings and also an excellent way to prepare for a multiple-choice exam. I also think that the process is helpful in building effective classroom teams and encouraging each team to encourage all its members to do the reading before class. I would reintroduce that process if I were to repeat the course.

8. **My university's team-developed principles of management course.** At the very end of these reflections, on what I might do differently, if I were to teach the same course again, and perhaps what should be the starting point of these reflections, I would look into the course my colleagues in the Leading People and Organizations group at Fordham have developed and delivered. They have developed an excellent principles of management course that includes the need to create a sustainable world. I would investigate that course more deeply to see how it fits with the goal of teaching a first management/OB course, fully aligned with the need for a sustainable world.

Kind of a postscript

My own biases and tendencies: As I started capturing my reflections on this course, it became clearer and clearer to me that it's worthwhile to say at least a little bit about my own biases and tendencies and the personal/professional situation I was in when I embarked upon this course adventure – especially because of the unusual way I allowed the course to unfold. I love what we did in the course, and I found doing it was fun if a bit stressful at times – especially when copy machines were throwing tantrums.

However, as much as I enjoyed this adventure and feel good about the results, I would be reluctant to recommend to anyone *the way* the course was cobbled together at the last minute. Although I am more than comfortable urging all of us to align our courses with the realities and challenges of the 21st century, I would not urge everyone to follow the last minute, class-by-class path I trod. Especially anyone without the extremely, virtually off-the-scale, tolerance for ambiguity, that I seem to have and anyone who is not a tenured full professor, who can afford to crash and burn with no real consequences, or anyone who really does not want to take a big risk of failing. I'm not sure I would have followed the path I did in this course if I were an assistant professor hoping to get my contract renewed or get tenured.

In terms of the syllabus we came up with, I think it's important that each faculty member bring into this adventure his or her full career and way of being. It is clear to me that this course is an awful lot of Jim Stoner. In attempting to bring sustainability into a core-required course in management I was influenced greatly by having the privilege of sitting at feet (literally and actually at the feet) of such sustainability and quality leaders as L. Hunter Lovins, Amory Lovins, John Ehrenfeld, Joseph Juran, W, Edwards Deming, and Blan Godfrey.

For me, the point is that, as we transform our teaching, researching, and positive activism, we are each unique, what we produce will be unique and will reflect what we are and who we wish to be. What my students and I did in 2019 offers no "cookie cutter" answer to the questions "What should we teach?" and "How should we figure out how to teach it?" The magic in what we do comes from our doing our own thing in our own way.

I wish you joy and success in your journey and I look forward to reading the story of that journey.

References

Chapman, B., & Sisodia, R. (2015). *Everybody matters: The extraordinary power of caring for your people like family.* Portfolio/Penguin.

Dauten, D. (1990). *The max strategy.* Morrow.

Humanistic Leadership Academy (undated). https://humanisticleadershipacademy.org. Accessed May 28, 2024.

Quinn, R. E. (1996). *Deep change: Discovering the leader within.* Jossey-Bass.

Rimanoczy, I. (2014). A matter of being: Developing sustainability-minded leaders. *Journal of Management for Global Sustainability, 2*(1), 95–122.

Rimanoczy, I. (2016). *Stop teaching: Principles and practices for responsible manage-ment education.* Business Expert Press.

Rimanoczy, I. (2020). *The sustainability mindset principles: A guide to developing a mindset for a better world.* Routledge.

Scharmer, O. (undated). *Otto Scharmer on the four levels of listening.* https://www.youtube.com/watch?v=eLfXpRkVZaI. Accessed May 28, 2024.

Stoner, J. A. F. (2023). Gratitude, thanks, and almost "curing cancerous capitalism". *Journal of Management for Global Sustainability, 11*(1), 1–11.

Stoner, J. A. F., & Peregoy, R. (2021). Introduction to: Management perspectives at the convergence of eastern wisdom and quantum science. *Journal of Management, Spirituality, and Religion, 18*(6), 1–6.

Turner, E., & Tan, S. H. (2023). *Shared leadership disciplines: A better way to lead & coach.* Candid Creation Publishing.

Additional Resources

Documents, cases, readings and resources created to support this course are available for open-source use at the Global Movement Initiative website. www.globalmovement initiative.com

INDEX